COMPUTERS
ECONOMIC PLA
THE SOVIET EXP.

COMPUTERS AND ECONOMIC PLANNING: THE SOVIET EXPERIENCE

MARTIN CAVE

CAMBRIDGE UNIVERSITY PRESS
CAMBRIDGE
LONDON · NEW YORK · NEW ROCHELLE
MELBOURNE · SYDNEY

Published by the Press Syndicate of the University of Cambridge
The Pitt Building, Trumpington Street, Cambridge CB2 1RP
32 East 57th Street, New York, NY 10022, USA
296 Beaconsfield Parade, Middle Park, Melbourne 3206, Australia

First published 1980

Printed in Great Britain
at the University Press, Cambridge

Library of Congress Cataloguing in Publication Data
Cave, Martin.
Computers and economic planning, the Soviet
experience.

(Soviet and East European studies)
Bibliography: p.
Includes index.
1. Russia – Economic policy – 1966–1970 – Data
processing. 2. Planning – Data processing.
3. Industrial management – Russia – Data processing.
I. Title. II. Series.
HC336.23.C38   338.947   79–7659
ISBN 0 521 22617 1

CONTENTS

PREFACE

This book describes the effect which the application of computer technology has had on the system of economic planning and management in the Soviet Union. The potential impact of computers on economic planning is enormous. To appreciate this one only has to recall one of the arguments made in the debate in the 1930s on the feasibility of central planning. It was asserted then that an efficient allocation of resources in a centrally planned economy was inconceivable, because such an allocation would require the solution of 'millions of equations'. At that time, of course, no electronic computers were available. Today the situation is quite different and the computational objection would have much less force.

Interestingly, Oscar Lange, the author of the famous 'competitive solution' of the planning problem in the 1930s, turned in his last article, published in 1967, to the potential impact of computers on economic planning. There he reinterpreted the market as a 'computer *sui generis* which serves to solve a system of simultaneous equations' by the tâtonnement process, noting that the solution mechanism operated not via a physical process, as in an analogue computer, but by a social process. He then went on to compare the merits of the 'two instruments of economic accounting' available to managers in socialist economies, the electronic computer and the market (Lange (1967), p. 159).

In his article Lange was concerned with the potential impact of computers when they had been fully assimilated into planning and when technical difficulties had been overcome. The aim of this book, in contrast, is to establish in detail what changes computers have brought to the actual operation of the Soviet economy, in which neither of these two conditions has been fulfilled. We begin by examining the history of the Soviet efforts to use computers for management purposes. The second chapter gives an account of alternative basic approaches to adapting the planning system to take advantage of computers. This is followed by four chapters describing the use of computers at four major organisations or levels of industrial management: the State Planning Commission (Gosplan); the State Committee for Supply (Gossnab); ministries; and enterprises and production associations (*ob'edineniya*). A final chapter offers an overall assessment and some conclusions.

The book is organised so that a reader with a general interest in the Soviet economy can get a fairly self-contained account of the background and implications of Soviet work in computer-based planning systems by looking at Chapters 1 and 7. The reader interested in the more abstract aspects of economic planning may find Chapters 2 and 3 of most interest. The remaining chapters describe the impact of computers on particular organisations and the special problems of modelling and implementation encountered there.

The materials for this study are largely Soviet publications supplemented by a visit to the Soviet Union in 1973. Soviet sources have seemed to me to be relatively open and frank in discussing the successes and failures of computer use. However, I recognise that they are no substitute for direct access to practitioners in the field, which was not available to me. I am aware, moreover, that an outsider can capture only imperfectly the atmosphere of an ambitious programme such as the one described here.

A large number of people have helped me to complete this study. I am especially indebted to Francis Seton of Oxford University who supervised the thesis from which the present book is derived. Most of the research was done at the Centre for Russian and East European Studies at Birmingham University, and I owe a great deal to the encouragement and help of many individuals working at or attached to the Centre, in particular R. W. Davies (then Director of the Centre), Philip Hanson, Julian Cooper, and Chris Siemaszko. The help of the Centre's librarian, Jenny Brine, was invaluable. I am also grateful to Paul Hare of Stirling University for reading successive drafts of many chapters. Mrs C. Newnham typed the manuscript with her customary speed and efficiency.

GLOSSARY

*Glossary of terms used in connection with automated planning
and management systems in the USSR*

ABD   (*Avtomatizirovannyi bank dannykh*) A bank of data stored in a computer. TsSU is developing such a bank as part of ASGS (q.v.).

AIUS   (*Avtomatizirovannaya informatsionno-upravlayushchaya sistema standartizartsii i metrologii Gosstandarta SSSR*) The automated system for the State Committee on Standards.

ASFR   (*Avtomatizirovannaya sistema finansovykh resursov*) The automated system covering the activity of the Ministry of Finance.

ASGS   (*Avtomatizirovannaya sistema gosudarstvennoi statistiki*) The automated system dealing with the functions of TsSU.

ASN   (*Avtomatizirovannaya sistema normativov*) The automated system with the function of collecting and preparing data on normatives (input coefficients) of various kinds for use in planning. Though it is sometimes referred to as a subsystem of ASPR (q.v.), ASN also has connections with enterprises and ministries.

ASOI tsen   (*Avtomatizirovannaya sistema obrabotki informatsii po tsenam*) The automated system which processes information used by the State Committee on Prices of the USSR Council of Ministers.

ASPR   (*Avtomatizirovannaya sistema planovykh raschetov*) The automated system designed to assist Gosplan USSR and Union Republic Gosplans in the performance of planning functions.

ASU MTS   (*Avtomatizirovannaya sistema upravleniya material'no-tekhnicheskym snabzheniem*) The automated system which covers the activity of Gossnab.

ASUNT   (*Avtomatizirovannaya sistema upravleniya nauchno-tekhnicheskym progressom*) The automated system dealing with the planning and control of research and development at the State Committee for Science and Technology.

ASUO   (*Avtomatizirovannaya sistema upravleniya ob'edineniem*) These systems will be responsible for the management of (production) *ob'edineniya*.

ASUP   (*Avtomatizirovannaya sistema upravleniya predpriyatiem*) These systems are responsible for the management functions of individual enterprises.

ASU-pribor (*Avtomatizirovannaya sistema upravleniya Ministerstvom proborostroeniya*) The management system for the instrument-building industry. An example of an OASU (q.v.).

ASUS (*Avtomatizirovannaya sistema upravleniya stroitel'stvom*) The automated system concerned with the activity of Gosstroi, the State Committee for Construction.

ASUTP (*Avtomatizirovannaya sistema upravleniya tekhnologicheskim protsessom*) These systems are concerned with controlling complex physical processes in, for example, the chemical industry, rather than with planning and management.

ASVT (*Agregat sredstv vychislitel'noi tekhniki*) A family of second and third generation computers used both in process control and in management.

EASS (*Edinaya avtomatizirovannaya sistema svyazei*) The overall automated communications network for the USSR.

EMM (*Ekonomiko-matematicheskii model'*) Mathematical economic model.

ES EVM (*Edinaya sistema elektronno-vychislitel'nykh mashin*) A family of third generation computers, produced under a Comecon co-operation agreement; also known as the Ryad series.

EUSPD (*Edinaya unifitsirovannaya sistema planovoi dokumentatsii*) A unified system of planning documentation specially designed for ASPR (q.v.).

EVM (*Elektronno-vychislitel'naya mashina*) An electronic computer.

GSVTs (*Gosudarstvennaya sistema vychislitel'nykh tsentrov*) A grid of computer centres serving enterprises, ministries and higher-level organs (Gosplan, Gossnab, TsSU). Transfer of information between them is handled by the EASS (q.v.) which together with GSVTs forms the technical base of OGAS (q.v.). Initially, the management automation programme in general was referred to as the building of GSVTs.

IPU (*Institut problem upravleniya*). The institute of control problems, a research institute subordinate to the Ministry of Instrument Building and the Academy of Sciences, and formerly known as *Institut avtomatiki i telemekhaniki*, the institute for automation and remote control.

ISKhOD (*Integrirovannaya sistema khraneniya i obrabotki dannykh*) An expression similar to ISOD (q.v.), but used in connection with the design of ASPR (q.v.).

ISOD (*Integrirovannaya sistema obrabotki dannykh*) The outcome of a reorganisation of information processing in a branch, enterprise or smaller unit, so that information collection and processing are co-ordinated and data needs are met without redundancy of information.

KIP (*Kustovyi informatsionnyi punkt*) An information collection and processing centre serving several users, usually enterprises.

KIVTs (*Kustovyi informatsionno-vychislitel'nyi tsentr*) An information centre equipped with a computer and serving several users, usually enterprises.

MSS   (*Mashino-schetnaya stantsiya*) A centre organised by TsSU and equipped with calculating machines (sometimes computers), which carries out data processing for enterprises on a contract basis as well as TsSU work.

NIIMS   (*Nauchno-issledovatel'skii institut ekonomiki i organizatsiya material'no-tekhnicheskogo snabzheniya*). The scientific research institute for the economics and organisation of supply, a part of Gossnab USSR.

NIISU   (*Nauchno-issledovatel'skii institut sistem upravleniya*). The scientific-research institute for management systems of Gossnab USSR.

OASU   (*Otraslevaya avtomatizirovannaya sistema upravleniya*) An automated system for performing the functions of planning and management at ministry or branch level.

OGAS   (*Obshche-gosudarstvennaya sistema sbora i obrabotki informatsii (dannykh) dlya ucheta, planirovaniya i upravleniya narodnym khozyaistvom*) A comprehensive expression for the link-up of all the automated systems operating at different levels in economic planning and management. The hardware, or technical base of OGAS is the GSVTs (q.v.).

OGSPD   (*Obshche-gosudartstvennaya sistema peredachi dannykh*) The automated system which organises data exchanges between computer centres; a component part of EASS (q.v.).

OKP   (*Obshchesoyuznyi klassifikator produktsii*). The union-wide product classifier; a commodity classification system being developed in the USSR.

SGK   (*Soyuzglavkomplekt*). A chief administration for supplying enterprises under construction with equipment of a certain kind; part of Gossnab's product distribution system.

SGSS   (*Soyuzglavsnabsbyt*). A chief administration for the supply of a group of products; part of Gossnab's distribution system.

SKP   (*Sistema kompleksnogo planirovaniya*) The system of integrated planning; a system of plans linking long-term, five-year and annual plans and incorporating the construction of programmes for regions and sectors of the economy.

SOFE   (*Sistema optimal'nogo funktsionirovaniya ekonomiki*) A general conception of the operation of the economy originating in TsEMI in the 1960s and developed in the 1970s. SOFE envisages the construction of a plan by a computer-based iterative procedure and its implementation at least in part by a market system.

TsEMI   (*Tsentral'nyi ekonomiko-matematicheskii institut*). The central mathematical economics institute; a research institute of the USSR Academy of Sciences.

TsSU   (*Tsentral'noe statisticheskoe upravlenie*). The central statistical agency.

VTs   (*Vychislitel'nyi tsentr*) A computer centre.

VTsKP   (*Vychislitel'nyi tsentr kollektivnogo pol'zovanina*) A computer centre set up to serve several users.

1

THE HISTORICAL BACKGROUND

1 INTRODUCTION

Proposals to use computers on a large scale for economic planning and management first gained currency in the USSR in the late 1950s and early 1960s. For such proposals to be acceptable and for their implementation to be feasible it was necessary that a set of preconditions be fulfilled; by the early 1960s these conditions were largely met.

The first of them was the acceptance of cybernetics in the USSR as a science not at odds with dialectical and historical materialism.[1] The ideas of Norbert Wiener and his fellow cyberneticists originally received a hostile reception in the USSR, expressed in the famous article 'Whom Cybernetics Serves', published in *Voprosy Filosofii* in 1953 above the name of 'Materialist' (Materialist (1953)). This article and the entry on cybernetics in the 1954 edition of the *Short Philosophical Dictionary* denounced cybernetics as a tool of the reactionary bourgeoisie and as inimical to Marxism. But subsequently a body of opinion grew up in favour of cybernetics, and it was even argued that the earlier denunciations of the science had unwittingly accepted a false view deliberately propagated by reactionary interests to conceal the true potential of cybernetics from Soviet scientists.

This more favourable assessment of the new subject gained ground. In 1956 a seminar on cybernetics at Moscow University heard papers on a wide range of subjects, including a paper by Kantorovich on 'Mathematical Methods in Economic Planning'. In 1958 the importance of cybernetics was recognised by the establishment of a Scientific Council of the USSR Academy of Science on Cybernetics, under the direction of A. I. Berg, an admiral with interests in all aspects of cybernetics, including military and economic applications. Cybernetics became officially accepted as a science of rationality which was not at variance with Marxism, but which operated on a different plane. Indeed Graham observes that during the 1960s cybernetics enjoyed more prestige in the USSR than in any other country in the world (Graham (1973), p. 324).

Even the early opponents of cybernetics had recognised the potential of computer technology, and the 1950s saw the laying of the technical and engineering basis for the later development of the Soviet computer industry. A brief survey of Soviet computer technology, especially in recent years, is given in Appendix 2. After an initial period of rapid development, which kept pace roughly with that in the USA, Soviet computers lagged behind in the late 1950s. However, at the beginning of the 1960s the Soviet computer industry made the important breakthrough into second generation computer technology using transistors instead of valves, which not only made possible higher speeds of operation but also created the technical conditions for greater reliability.

The automation of production itself took precedence in the USSR over the use of computers for management and planning. It was natural for the Soviet government, as it began to pay more and more attention to technical progress in the period beginning in the middle 1950s, to devote resources to the automation of technological processes. A series of decrees dealing with the introduction of technical advances into the economy mentioned the scope for automation, and in the early 1960s a number of process control computers were developed (Ware (1965)). At the same time the possibilities for mechanisation of economic data processing received attention. The Central Statistical Administration (TsSU), its powers enhanced by the 1957 management reform which provided for a reorganisation of control on regional instead of ministerial lines, installed mechanical data-processing equipment in a number of machine accounting stations (*mashino-schetnaya stantsiya* – MSS). From a base of 70 MSS in 1957, equipped with about 4,000 machines (presumably fairly primitive punch-card and adding machines) the network grew by 1968 to about 1,000 stations with 35,000 machines (Treml (1972), pp. 24–7). Initially these MSS worked largely on a contract basis for enterprises in their neighbourhood. Later, as we shall see, they played a role as a basis for TsSU's campaign to control the state network of computer centres.

Finally, in the period beginning in 1960, mathematical economics, and more specifically the mathematical formulation of planning problems, enjoyed a revival in the USSR. The history of this revival has been told by a number of authors (Zauberman (1975), Ellman

(1973)). For our purpose its importance was that it made it possible and necessary to use computers for economic decision making at exactly the opposite pole from TsSU's attempts at low-level mechanical data processing, at the level of Gosplan USSR and the Sovnarkhozes or regional economic councils. The Central Economic Mathematical Institute (TsEMI) was formed in 1963 out of a number of previously existing organisations in the field. Its programme of research, outlined by N. P. Fedorenko in 1964, included the design of a state network of computer centres which would serve as the 'technical base' of the system of optimal planning and management which was the main focus of the Institute's research.

Thus at the beginning of the 1960s, conditions had been created in which proposals to use computers for planning and management of the economy would be seriously entertained. But at this stage not much importance was attached to this aspect of economic management. The 1961 Programme of the CPSU devoted a single paragraph to automation, in which management applications were the last to be mentioned (**XXII S'ezd** (1962), p. 220).

2 EARLY PROPOSALS

The first developed proposal for the automation of economic management was made by Berg, Kitov and Lyapunov[2] at the Cybernetics section of an all-Union Conference on Computer Mathematics and Technology held in 1959. The authors considered five primary areas for the application of computers in economic management:

1 the system of national-economic accounting and statistics
2 the system of state planning
3 the system of material-technical supply
4 the financial and banking system
5 the system of transport management.

We can see how ambitious the scheme was from the list of applications under heading (2). These include the preparation and use of input–output tables, a system of price formation, investment efficiency calculations and a set of lower-level optimising calculations (Berg (1961), pp. 87, 89–90).

The authors recommend a gradual implementation of their programme, starting with the installation of computers in large enterprises and government departments and progressing through regional link-ups to the establishment of a unified state network of information and computing centres which would ultimately supply the needs of all organisations in information and data processing. An experimental system to operate in a single region was recommended, with the advantage that 'concentration of Gosplan, Gosbank, TsSU and corresponding *Sovnarkhoz* organs in a single information and computer centre of a given region would ensure more operational contact in work'. The network was intended to amalgamate the separate data-collection systems then functioning.

In 1963 considerable impetus to work in this field was given by a decree of the Central Committee and the Council of Ministers 'On improving the guidance of work on introducing computer technology and automated management systems in the economy'. The text of this decree is not available to me, but one of its important consequences was the foundation of a Chief Administration for the introduction of computers and management systems, within the State Committee of the Council of Ministers for the co-ordination of scientific research work.[3] According to one source the Chief Administration was assigned the following tasks (Makhrov (1974), pp. 12–13):

1 building and installing automated information processing and management systems at all levels of management, from the Statewide level down through ministry and enterprise level systems to the level of controlling technological processes
2 designing high capacity computing systems, suitable for processing economic information
3 building a state network of computer centres servicing local organisations
4 developing coding and classification systems and software
5 preparing recommendations for the education of specialists.

It is not clear which items in this extensive agenda were imposed upon the Chief Administration by the 1963 decree, and which were assigned subsequently. From contemporary discussions it appears that there was little clarity in the proposals, and little agreement about how they were to be realised. In 1964 a joint article by Doroditsyn, Fedorenko and Glushkov[4] considered some organisational problems of establishing a computer grid (Doroditsyn (1964)). The article proposed a three-tier system of computer centres, ranging from a few centres at the highest level, equipped with very powerful computers, to the lowest tier, numbered in thousands and equipped with more modest machines. To build the system a cybernetics industry would be created, and the authors proposed that responsibility for it should be divided among TsEMI, a newly-created Institute of Systems Techniques and the computer industry. The authors specifically ruled out TsSU's Scientific Research Institute (NII TsSU SSSR) as a candidate for the role of reorganising the existing system of primary information on the ground that it was too busy and in no condition to understand the problem in all its complexity. Finally the authors proposed that the Chief Administration for the introduction of computers be given enlarged powers and made responsible for the development and application of computers.

Inevitably the question of the role of a network of computer centres became inextricably mixed up with discussion of the proposed economic reform. The final period of debate over the reform was inaugurated by an important article in *Pravda* by V. A. Trapeznikov[5] (Trapeznikov (1964)). After arguing for certain changes in the Soviet management system, some of which – the capital charge, increased use of profit as an indicator – were subsequently adopted in the reform, Trapeznikov noted: 'In the recent period, a series of articles has been published about the need to establish a network of computer centres for planning the economy. We must in every way support the large-scale use of computers for economic calculations, in which we have considerably fallen behind the leading capitalist countries. However it would be self-deception to think that it is possible with the help of computers alone to solve the problem of optimal planning and management. It must be based on *correct economic criteria which will stimulate the purposeful development of the economy*' (emphasis in original). The influential mathematical economist Nemchinov, in a well-known article supporting reform proposals, attached a similar role to computer centres, as something complementary to the extension of *khozraschet*, or independent accounting at enterprise level. 'Automated electronic systems of management,' he wrote, 'are intended to give priority to directives and the control figures of the national economic plan and simultaneously to promote the broad use of *khozraschet* and economic levers in the form of a system of social funds, prices, profits and credits' (Nemchinov (1964), pp. 84–5). After the announcement of the reform Starovskii, the head of TsSU, argued that it went against the spirit of the new system of management to represent scientific planning as merely carrying out a set of highly centralised calculations, the results of which were dispatched by computer centres to subordinate units (Starovskii (1965)).

In the midst of the uncertainty which characterised the pre-reform period, work continued on a modest scale on the design and use of automated planning and management systems. In 1963 Glushkov's Institute of Cybernetics began the task of developing an automated management system for the L'vov television factory. Nemchinov's Laboratory for the application of mathematical methods in economic research and planning designed an integrated series of matrix models of the input–output type (Pirogov (1963), p. 50; Modin (1963)). The Moscow Sovnarkhoz had a dispatching centre which operated on such a system (Chernyak (1963)). A model was developed by TsEMI showing how, using thousands of computers, the economic planning process could be represented as and solved as a gigantic extremal problem (Pugachev (1964)). But all this scarcely amounted to a design for a state network of computer centres or a unified information system. In the event the delay was advantageous. In 1965 the economy's organisational framework was changed, being restored from a regional to a ministerial basis. A Soviet economist later caustically observed that had lines of communication for a state network of computer centres been laid before the change, they would have had to be pulled up after it, and that before the reform there was no integrated economic framework within which the network would operate (see pp. 45–6 below).

3   THE 1966 DECREE AND ITS CONSEQUENCES

The details of the reform of September 1965 and the simultaneous reorganisation of management are too well-known to need description here (see Zaleski (1967)). What concerns us more closely is the decree of the Central Committee and the Council of Ministers of March 1966, which established the responsibilities of different organisations for developing automated management systems and using computers for planning (Resheniya (1968), pp. 21–7). The allocation of responsibility was as follows:
1 Ministries were charged with establishing automated systems at branch and enterprise level, according to plans approved by Gosplan in conjunction with TsSU and the Ministry of Instrument Building (Minpribor).
2 Minpribor was to be responsible for maintaining technical standards, for the compatibility of the various branch automated

management systems, and for the production of certain computers and peripherals.

3 The Ministry of the Radio Industry (Minradprom) was to be responsible for constructing the state network of computer centres according to TsSU specifications, for the production of computers and peripherals for the system and for software design.

4 TsSU was to be responsible for directing the construction and operation of the network, for laying down the specifications for it jointly with Gosplan, the Academy of Sciences, Minradprom, Minpribor, Gossnab and Gosstroi (the State Committee for Construction), for organising the information system, and for certain other functions.

5 The Academy of Sciences was to be responsible for developing a system of optimal planning, with the assistance of appropriate organisations.

6 Gosplan was assigned responsibility for overall (*svodnyi*) planning of work on the state network and on automated management systems; for overall planning and allocation of computers; for the use of mathematical planning models at Gosplan level and for supervising implementation of the plan for constructing the network.

7 The State Committee on Science and Technology and the State Committee on Standards were assigned certain responsibilities. A division, later a Chief Administration, for computer technology and management systems was created in the former (Makhrov (1974), p. 21.

Plans for the state network were to be prepared by the third quarter of 1966.

The decree had the unfortunate consequence of dividing responsibility for the network so widely and combining so many organisations in work on identical or closely related aspects that it opened the door for dispute over which organisation could claim the major responsibility. As far as production and distribution of hardware is concerned, the decree confirmed a division of responsibility between two producing ministries and three distributing organisations which was later to hamper both the development of computers and the equipment of computer centres. A more important failing was that the phrasing of the decree permitted two organisations, TsSU and Gosplan, to dispute the role of principal organiser of the network. This problem was never really solved until the end of the eighth five-year plan in 1970.

Immediately after the announcement of the reform in September 1965, Starovskii, the head of TsSU, was arguing for an extended role for his organisation in the new conditions (Starovskii (1965)).

The reconstruction of the management of industry does not mean a return to the old pre-Sovnarkhoz order of carrying on statistical work ... Ministries have the opportunity to get statistical data through the unified network of TsSU organs, without having recourse to their own economists and engineers to work out statistical data. In the new conditions state statistics will build a system of accounting in such a way as to provide the central planning organs and ministries with all necessary data on industrial branches while maintaining at the same time regional calculations for local party and government economic organisations.

However TsSU had powerful opponents who doubted its abilities to operate a centralised data processing system. Glushkov and Fedorenko emphasised the failure of TsSU to handle primary data properly and to use the information collected to the full (O rabote (1964), pp. 6, 10). The alternative possibility was for Gosplan to stand at the head of a system of information transfer along the lines established by the 1965 reorganisation of management (i.e. Gosplan, branch, enterprise), relying on TsSU-collected data as a starting point for planning and as a check on plan fulfilment. The argument along these lines was continued for several years in the middle 1960s and was overlaid with the question of whether information should be collected on a ministerial or on a regional basis. TsSU favoured the latter method and use of its re-equipped machine-accounting stations for the purpose; Gosplan preferred a ministerial system.

The dispute was made possible by the ambiguity or contradiction in the 1966 decree. It assigned to TsSU the responsibility for 'accounting for [*uchet*] and planning the work of the computer centres, which will carry out the calculations necessary for the national economy, *irrespective of their department subordination*' (Resheniya (1968), p. 24). What then would be the role of the 'branch systems for planning, accounting, management and data-processing' mentioned in paragraph one of the decree as the responsibility of the ministries? It is possible to conceive a system in which computer centres both relayed information from enterprises to Ministries and carried out the necessary calculations for the latter on a *khozraschet* basis, in the way that MSS worked for enterprises. In such a system the relaying agent would be free from any self-interested motive to distort the data. But in the practice of imperfect organisations it is usually found necessary for the user to be in direct contact with the supplier if necessary information is to be transmitted on time. And it is very doubtful, in any case, if TsSU did in fact collect the right sort of information. A further argument against TsSU is that its leaders were not of the dynamic innovative sort necessary to carry out an important new project like the construction of a national grid of computer centres.

At the same time that this organisational question was in dispute an argument was raging on the more fundamental issue of what the system of economic management should be in the post-reform period. The years between 1965 and 1968 marked the high point of confidence of mathematical economists in the USSR, the period in which a group at TsEMI advanced the claims of their 'constructive' political economy in opposition to the 'descriptive' political economy of their conservative rivals. The 1965 reform had been noticeably conservative, extending the rights of enterprises to only a limited degree; it was to be implemented gradually, and it did little to alter the allocation of authority at the higher levels. But it was noticeable that the reform did contain proposals, not elaborated in Kosygin's speech outlining the reform, for further development at these higher levels. Moreover Kosygin did refer to measures envisaged to raise the scientific level of planning, and a number of exegeses on the reform emphasised the potential role of mathematical methods in the search for an optimum.

Thus although the conservative nature of the reform was a disappointment to TsEMI, some of Kosygin's remarks indicated that further more radical changes were not necessarily forestalled. In some respects the reform created an atmosphere favourable for TsEMI to advance its wide-ranging proposals for a system of optimal functioning of the economy. These relied in the main on multi-level models of iterative plan formation; the plans would later be implemented by decentralised means, using the price mechanism and profit-seeking as the chief incentive.

In relation to the proposals for building a state network of computer centres the implication of TsEMI's approach was that the computer centres would be used chiefly in plan formation at a fairly aggregate level and that the organisational structure of the network would correspond to the manner in which the economy was decomposed in a multi-level planning algorithm. In a discussion of attitudes towards man–machine planning prevalent in the USSR in 1968, Siroyezhin, the Leningrad economist, characterised TsEMI's conception of the role of the state network of computer centres as being 'both of the technique information[6] type and of the economic type' (Siroyezhin (1968), pp. 7–8). Whereas other views emphasised that useful economic results from computer use can be achieved by partial improvement in information-processing techniques, TsEMI attached more importance to a change in the economic mechanism itself. This approach helped to determine TsEMI's attitude on another organisational question concerning the computer network – whether to start implementing the system at the higher or the lower levels in the management hierarchy. Given TsEMI's view, quoted by Siroyezhin, that partial models of enterprise behaviour would yield insignificant results, the Institute naturally favoured an approach which started at the upper levels.

However this view of the role of computers in economic management did not go uncontested. Siroyezhin identified two competing views, one of which he associated with Glushkov's Institute of Cybernetics. 'In all the Institute [of Cybernetics] publications on management automation,' Siroyezhin wrote, 'it is the processing of primary economic data by means of modern computing techniques which is called an automated system of enterprise management. And such systems are applicable to the requirements of virtually any economic system. (Economic reform and the opportunities offered by it are not taken into account here).' Again: 'the essential feature of the ideological base (of the Institute of Cybernetics) is that no major change is involved in the application of electronic computer techniques. Computer systems are created which do not qualitatively transform the management process' (ibid., pp. 6–7).

The third view of the role of the state network of computer centres in the management process was held at this time by the Institute of Automation and Remote Control, under its director V. A. Trapeznikov. If Glushkov favoured an approach to management automation starting at the bottom, or enterprise level, and TsEMI an approach which began with a reorganisation of management at the higher levels, then Trapeznikov proposed an advance on all fronts simultaneously. Viewing management as a struggle against disorder (entropy) and identifying information with the opposite of disorder (negentropy), he saw the need to do battle with disorder at all levels simultaneously, thereby getting the best economic return to investment in management automation (Trapeznikov (1966)).

Thus the 1966 decree introduced more uncertainty into an already fluid situation. There was, in any case, extensive discussion of the wider issue of the development of the reform; the outcome of this would affect the very purposes for which the state network of computer centres should be built. The main organisational question concerning the network, whether Gosplan or TsSU should play the principal role in developing it, was itself related to subsidiary disputes over whether to start at the upper or lower levels of management, and whether the network should be based on regions or ministries. While these issues remained in doubt the haphazard development of automated planning and management systems continued. This had certain advantages. It permitted a period of trial and error during which successful systems, such as the automated system of management for the L'vov Television Factory, were developed. Of course there were costs as well. Even some of the locally successful systems were bound to develop along incompatible lines. But the extent of these losses was restricted by the availability of computers in the USSR which was then very limited. Moreover in 1968 less than one quarter of that restricted amount of computer time was used in economic or management applications.

In August 1966 the USSR Supreme Soviet noted that Gosplan and TsSU were preparing measures to organise a state network of computer centres. A preliminary draft, worked out by TsSU, the Ministry of the Radio Industry and the Academy of Sciences was ready by mid-1967, but after that the design seems to have gone into abeyance until after the XXIV Party Congress in 1971. Meanwhile TsSU was developing its machine accounting stations: they grew in number to 700 in 1967, servicing more than 12,000 organisations and to 1,000 in 1968. In 1966 Gosplan began work on its automated system of planning calculations, and automated management systems were designed for ministries and enterprises. In 1967 the national plan contained for the first time a section for the introduction of computers, and a three-year plan for the installation of automated management systems was prepared in the same year (Lapshin (1977), pp. 90–1). Of the ministry-level systems, that for the Ministry of Instrument Building, named ASU-pribor, was the first to be developed. Conspicuous among enterprise level systems were those for the L'vov TV factory, and for the Frezer factory in Moscow, which was developed by the Ordzhonikidze Engineering-Economic Institute. A number of temporary guidelines were also prepared, covering the design of automated management systems in enterprises of various kinds. By the end of the eighth five-year plan, a total of 417 automated management systems were installed, including 19 branch automated management systems.

4   THE EMERGENCE OF OGAS

The Plenum of the Central Committee of the Communist Party, held in December 1969, put a brake on some of the more adventurous proposals and speculations for an optimally functioning economy. The political background to the Plenum, which was importantly affected by recent events in Czechoslovakia, needs little elaboration here. Brezhnev emphasised in his report the need for Soviet party discipline and for moral rather than material incentives in the economic sphere. At the same time TsEMI's proposals were forcefully attacked by Gosplan officials (Bachurin (1969)). Although this recentralising, or more precisely, anti-decentralising, tendency ran counter to the views of some mathematical economists, paradoxically it made the economic management system if anything more reliant on their techniques and on those of the computer specialists, even if this consequence was not foreseen at the time. Kossov observed in 1971 (Kossov (1971), p. 328):

The December (1969) Plenum of the CC CPSU set the planning authorities the task of raising the quality and operational efficiency of their work by introducing scientifically based methods of planning and decision-taking, and by improving their work in the area of the collection, processing and analysis of information, on the basis of the integrated use of mathematical economic models and computer technology.

This attitude was underlined at the XXIV Party Congress held in April 1971. The essence of the December 1969 decision, Brezhnev observed, was to pose the question of improvement of management as an 'important constituent part of all activity of the party in directing the economy'. He went on: 'Science has substantially enriched the theoretical arsenal of planning, by developing methods of mathematical-economic modelling, systems analysis etc. We must use these methods more widely and establish branch automated management systems more quickly, bearing in mind that in the long-run we must establish the statewide automated system of information collection and processing. This makes it important not only to produce the corresponding technical equipment but also to train a substantial number of qualified personnel' (Materialy (1971), pp. 65, 67–8). In practical terms the Congress set a target of installing as many as 1,600 automated systems of management in the course of the ninth five-year plan. This target would be achieved on the basis of expanding computer production by 2.6 times in the course of the plan (ibid., pp. 174, 176).

The form of words used by Brezhnev in describing the statewide automated system suggested that the disputes recounted above had been largely resolved. This became clearer at an important conference on automated management systems held in Moscow at the end of 1971. The full title of the global system was 'the state-wide automated system for collection, storage and processing of data for national-economic planning, management and accounting', known by the acronym OGAS. Whereas previously the management automation programme was sometimes known as the construction of the state network of computer centres, the new formulation reduced the latter to the role of 'technical base' of the system on a par with a unified system for information transfer. The effect of this was to make the whole project more central to the process of economic management, rescuing it from the marginal status it may have occupied as, so to speak, part of a building programme. The new formulation also implicitly rejected the claim of TsSU to have control over the project as a whole, for while that organisation could plausibly be entrusted with control of computer centres, it could scarcely be responsible for a system which, as we shall see, incorporated automated systems of management for ministries and enterprises, as well as Gosplan's automated system.

The wide-ranging strategy of automation was evident in the architecture of OGAS as revealed at the conference. Scarcely any organisation involved however marginally in economic planning and management was untouched by the design. The most important elements in the system, moving upwards in the structure of management, were: automated systems for the control of technological processes (ASUTP); automated systems of management of enterprise (ASUP); branch automated management systems (OASU); Gosplan's automated system of planning calculations (ASPR); TsSU's automated system of the state statistics (ASGS); and Gossnab's automated system for management of material–technical supply (ASU MTS).[7] A diagram showing basic information flows by connecting lines is given below (figure 1).

It was proposed to establish OGAS in two stages. Initially development would be concentrated on branch and departmental systems and on the highest level systems, and a link would be

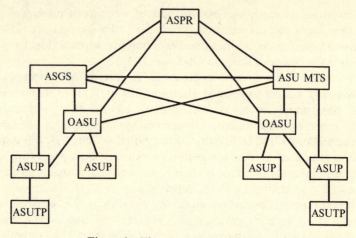

Figure 1   The structure of OGAS

forged between them. The second stage involved the development of regionally based systems and consolidation of all systems into a single whole. Coverage would be progressively extended as more automated systems were brought into use (Zhimerin (1972), p. 13). Effectively the core of OGAS as described at the 1971 conference was the central management link of Gosplan–ministry–enterprise. Regional systems were relegated to a second stage and the automated system of state statistics played a subsidiary role, but one still pressed by TsSU officials (ibid., pp. 13, 105). The conference was followed by a meeting of the interdepartmental council for improving management of the economy.

1971 also saw the establishment of a new organisation intended to co-ordinate activity in the development of OGAS. The new institute, the All-Union Scientific Research Institute on Problems of Organisation and Management, would serve as head (*golovnaya*)[8] scientific organisation in the field of improving economic management and was attached to the State Committee on Science and Technology. Its director, D. G. Zhimerin, a former specialist in power, was first deputy chairman of the committee. Participants at the conference on automated management systems in 1971 were much exercised by problems and failures of co-ordination which had been a feature of the previous five years and which are, in fact, inevitable in a project involving many hundreds of research organisations. However the Institute's powers are limited to research and development, and Gosplan is still empowered, as under the 1966 decree, to plan the installation of computers in the economy and to allocate investment for this purpose. Nor does the institute have power, beyond that of criticism, over the two ministries responsible for computer manufacture, both of which in 1971 emphasised their own importance in the development of OGAS (ibid., pp. 27–41). This question of co-ordination is one to which we shall pay special attention throughout this study. It concerns not only the compatibility of computers and different types of peripheral equipment and software but also the possibility of forging a single overall system out of the several links which are considered in the following chapters.

5 THE NINTH FIVE-YEAR PLAN

As we have seen, the XXIV Party Congress set an ambitious target for the automation of management in the USSR. The initial target of a total of 1,600 automated management systems over the five years to 1975 was broken down and apparently extended after the Congress. According to one source, the target for automated management systems in industry alone became 1,583, compared with 329 in 1966–70. In construction 417 were to be installed (33 in 1966–70); in agriculture 129 (4 in 1966–70); in transport and communications 129, compared with 9 in 1966–70 (Samborskii (1974), p. 79). This revision of the target seems to have taken place before the Conference on ASU held in December 1971.

The implementation of the plan was influenced by a number of changes of circumstances, not all of them foreseen in 1971. One change that was foreseen – was overdue, in fact – was the appearance on the scene of third generation computers. Computers of the M-series, and ES or Ryad computers became available in small numbers from 1972–3, and some of the systems installed or extended after that date incorporated features made possible by the enhanced capacity of third generation machines. At the same time the number of computers available was limited, and the overwhelming majority of systems installed from 1971–5 used second generation series of computers, such as the Minsk 32.

Another change deserves more extensive examination. This was the decree published in April 1973 which required a reorganisation of the industrial management system. The changes altered the circumstances in which the management automation programme would be implemented. At the XXIV Party Congress separate

sections of Brezhnev's speech and of the ninth five-year plan directives were devoted to problems of management. Automation of
management played an important role in these sections, but only
as part of a number of changes and developments in economic
management. Indeed a commentary on the congress by Afanas'ev
noted the danger of exaggerating the impact of automation, observing that social as well as scientific factors play a role: 'management
of society, as of its individual links, is primarily an economic,
socio-political and ideological problem, not a cybernetic, natural
science, technical or other problem' (Afanas'ev (1971), p. 16).

The April 1973 management changes foreshadowed at the 1971
Congress were clearly 'economic and socio-political' rather than
'technical' in nature. The reorganisation required industrial ministries to establish a system of management based on one of two variants:
a two-tier system wherein production *ob'edineniya*, newly formed
where necessary by amalgamation of enterprises, are directly
subordinated to the ministry; or a three-tier system formed by
interposing an industrial *ob'edinenie*, the successor to the *glavk*,
between the ministry and the production *ob'edinenie*.

The amalgamation of enterprises into production *ob'edineniya*
is a feature of both variants. Piecemeal formation of this kind of
ob'edinenie has been continuing since the Sovnarkhoz period.
By 1973 their number amounted to 1,000, accounting for 12%
of industrial output. Industrial *ob'edineniya* are a greater but not
unprecedented departure. *Glavki* in the Ministry of Instrument
Building (Minpribor) were transferred in 1968 to the same status
that industrial *ob'edineniya* are to have under the 1973 changes,
and renamed industrial *ob'edineniya* in 1971. In the case of Minprib-
or the *glavki* were put on a *khozraschet* basis after the change, on
lines similar to the enterprise reform of 1965. Funds were set up
for material incentives for employees, for production development
and for use as reserves; at the same time the rights and responsibilities of the *glavki* in allocating funds among subordinate enterprises
were increased (Mergelov (1972), (1975); Karnovskii (1976)).
This arrangement was, with minor variants, repeated in the 1973
decree, which also provided for a board of directors of the industrial
ob'edinenie to be established consisting of the directors of constituent productive *ob'edineniya* under a ministry-appointed general
manager with the power of veto (Smolinski (1974), p. 28).

Meanwhile the experiment at Minpribor had gone further to
embrace the ministry as a whole. The crucial step was to apply

incentives in the *glavki*, to administrative personnel divorced from the production process. If that were possible, then nothing prevented the ministry being put on a *khozraschet* basis as well. In 1970 this was done. The main features of the change were: greater reliance on five-year planning; financial independence of Minpribor, with a guaranteed annual payment from the ministry to the state budget, irrespective of results; a general extension of the ministry's rights; and the use of an incentive system for ministry personnel. The new system received a favourable assessment at the ministry. In 1972, Drogichinskii, an important Gosplan official, recommended that it be extended to other ministries (Drogichinskii (1972)).

The 1973 decree called for plans to be prepared within six months and for implementation by the end of 1975. The reality was different. Drogichinskii observed in early 1975 that 'the elaboration of general schemes of management has been completed in almost all ministries' (Drogichinskii (1975), p. 8), yet in the spring of that year only eight of twenty-five schemes had been approved, though by mid-1976 twenty-one schemes had been accepted (Ishkov (1976)). A number of difficulties contributed to the delay. In the first place each ministry has its own special features requiring adaptation of the general schemes. Secondly, there is some opposition to the reorganisation. Ministries try to maintain the independence of their enterprises, a deviation permitted by the 1973 decree only in exceptional circumstances. The fact that enterprises producing the same products are often subordinate to different ministries or, if they are within the same ministry, are often dispersed geographically creates serious problems of amalgamation. Moreover ministries are reluctant to reduce employment centrally or to loosen their ties with the industrial *ob'edineniya*, and show a tendency to regard them as rechristened *glavki*.

The programme of management automation was a secondary factor in the decision to make the management reorganisation.[9] The reverse influence is more significant. This is because enterprise-level automated management systems already in existence have had to be redesigned or at least adapted when the enterprise is incorporated in a production *ob'edinenie*.[10] As for the decision to create industrial *ob'edineniya* to replace *glavki*, it is clear that the new system and automation of branch management are by no means incompatible. Indeed, the same ministry, Minpribor, has been chosen as a proving ground both for branch automated management systems and the experiment in ministry-level *khozras-*

chet, a coincidence which supports the proposition that automation of management and the 1973 changes jointly represent a new pattern of Soviet economic planning and management. We return to this point in the concluding chapter.

As noted earlier the 1971 Conference on automated management systems prescribed a two-stage development of the Statewide Automated Systems (OGAS), in which the first stage would be departmental, the second stage regional. In the years since 1971 the regional or territorial aspect has been given progressively more prominence by Soviet writers. Part of the reason for this change of emphasis has been the low level of utilisation of computers in enterprises and organisations in which automated management systems have been installed. Myasnikov, the head of the Chief Division for computers and management systems at the State Committee for Science and Technology argued strongly for computer centres independent of departments, as a means of improving utilisation (Myasnikov (1974), p. 93).

In 1973 Gosplan issued a decree which required its division for planning and installing computers to prepare jointly with TsSU recommendations for setting up as an experiment in 1974–5 three territorial computer centres for joint use, servicing enterprises and organisations of different ministries and using TsSU computer centres as a basis (V Gosplane (1973), p. 158). The Ministry of the Machine Tool Industry seems to have set up a computer centre serving several of its own enterprises within a region (Maksimenko (1974)). Such centres are known as computer centres for collective use (*vychislitel'nyi tsentr kollektivnogo polzovaniya*–VTsKP) or group information and computer centres (*kustovyi informatsionno-vychislitel'nyi tsentr*–KIVTs). The existence of such centres greatly reduces the demand for computers within the economy, and no doubt forms the basis for the forecast that the total number of computers needed in the USSR in the 1980s will not exceed 'several tens of thousands' (Kozlov (1973)). Other writers have estimated that a centralised approach, using a system of computer centres for joint use, will make an enormous saving compared with a decentralised or departmental approach (Samborskii (1974), pp. 81–3).

However the argument for joint use of computer centres goes beyond simple economy in the use of computers. The same authors argue that the Statewide Automated System (OGAS) must not run parallel to nor be superimposed upon departmental systems, but must be a development and extension of them. Forcing the departments and ministries to use the same computer centres is therefore a powerful means of ensuring compatibility and unity in the system as a whole.

The argument for a territorial approach has received backing from Glushkov, Zhimerin and Myasnikov (Glushkov (1973)). The authors draw an interesting parallel between the development of an electricity generation network and of a network of computers. In each case the alternatives are either to develop a connected system or to permit a number of isolated systems to come into being. In each case, they argue, the former variant is the correct one. In a computer system it is more economical in reducing capacity by spreading peak loading, and it ensures compatibility of the component automated management systems.

The structure the authors propose for the Statewide Automated System is illustrated in the following diagram (Figure 2). There are three levels. The highest level comprises State Committees of the USSR Council of Ministers, State Committees attached to the Council and Union Ministries. These have their own computer centres linked to the Chief Computer Centres of OGAS. The second level consists of computer centres of republican automated management systems and territorial computer centres. The third level would be enterprise automated management systems (the proposal was made before the 1973 management changes). These would communicate with their ministry via the territorial computer centre or a special message switching centre (*tsentr kommutatsii soobshcheniya* – TsKS), rather than directly as under present arrangements.

The overall number of computer centres at the territorial level required in this scheme is not stated. Zhimerin has asserted elsewhere that about 200 territorial computer centres for joint use should be built, linked with ministerial and departmental computers (Zhimerin (1974c)). Glushkov proposed the same number in a later article in which he argued that since OGAS is more than just the sum of a number of sub-systems, and since the management system may well change in the course of constructing OGAS, the structure must above all be flexible (Glushkov (1974), pp. 7–8, 13).

In practice there was little flexibility during the ninth five-year plan. Problems of administration and of finance hampered the development of computer centres for joint use. According to Rakovskii, the deputy-Chairman of Gosplan in charge of the

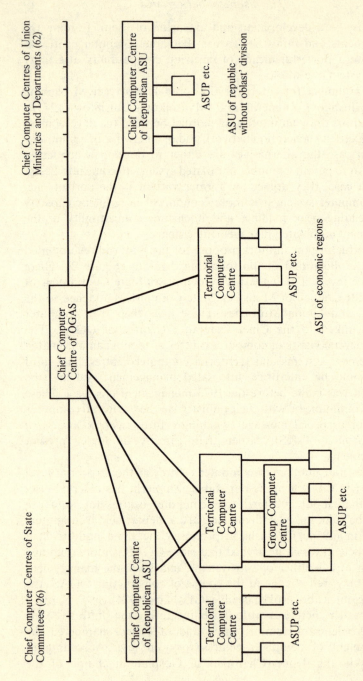

Figure 2 An outline of a possible system of data flows in OGAS
Source: Glushkov (1973), p. 11 (slightly adapted)

Table 1 *Installation of automated management systems in the USSR 1966–78*

	1 1966–70	2 1971–2	3 1973	4 1974	5 1975	6 1971–5 (Plan)	7 1971–5 (Fulfilment)	8 1976–8	9 1966–78
Automated management systems for									
1 Enterprises	151	192	161	229	256	1,800	838	210	1,199
2 Technological production processes	170	94	126	206	193	700	564	590	1,324
3 Territorial organisations	61	96	110	162	263	—	631	180	872
4 Ministries and departments	19	23	22	21	102	212	168	45	232
5 Automated systems for information processing	13	15	17	30	46	—	108	55	176
6 Total	414	420	436	648	860	—	2,309	1,080	3,803

Sources: Columns 1–5, 7–9: *Narodnoe Khozyaistvo SSSR* (various years), *SSSR v tsifrakh* (various years).
Column 6: Zhimerin (1972), p. 11.

Ryad computer project, of the twenty large-scale computer centres for joint use planned for construction in the ninth five-year plan not a single one had been built by the beginning of 1977. Rakovskii attributes the delay to deficiencies in the production of computers (Rakovskii (1977)). For the tenth five-year plan the target has fallen to six (Zhimerin (1978)).

Thus the development of automated systems of management has followed the pattern laid down at the 1971 Conference, rather than the line subsequently promoted by Glushkov, Zhimerin and Myasnikov. The figures for completed automated management systems have been published in statistical handbooks since 1973. The data are presented in the preceding table, together with the targets for the ninth five-year plan. The data for the ninth five-year plan indicate near-fulfilment of the plan for ministry and departmental systems, and substantial underfulfilment (slightly less than half) of the plan for enterprise systems. However in the last case the 1973 management reorganisation has altered administrative divisions at the level of enterprises, and this makes comparisons of targets and achievements of doubtful significance. Bearing this in mind it is clear that substantial progress was made up to the end of 1975, even if, as we shall see later, some of the data may be questioned.

Since 1976, the pace seems to have slackened. The directives of the XXV Party Congress of April 1976 contained an instruction to ensure further development and increase in effectiveness of automated management systems and computer centres, subsequently combining them into a unified statewide system for the collection and processing of information for accounting, planning and management (Materialy (1976), p. 174). In May 1978 a second conference on the use of computers for management was held, attended by a Politburo member A. P. Kirilenko. A number of important systems begun in the years 1966–75 have first come into operation since that time. Generally however the focus of attention has moved from automated management systems and work continues now in a more routine way.

After this historical outline, the succeeding chapters examine the automated systems in more detail. Chapters 3 and 4 discuss the automated systems developed by Gosplan and Gossnab. Chapter 5 is devoted to ministry systems, and Chapter 6 to automated systems operating at enterprise level. Chapter 6 also includes a note on process control systems, though less attention is given to these than to automation of economic and administrative functions. First however we consider a number of different approaches to the issue of how computers affect management and planning in a socialist economy.

2

THE IMPACT OF COMPUTERS ON PLANNING AND MANAGEMENT: SOME APPROACHES

If we consider the problems of planning and managing the economy in very broad terms, then we might set up the objective of maximising the output of the economic system, defined in some appropriate way, minus the costs of running the system. (This approach is taken in Hurwicz (1972a) p. 299.) Of course such a statement of the problem is both imprecise and controversial: imprecise because an operational way of evaluating output has not been proposed and controversial because it is quite plausible to include the mechanism under which the economy operates ('competition', 'planned economy') as one of the variables on which the assessment is made. Indeed Koopmans and Montias, in their enumeration of goals of an economy, include for socialist countries (in their terminology, East) a preference for central direction, and for capitalist countries (West) a preference for freedom from central control (Eckstein (1971) p. 47), and they in their turn are basing their inclusion of the features of the economic mechanism itself as an independent objective on the explicit statements of numerous economic and political writers. However, by overlooking these objections we can use the above formulation as a starting point from which to consider the effects of widespread introduction of computers and data processing equipment into planning and management of the economy. Computerisation may affect the objective in both its aspects. Clearly the introduction of an enormously greater capacity for computation and data-handling will vary the costs of running the pre-computer management system. (In fact some evidence from both Western and Soviet experience suggests that the variation would be upwards.) But it will also expand the set of possible mechanisms to include those for which both output and costs will be different from pre-computer days.

This immediately raises the issue of what Soviet specialists have called metaplanning, the selection of and, where necessary, the transfer to a new planning and management system (Problemy (1974) p. 33). This involves establishing a system of hierarchical relations within the framework of which exchanges of information, computations, and finally the material processes of production and distribution take place.

The object of enquiry and depth of treatment in the metaplanning process will vary according to circumstances: the planning and management process in a factory, a ministry or the entire national economy may be considered. An organisational change or repartitioning of the economy may lead the investigator to ignore procedures internal to some newly established unit. This process of re-examining and recasting the economic system takes place in response to changes in the technologies of production or of planning or to changes in tastes. Thus it is common for the 1965 economic reform in the USSR to be explained in part as a response to the proliferation of information flows as production processes became more complex and interrelated and consumer demand became more diverse.

There is a feature of the large-scale introduction of computers, a change in the technology of planning, which makes it especially natural to aim for a description of changes in the system of management that computerisation brings about. Computers need explicit instructions: they cannot rely on intuition built up by a planner or manager over a period of years. The way in which a computer reaches a decision may be described quite unambiguously, and when a series of computers is involved, communicating with one another in the management process, we should have a much more precise idea of what is going on than we would if the same decisions were made on the intuition and memory of human planners.

We shall see that it is precisely this need for formalisation which rules out ideas such as that of 'perfect computation', and ensures the continued participation of human agents in what is essentially a man–machine system. We shall also examine the relevance to the current discussion in the USSR on the impact of computerisation of two approaches: namely, the planning algorithms developed in the 1960s for implementation on computers, and statistical communication and information theory. It is my argument that recognition of the limited utility of these approaches, which may spring in part from reluctance to accept the changes they would entail, has led those engaged in introducing computers into the economy to adopt the pragmatic approach which is discussed in the final section.

1   THE PLANNING ALGORITHMS APPROACH

This section is devoted to a discussion of formal planning procedures, and to assessing their suitability as a basis for restructuring the planning and management system to incorporate computers. It scarcely need be said that this approach has been the inspiration of much of the discussion of the automation of planning and management in the USSR. Several authors or groups of authors have made proposals using this basic approach, but the most influential has been a proposal originating from TsEMI, under the name of the 'system of optimal functioning of the economy' (SOFE). (See Fedorenko (1968).)

The concept of SOFE has gone through various changes since it first appeared in the middle 1960s, and its elaboration is still provisional or incomplete. Essentially SOFE is a system which seeks to treat the process of compiling and implementing the plan as a whole. At its simplest, preparation of the plan would be done by a decomposition algorithm, yielding (together with a solution for quantities) a set of prices which could be used for implementation of the plan through a market with plan executants having profit as an incentive. This basic scheme can be supplemented by more elaborate procedures for compiling the plan, some of which are discussed in Chapter 3 below, but the key element in the stage of plan compilation is a computer-based planning procedure.

However, this section is devoted to a discussion of planning algorithms in general and not to SOFE in particular. There is no necessary connection between compiling a plan using a formal decomposition method and implementing it through a market. Accepting one plank of SOFE does not entail acceptance of the other. As a result the detailed description of particular models specifically presented as part of SOFE is postponed until the next chapter, which also gives an account of Gosplan's objections to SOFE. This section is devoted to a discussion of planning algorithms in general and an examination of their usefulness and limitations; an account of the Soviet debate in particular is deferred until the next chapter.

Several writers have noted and regretted the gulf existing between two groups of investigators of economic mechanisms, the one group formulating abstract models of economic systems, the other studying existing systems. The reasons for this gulf are worth examining, and I shall try to do so using a general formalised description of the process of planning and management, which is due to Hurwicz (Hurwicz 1972b); this gives a context for a discussion of certain salient features of an economic mechanism. I shall then attempt, using the language of Hurwicz's description, to outline and examine three planning algorithms and the current practice of annual production and supply planning in the USSR.

In the model of the economic process there are two phases: first an exchange of messages by economic agents, and second the translation of messages into plans of action and into decisions which are then implemented.

To define the first phase we need to specify the language in which the exchange of messages takes place. Hurwicz notes a range of complexity increasing from the price vectors of the perfect competition model to the elaborate exchanges of technological information required in some models of centralised planning. (Ideally our specification would be even more complex, including, for example, such 'messages' as hints of possible compromises in bargaining situations, a complication which goes beyond even the exchange of information in probabilistic terms.)

With a language established we move on to the exchange of messages. Labelling the agents $1, \ldots, n$, at each stage $s (s = 0, 1, \ldots, T)$ an n-tuple of messages is sent out. We need to establish how the initial message, m_0, and all subsequent messages are formed. We suppose them to be formed on the basis of a response function f_s^i, $i = 1, \ldots, n$, $s = 1, \ldots, T$ depending both on previous messages and on the agents' perception of the environment. Agent i has a partial knowledge e_i of the total environment e.

The sequential process of message formation can be expressed in the following system of equations:

$$m_s^i = f_s^i(m_{s-1}, m_{s-2} \ldots m_0, e_i), i = 1, \ldots, n; s = 1, \ldots, T \qquad (1)$$

$$m_0{}^i = f_0{}^i(e_i), i = 1, \ldots, n \qquad (2)$$

However, as Hurwicz is quick to emphasise, this is not the end of the process. 'The message n-tuple m_T produced in the terminal stage serves as a basis for decisions as to actions to be taken. The language of the terminal message may or may not be that of possible actions. If not one must, as it were, decode the terminal message. Ideally the decoded terminal message should provide for a feasible action plan but in many cases it may turn out to be a set of mutually inconsistent action proposals, which we may call the paper plan' (ibid., p. 93).

Denoting the decoding function by d, we have the relation:

$$b = d\,(m_T) \qquad\qquad (3)$$

Finally, the real plan, a, emerges by a transformation of the paper plan, b:

$$a = r\,(b) \qquad\qquad (4)$$

The last two equations can be condensed to

$$a = \Phi(m_T) \qquad\qquad (5)$$

an expression which Hurwicz calls the outcome function. Most planning procedures are concerned, as their name suggests, with the process as far as the decoding function. They ignore the implementation stage expressed in the transformation of plan into actuality.

We now consider certain important aspects in which planning procedures may differ:

Language and message space

Typical examples of 'languages' are those of production quotas, resource allocations or prices. Other more complicated languages include that in which a firm's whole production set is transmitted to a Central Planning Board. There is no reason why the language of successive messages should be the same; two instances where this is not the case appear below.

The message space indicates the length of any message and may, of course, vary between messages. Restrictions on the message space have been discussed as a means of defining the concept of informational decentralisation. Those processes have been defined as informationally decentralised which restrict messages to vectors whose dimensionality is the same as that of the commodity space, a restriction based on the properties of the perfectly competitive model. (The weaknesses of this definition are discussed in Hurwicz (1969), p. 515.) Some messages have the additional property of relaying information of a directive nature. This property relates to the different concept of decentralisation of authority. (See p. 200 note 1 below.)

The response function

This has two aspects: freedom of choice of response function and properties of response functions. An agent may be free to choose his own response function from those naturally available to him, or he may suffer restrictions from other agents on his choice, up to and including restriction to a single behaviour rule. (In some models it is assumed that all agents voluntarily follow such a rule as maximisation of utility, and this assumption may then be used to demonstrate, for example, the difficulties occasioned to perfect competition theory by the existence of public goods.) Not all agents need be equally restricted, and restrictions may be imposed by diktat or sustained by a system of incentives.

Mechanisms may also differ in the arguments entering into the response functions. Hurwicz distinguishes first-order, finite-order and infinite-order response functions. First-order functions depend only on the immediately preceding messages and may therefore be written:

$$m_s^i = f_s^i(m_{s-1}, e_i), \quad i = 1, \dots, n$$
$$s = 1, 2, \dots, T \tag{6}$$

The distinction between finite and infinite-order functions is of relevance if we want to define as informationally centralised any process in which one agent acquires full knowledge of the environment of all other agents. Infinite accumulation of messages may bring about such a situation, regardless of any restrictions on message size. Moreover, the order of the response function influences the costs of the process by determining the memory capacity needed by each agent.

Response functions may be the same at all stages (except the first) or may differ. Special cases of processes involving response functions of the second category are those with cyclical response functions such as are found in models of multi-level planning. The simplest case is that in which two fixed response patterns alternate as in two-level planning so that

$$f_s^i = f_{s-2}^i, i = 1, 2, \dots, n$$
$$s = 3, 4, \dots, T \tag{7}$$

More complex patterns may occur when there are three or more levels.

The decoding function

Properties of this function can reflect relationships of sub- and super-ordination or of autonomy. According to Hurwicz the ith unit has autonomy if:

$$b^i = d^i(m_T^i) \tag{8}$$

In contrast we speak of a centre, 1, and subordinates i $(i = 2, \ldots, n)$, if

$$b^i = d^i(m_T^1) \tag{9}$$

(In addition, other conditions must be fulfilled: the decoding functions may not be independent of m_T and m_T^1 may not be dictated by m_{T-1}^i, i.e. it must be sensitive to e_1).[1]

Incentive systems and enforcement

On the theoretical side the problem of enforcement has been prominent since early discussions of Lange's proposed model of market socialism, which lacks any obvious method for inducing managers of firms to behave as the model requires them to, short of detailed supervision by the centre, which would destroy the decentralisation property. The question is treated at some length by Hurwicz who shows that in certain environments (characterised by a small number of agents) particular mechanisms may be incentive-incompatible as it will be in the interests of agents to falsify their tastes or their production possibilities (Hurwicz (1972a), pp. 320–34).

These problems cause little surprise to those familiar with Soviet planning practice. The problems of enforcement there are treated below. For the moment we notice its two related aspects: enforcement of response functions laid down from above, and enforcement of plan instructions derived from the 'decoding' of the final message from the centre.

We now consider four specific planning processes.

Kornai–Liptak two-level planning[2] The response functions are cyclical in character involving a dialogue between the centre, agent 1, which issues message 0 and even-numbered messages, including the final message, and the branches, agents $2, \ldots, n$, which issue odd-numbered messages. The environment observed by the centre comprises certain upper-level constraints restricting the whole economy. Agents $2, \ldots, n$ observe $e_2, \ldots, e_n$, the respective lower-level constraints which apply to them alone. The language of even-numbered messages is that of vectors of resource flow, of dimensionality equal to that of the upper-level constraints. The language of the odd-numbered messages is that of price vectors, of the same dimension.

The initial response function is either an arbitrary allocation by the centre of centrally constrained resources among the branches, or it may be last year's allocation. The branch response functions yield messages which are the shadow prices of centrally constrained resources, found with the solution of branch linear programming problems, with values of centrally constrained resources as given in the previous message. The centre, on the basis of these messages, redistributes its resources. Response functions of the branches are first-order processes, while the centre recalls earlier messages.

The decoding function specifies branch output levels as the solutions of branch programming problems solved on the basis of the final distribution of central resources contained in m_T, the final message from the centre.

Dantzig–Wolfe decomposition algorithm (Dantzig (1961)) The division of agents into centre and branches, the cyclic quality of response functions, and respective observations of environment by centre and branches is the same as in the Kornai–Liptak process. The language of successive messages is reversed: m_0 and even-numbered messages sent by the centre are vectors of prices of centrally constrained resources; odd-numbered messages sent by the branches are the quantities of those resources which would be demanded at the prices in the previous message, obtained by the solution of branch linear programming problems. Odd-numbered functions are, therefore, first-order processes. But the centre's even-numbered messages, which are products of a response function which recalculates centrally-constrained resource prices on the basis of demands expressed in the previous message, are not first-order: they depend on all previous odd-numbered messages.

The final message m_T (T even) gives output targets to all branches, and is decoded by the branches as such. Implementation is not considered, but it is worth noticing that the plan is probably not sustainable by a price system (Baumol (1964) pp. 15–17).

Weitzman's model of iterative multi-level planning with production targets (Weitzman (1970)) Again we have cyclic response functions with a dialogue between centre and branches. The latter, agents $2, \ldots, n$, observe their own production sets and progressively transmit more information about them to the centre, agent 1.

The initial message m_0 is an allocation by the centre of production targets, calculated by solving a programming problem incorporating as constraints the centre's original, and by assumption optimistic, assessment of branch production possibilities. Each branch replies (odd-numbered messages) by scaling down its quota to a feasible level and by transmitting to the centre that feasible point and the tangent to its production set at that point. (The production set is assumed to be convex.) The centre's second and subsequent messages are production quotas found as the result of further solutions of its original problem, now incorporating the restrictions on branch production possibilities implicit in the branches' successive messages. The language of even-numbered messages is thus that of vectors of production targets; odd-numbered messages are output vectors, supplemented by vectors of relative prices (the tangent to the production set). The procedure stops if all branches transmit to the centre the message that production targets received in the previous message are feasible. The final message m_T is a reiteration of these feasible production quotas, to be decoded as an instruction to produce these outputs. Whether the process converges in a finite number of steps depends on properties of branch production sets and on the precise method of scaling down infeasible production quotas.

It is an interesting feature of this procedure that it was designed to capture properties of actual planning procedures in centrally planned economies, with the qualification that 'needless to say, a theoretical study of this sort cannot purport to reflect planning as it is practiced in any real organisation' (ibid., p. 51). Yet Portes has noted an important descriptive failure: each branch is assumed to return to the centre a series of efficient counter-proposals on the frontier of its production set, yet we know from many sources of the tendency for lower-level units to maintain a 'safety margin' by returning proposals strictly within their production possibilities (Portes (1971), p. 423). The strength of this criticism is partly mitigated when we consider another deviation of the model from reality. The model yields a feasible plan while in reality enterprises may only conceal their true capabilities in order to be able to fulfil inconsistent plans which are the product of the present inadequate planning procedures.

Soviet annual production and supply planning For comparison purposes, a simplified account of the most important aspect of

Soviet annual planning is given. The relations of super-ordination and sub-ordination of the agents involved are much more complex, information flows are far more numerous and specification of planners' or other agents' response functions presents great difficulties.

The sequence of forming the plan of production and material–technical supply of an industrial enterprise is shown in Figure 3, which illustrates 1972–3 procedure (Makhnova 1973). The figure gives a highly simplified representation of actual practice, ignoring, for example, complications arising from which organisation is charged with distribution of particular commodities (see Chapter 4 below). But it does give a starting point for considering the complexity of planning practice.

The language of the planning process is that of vectors of output targets or enterprise counter-proposals (on the production side) and of input requirements or allocations (on the supply side). The message space is reduced through aggregation at upper levels in the hierarchy. Prices appear in messages, if at all, only at stage 7 of the supply (upper) section of the figure, when contracts are exchanged between supplier and customer.

We consider only the response function of enterprises at stages 2, 3, and 4 of the production planning process. What arguments are likely to enter into the response functions? Obvious candidates are the output targets expressed in the control figures sent down from above, the production possibilities of the enterprise, the bonus structure, the desired safety margin of the enterprise, recollections of the course of the planning process in recent years and expectations of the future course of this year's planning process. Supply planning is the subject of an equally complex system of message exchanges predicated upon non-formalisable response functions.

Two related features of the process are specially noteworthy: (1) indents are initially submitted on the basis of preliminary output targets and are not usually corrected as targets are altered. This practice is a guarantee of ill co-ordinated supply and production planning and inevitably influences the response functions of enterprises. (2) Consequently the final stage of the production planning process, in which the last message, 10, is 'decoded' by the enterprise as a production target, yields an infeasible paper plan which is subsequently adapted, corrected, ignored or circumvented in the actual production process. The same goes for the supply plan (witness the *tolkachi*). A further complication is shown by 11 in

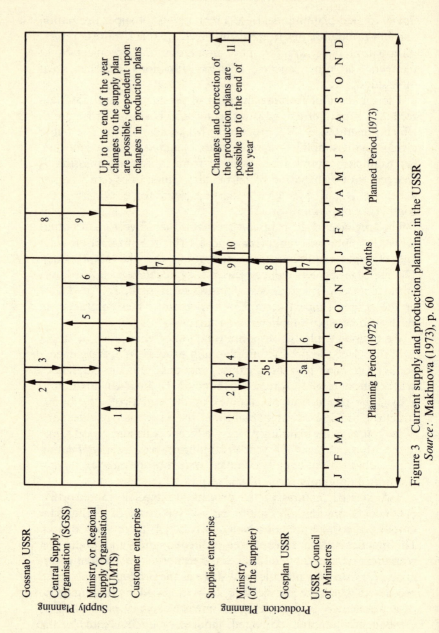

Figure 3 Current supply and production planning in the USSR
Source: Makhnova (1973), p. 60

The procedure for forming production and supply plans for an industrial enterprise (based on practice in 1972–3).

A   *The production plan*
1   Control figures for basic products are issued.
2,3,4 Variants of the plan are prepared and corrected.
5a   The Ministry's draft plan goes to the USSR Council of Ministers by 10 July.
5b   A copy of the Ministry's draft goes to Gosplan USSR by 10 July.
6   A draft of the plan worked out by the ministries is submitted by Gosplan USSR to the USSR Council of Ministers by 15 August.
7   The Decree of the USSR Council of Ministers on the plan for the coming year is issued by 15 December.
8   Gosplan USSR hands down the production plan to ministries by 25 December.
9   Targets for raw materials savings and norms of expenditure of raw materials are issued by 1 January.
10   The plan is passed down to enterprises by 10–15 January.
11   The final version of the plan.

B   *The plan for material–technical supply*
1   Indents (*zayavki*) are collected for centrally distributed commodities.
2   Indents are aggregated.
3   Preparatory distribution plans are issued.
4   Allocations are notified.
5   Specifications are submitted.
6   Orders (*naryady*) for shipment are issued.
7   Contracts are concluded between customer and supplier.
8,9   Final allocations are notified under the approved plan for material–technical supply.

Note: Some of the early stages of production planning are not included in the figure.

the figure: the final corrected plan may only be available after it has (or has not) been fulfilled.

Having counterposed a simplified version of planning practice with some well-known formal planning procedures, we can now examine the problems of adapting the former to the latter. First, however, it is worth noting that Soviet assessments of the formal processes outlined above have often been favourable, and the conclusions drawn from them have been far-reaching. The point is illustrated by the following quotation from an economist then at TsEMI, taken from a discussion of methodological problems of controlling complex (S-) systems (Problemy (1970a), p. 93).

Besides, the application of mathematics in economic research has shown that here a most important role is played by the use of mathematics as an instrument of control: interpretation of the algorithm gives a mode of functioning of the system. Such an application of mathematics in economic research has a most important methodological significance. It shows that in the limit it is possible to go over to establishing a deductive theory of S-systems, based on their strict mathematical analysis.

Soviet enthusiasm for such models reached a peak in the late 1960s, with the publication of a book edited by Fedorenko, the Director of TsEMI. The national economic planning mechanism proposed there is, as Dr Ellman notes, a three-level tâtonnement process in both quantities and prices. He goes on to argue that such proposals were rightly rejected by the Soviet government as being of doubtful 'feasibility, desirability and acceptability' (Ellman (1971), p. 161).

If we examine the reasons for this official scepticism we will also gain some insight into the difficulties faced by Soviet specialists trying to devise changes in the planning and management process made appropriate by the widespread use of computers. These relate to the difficulty of establishing the planning process as an optimal problem, the difficulty of co-ordinating the structure of management of the economy and the planning process, and the difficulty of grappling with the complexity of the existing planning system.

We should straightaway acknowledge certain technical drawbacks of the planning algorithms discussed. Convergence to the optimum may be a doubtful or lengthy procedure; should the process be interrupted before an optimum is reached the resulting plan may not be feasible; there may not be monotonic improvements in successive iterations. The preparation of the plan may be an enormously costly business, requiring large computational and data-transmission facilities. (All these points are made in Portes (1971).) These are important objections, but if we take a long-term view of the development of computational equipment, we may reasonably expect technical problems of feasibility to be overcome. Accordingly we shall concentrate here on other more fundamental difficulties in the way of using such procedures in planning practice.

First of all there is the question of goals. The national economic planning interpretation of the decomposition algorithms, as indeed any formulation of the problem susceptible to mathematical programming, assumes certain goals at the national level. Yet how are these goals to be selected? There is, of course, a voluminous literature on this subject. Leibkind in his classification of national planning models lists sixteen goals, ranging from the achievement of maximum labour productivity in the last year of the plan to maximisation of rents on the use of land and labour resources (Fedorenko (1972a), p. 237). Kornai has even argued that it is incorrect to see the planning process as a standard optimisation problem, preferring to look at it as a process of compromise between loosely expressed aspirations and imprecisely known possibilities, a process more likely to result in an acceptable than an optimal plan (Kornai (1970)).

More recent Soviet thinking on the question of goals has emphasised the construction of the so-called tree of goals. Social goals, stated very broadly, are broken down into their constituent parts, which themselves are successively sub-divided. Establishing the tree of goals is part of an approach to economic planning developed by TsEMI and named the 'system of integrated planning' (SKP). The breakdown of goals is accompanied by an analysis of resources, and programmes are devised which use particular resources and satisfy particular goals in varying degrees. Examination of alternative programmes precedes the construction of the plan. The system has been proposed as the methodological basis of the automated system of planning calculations (ASPR) which is being designed to fulfil the planning functions of Gosplan USSR and the republican Gosplans. A fuller account of this proposal is given in Chapter 3. It is evident, though, that the more flexible and realistic approach to the selection of national economic objectives contained in SKP is not compatible with the simple planning algorithms outlined above, though the latter may be of use at later stages of the process.

A second point which can be made is that the planning algorithms are incomplete in that they are only a second stage in the planning process. The first stage is the partitioning of the economy into agents who will then act in the planning process in accordance with the algorithm. This first stage is important. Portes has noted that 'planners in a centrally planned economy have a great degree of latitude in this regard. ... They are relatively free to reshuffle ministries, dissolve or create industrial associations, break up or amalgamate enterprises and reorganise the hierarchy' (Portes (1971), p. 425).

A few attempts have been made in Soviet literature to define and solve the problem of forming a hierarchy of management in ways which link the twin problems of structure and operation of the system. However attempts to formulate the two problems together have been sparse and either impractically abstract or, where concrete, inadequately formulated. The best Soviet planners can aspire to is some kind of intuitive groping for a satisfactory solution to the problem of finding a hierarchy, which must take into account not only changes in the technologies of planning and production but also general social aims. As an illustration, some authors have cited the increasing use of computers for management as one of the factors influencing the decision to adapt the management hierarchy by the 1973 management changes (Bachurin (1975b), p. 10). From this standpoint the highest level organisations were able, as it were, to legislate out of existence thousands of agents in the planning process. Of course a simple repartitioning of the economy into less fine units does not eliminate the need for many of the planning calculations necessary before the change; this would require a change in the planning procedure as well. But after such a repartitioning the planners can confine their attention to a smaller part of the process. This example is clearly a far cry from a proper theoretical formulation and so far little progress has been made in jointly determining the partitioning of the economy and the planning algorithm. The algorithms discussed above offer no guidance on this issue.

The third and most fundamental reason for scepticism of planning algorithms is that they do not, nor are they intended to, do justice to the complexities of a centrally-planned economy. There is a parallel between the centrally-planned economy and its representation by a planning algorithm and a capitalist economy and its representation in the general equilibrium analysis of perfect competition. The latter relationship is examined at some length by Kornai (Kornai (1971)). Some of his arguments are adapted in what follows.

Let us consider the system of information flows current in Soviet planning and management practice. Three aspects are of special interest: overlapping of planning procedures in the time dimension, the interconnection of planning procedures for different functions, and the apparently irrational multiplication of information flows.

Ignoring the long-term (15–20 years) general plans, there are three main time dimensions – five-year planning, annual planning and operational regulation (over periods less than one year).

Each of them has its own function in the planning and management process and each has, therefore, its own appropriate set of procedures.

We can illustrate the interlocking of plans covering different time periods, and the different functions they fulfil, by the example of a particular industrial ministry, the Ministry for Instrument Building, Means of Automation and Control Systems (*Minpribor*). This ministry is chosen because, among other reasons, we have fairly detailed knowledge of the planning procedures adopted in its branch automated management system (ASU-pribor), described in Chapter 5 below. The five-year plan is for investment planning purposes and intended to identify the optimal way of producing a given target output in the final year of the plan, by selection from a list of investment possibilities, some of which are mutually exclusive. Data are collected and processed centrally for a highly aggregated bundle of commodities. The annual plan serves the different function of distributing output targets among enterprises (or *ob'edineniya*) on the basis of detailed information on enterprise capabilities. The extent of aggregation and the degree of central-isation of the calculation are quite different from those in five-year planning. Finally, operational control consists in the correction of errors in the annual plan and of mishaps in the supply process. Since the functions of planning in the Ministry for different time scales are so very different we can expect no single planning proced-ure to be appropriate for all of them. The conclusion applies *a fortiori* when we consider planning links both higher and lower than the branch.

The second aspect can be dealt with more quickly. We have already noted in the case of supply and production planning the complexities which arise from separate and simultaneous treatment of the several functional aspects of preparing the annual plan. Of course, production planning plays the dominant role in enter-prise annual plan construction, but other sections of the plan, covering for example the financial side of enterprise activity, are prepared in a way which makes them not merely derivative from the production plan. In short, the complexities are such that it is difficult even to track down the process of plan construction, let alone adapt it to a planning algorithm without losing large chunks of the existing system.

The third line of argument parallels that of Chapter 5 of Kornai (1971). It is a common observation that far too much information is collected in the Soviet Union. It is not uncommon to find estimates for the proportion of redundant information as high as 80 or 90%. Before accepting this criticism entirely it is worth while considering the possible benefits of collecting apparently redundant information. The first is the elimination of accidental human error. The second is the elimination of deliberate misrepresentation. We well know the inadequacies of the Soviet incentive system and the encouragement it gives for distortion or misreporting. Part of the multiplication of information flows may be put down to an attempt to enforce official procedures and exercise double surveillance over lower-level units. 'It may be assumed that in an economy which is also composed of units functioning unreliably themselves, multiplication of information is both *necessary and useful*. Too much information will obviously not be necessary. It is however certain that the operation of a system with "maximum information thriftiness", relying on a single type of information flow, would soon get stuck' (ibid., p. 74).

These questions of a rational information structure are dealt with in more detail below. It is not my intention here to justify the existing system of information but merely to indicate certain features of the system which may be related to the inadequacy of the incentive system and enforcement rules. The same observations will apply in one form or another to any system which is not truly incentive-compatible.

The contents of this section can be summarised as follows. A language for describing planning systems has been established and used to define three planning algorithms with varying claims to descriptive accuracy and a simplified version of the existing annual planning system in the USSR. Arguments have been adduced to show the gulf between the existing system and the algorithms. The absence of an explicit objective function makes it impossible to define the planning process as an optimising problem. The existing system is multi-facetted in both the time and the functional dimensions, since different time periods require different planning procedures and equally the many functional aspects of existing planning practice cannot easily be integrated into an all-embracing single process. These many facets are not represented in the planning algorithms. Finally the problem of enforcement imposes certain limitations on the choice of a planning procedure. For these reasons Soviet specialists have not been able, or have been unwilling, to derive much inspiration from formal planning procedures in their adaptation of the existing system to large-scale computer-isation. We now turn to a less ambitious and piecemeal approach, attempts to calculate the costs and value of separate messages in the planning process.

2 THE CONTRIBUTION OF INFORMATION THEORY

Many of the problems discussed above arise from the oversimplifi-cations of the planning algorithms. Attempts to incorporate the greater complexity observed in actual planning experience led naturally to the adoption of certain concepts employed in cyber-netics, such as system, control and information. A full account of these developments is not possible or appropriate here. Instead I describe a particular approach to the analysis of information in planning which, though by no means so influential as the approach outlined above, nonetheless had a number of adherents and seemed to some to be of direct application in the design of computerised management systems. Special analysis of information flows for planning began in 1963, when a seminar was held in Moscow under the chairmanship of Nemchinov (Sistemy (1967)), but most of the work to be discussed below on the value of information was done in the late 1960s and early 1970s.

Much Soviet work in this area has been concerned with attempts to exploit the convenient body of theory concerned with the quantity of information contained in a message, to identify that quantity with the value of information, and then to introduce rationality into the information system by a cost–benefit analysis: the value of a message and the costs associated with its transmission would be compared and the continued existence of the information channel would depend on the results of this comparison.

The theory appealed to is Shannon's measure of information, which defines information as follows:

$$\text{Information received with a message} = \frac{\text{probability ex post}}{\text{probability ex ante}}$$

where probability ex post is the probability of the event after the message has been received and the probability ex ante is the probabil-ity before receipt of the message (Theil (1967), p. 10).

A special case occurs where the probability ex post is equal to 1. Then the information content of the message, $h(x)$, is conventionally defined as:

$$h(x) = \log \frac{1}{x}$$

$$= -\log x \qquad (11)$$

where x is the probability ex ante. It is customary to take two as the logarithm base. Then the information content is expressed in binary digits or bits.

Now we can consider the expected information in a message. We consider a set of n events, $E_1, \ldots, E_n$, mutually exclusive and exhaustive, occurring with probabilities $x_1, \ldots, x_n$. The expected information content $H(x)$ is given by.

$$H(x) = \sum_{i=1}^{n} x_i h(x_i) \qquad (12)$$

where $h(x_i) = -\log x_i$

Therefore:

$$H(x) = -\sum_{i=1}^{n} x_i \log x_i \qquad (13)$$

Using this measure it is easy to prove, for example, that uncertainty is at its greatest with equi-probable outcomes.

Can these concepts be applied to the planning and management process? Obviously, the Shannon results do show, if demonstration were needed, that there is no point in transmitting the same data twice. (We are assuming here that the information is known to be accurate and that the channel is non-distorting.) But we also note that no consideration is given to the question of whether the information is necessary to the receiver. As Maiminas puts it: 'In Shannon's theory it is assumed that the information transmitted through the channel from the source to the receiver is needed by the receiver. For this reason basic attention is paid in the theory to the inter-relation of the signal and the channel of communication in order to ensure transmission in an optimal manner of information known to be necessary'. But we are interested 'in the relation of the message and its receiver', or more precisely, 'the use of the message by its receiver' (Maiminas (1971), p. 246). The author gives two examples of cases where a message may be needed by various receivers yet be of enormously different importance. First, a weather forecast is transmitted to the directors of an agricultural enterprise, a pickling factory and a trolley-bus park.

In the second the director receives two messages containing the same quantity of information: 'the factory has over-fulfilled its profit plan by 5%' and 'the worker Ivanov has over-fulfilled his processing norm by 5%'.

Can anything be salvaged from the theory? Various attempts have been made. One involves an effort to get an ordering of information values by establishing the sequence in which simultaneously transmitted messages are selected – an impractical experimental procedure, but one which has analogies with the theory of consumer demand. Yasin extends this analogy by considering desirable qualities of a message other than the quantity of information contained therein: 'As a first approximation, the following properties may be proposed for inclusion in a list of desirable properties of data: (a) reliability, (b) urgency, (c) timeliness, (d) ease of perception, (e) degree of content' (*soderzhatel'nost* – a property reflecting the possibility of interpreting one piece of data in conjunction with another in such a way that the whole is greater than the sum of the parts) (Yasin (1971), p. 392). The five properties are said to reduce to two: (a) and (c), and the trick is then to minimise the sum of the costs of achieving a given degree of timeliness and reliability and the penalties for late arrival of information and inaccuracy (see also Zherebin (1968) and Issledovanie (1968), pp. 99–107).

In measuring the informativeness or quantity of information in a message, Yasin favours the Shannon measure. The information in an indicator is given as the sum of its impact on a number of independent decisions, each of which is given weight according to its importance: 'it is intuitively clear that establishing a national-economic plan eliminates more indeterminacy than establishing a plan for an individual enterprise' (Yasin (1971), p. 391). Undoubtedly true, but establishing an ordering is not the same thing as establishing a numerical scale. As we shall see, Yasin appears to have reversed his view of the feasibility of getting a meaningful measure of the quantity of information.

Other attempts to assimilate the quantity of information to its value revolve about the use of an explicit utility function. In one case it is simply profit, the 'value' of a precise estimate of demand being calculated as the increase in profit which it makes possible (Fedorenko (1972a), pp. 44–8). In another case the utility function is taken to be a logarithmic function of the probability of achieving a specified goal, which is P_0 before the receipt of the information and P_1 afterwards. The value of information, I, is then:

$$I = \log P_1 - \log P_0$$

$$= \log\left(\frac{P_1}{P_0}\right) \tag{14}$$

which is equivalent to the quantity of information. But this is a special case. Arrow has shown that only with a logarithmic utility function can the quantity of information be treated as its value (Arrow (1972), p. 134).

The conclusion to which we are drawn is well expressed by Maiminas. 'It has not yet proved possible to get a single, universal scale to compare evaluations of the utility of information in any information system. On the basis of current knowledge it is doubtful whether this is possible' (Issledovanie (1968), pp. 70–1). This last remark is developed by Yasin in his contribution to the same volume. Information must be studied at three levels: syntactic, semantic and pragmatic. The Shannon measure deals with the first aspect, while we are concerned mainly with the last, 'the relation of information to its user, its utility or value' (ibid, p. 109). All of the three aspects have their own appropriate measures, which should not be confused.

However there have been instances where an informal estimate of the quantity of information contained in statistical reports has led to revisions of reporting practice. For example the practice of reporting by exception was introduced in a limited way by the USSR Ministry of the Chemical Industry. After 1967, 179 enterprises restricted their reporting of daily output of 111 products to 'exceptions'. As a result the number of indicators collected fell to 6% and the cost of transmission fell to 7–8% of the original values. 'At the same time the level of informedness of the authorities was in practice not reduced' (Yasin (1970), pp. 98–9). Enterprises themselves were charged with defining an exception, and their judgement was fairly uniform. If we accept the assessment that there was 'in practice little change in the quantity of information transmitted', and the cost saving, then the change is worth while. But most situations will not be so clear-cut.

There are possibilities for the application of information theory in more restricted instances, where questions of coding or noise in transmission are at issue. The former question is of special interest as the USSR is currently engaged in introducing a state-wide system of product classification (see Appendix I). Information theory, more precisely the theory of optimal coding, may shed light on the relative advantages of using local codes with translation facilities or a single All-Union code, much of which will be redundant for any particular user, especially for those at the bottom of the hierarchy (Yasin (1970) and (1972)). This area of research has been christened 'economic semiotics'. But whether or not the new science will be as productive as some writers hope, the conclusion of the first part of this discussion stands: without a satisfactory method of assessing the value of information used for planning and management the cost–benefit approach cannot be applied.

3   PRACTICE

Given the failure or, at best, the limited utility of the approaches discussed in Sections 1–2 above, how have Soviet specialists proceeded in introducing computers into the planning and management system? It is my contention that Soviet work to date has been conditioned by two factors in particular. In the first place, implementation of the project for the State-Wide Automated System (OGAS) is a gradual process. The economy is not suddenly transformed into one that is fully automated. (The concept of a fully automated economy is a problematic one. Here I mean the stage at which the State-wide Automated System, as presently conceived, is complete.) We can expect certain problems to arise during the transitional period from incomplete and uneven coverage, both within units and between them. The second factor arises from the apparently contradictory properties of flexibility and rigidity which are present in the Soviet management system. Changes can be, and are, made in the system, but not necessarily the changes required by the introduction of computers into the process.

The second point is illustrated in an unusually outspoken account of early efforts to establish a unified State Network of Computer Centres (EGSVTs). Initially several regional councils (*sovnarkhozes*) were charged with the task of designing automated systems of management by 1964: 'and already this insignificant part of the EGSVTs gave rise to a complex problem. Does each factory need a computer centre? Or is a group computer centre better?... The EGSVTs required the solution of cardinal problems. The failure to solve them made a fiasco of the EGSVTs. But there is no need to worry. If part of the network had been established, then already in 1965 it would have been necessary to lay new cables, grouping factories by branches of industry.'[3] Popov went on: 'The pyramids of Egypt were one of the factors which turned that rich and ancient kingdom into a wilderness. A decision, which was senseless from the point of view of economics, would, if vigorously put into effect, have impoverished the country. According to the design for EGSVTs the computer centres would have littered the country as *sui generis* pyramids, designed by talented mathematicians and able engineers with the participation of unqualified economists.' This situation, Popov argued, arose from the failure to recognise the political nature of the problem of modernising the management system. What was needed was advance on the broad front of rationalisation opened up by the economic reform. Popov approvingly quotes E. G. Liberman: 'If enterprises, as now, have an interest in raising all input coefficients and thereby ensuring for themselves easy fulfilment of their plan in spite of any accidents or deviations in the process of planning and supply, then calculation on [computing] machines on the basis of these exaggerated norms would give you distorted results, though with great speed' (Popov (1967), pp. 157–61).

Soviet specialists concerned with the introduction of computers are thus obliged to operate within a matrix of institutional arrangements which is fundamentally rigid yet subject to shocks beyond their control. This both puts a premium on designing systems and using techniques which are flexible, and also encourages a certain limitation of view in the Soviet discussions reported below.

Essential distinctions drawn in Soviet work are those between what Kornai calls the real sphere and the control sphere of the economy, and between models based on a single one or on both of these spheres. The economic system can be regarded either as a combination of material processes, or in a purely informational aspect as a system of communication between agents, the material processes being taken as it were as given.[4] Using what is essentially this distinction, Soviet authors have identified two approaches, as follows:

a The first approach is to construct a management model based on an investigation of the purposes and modes of functioning of the unit in question. This will involve, where appropriate, an examination of the material processes of production (the real sphere of the economy). This formulation is conventionally known as 'from the problem' (*ot zadachi*), or as synthesis.

b The alternative is to short-circuit the fundamental analysis required above by accepting the existing system of management as being a reflection of the functioning of the unit, and to examine the existing management system (the control sphere). This approach is known as 'from the photograph' (*ot fotografii*), or as analysis.

These alternatives are contrasted at every level of the economy— enterprise, branch and Gosplan, whenever the question of redesigning the management system is raised.[5] The discussion invariably leads to the same conclusion: the first approach is to be preferred but the means of implementing it are lacking. The second approach is subject to the obvious drawback that the existing management model may not accurately reflect the nature of the problem being solved. But it does at least have the cardinal virtue of practicability. Fortunately, some kind of compromise or intermediate variant may be available. If so, this should be adopted, incorporating as much fundamental re-appraisal of the management system as possible.

A full account of the implications of the alternative variants for different levels of economic management will be found in the succeeding chapters, but it may be useful to illustrate the distinction further on the example of automation at Gosplan enterprise levels.

Gosplan is a unit belonging basically in the control sphere; its inputs are messages, as are its outputs, in the form of plan directives. The fundamental alternative (*ot zadachi*) is to formulate a programming problem, i.e. to maximise an objective function subject to constraints. The second alternative is to proceed from the existing system of planning, that is, to transfer traditional procedures onto the computer. Intermediate variants embody greater or lesser degrees of partial optimisation. The enterprise is a different case, combining elements of both the real and the control spheres. Hence the expression 'from the problem' implies establishing some correspondence between the real processes of production and a revised management system, a correspondence not mediated by the existing 'photograph' of the real system provided by the existing management system. The method will involve detailed analysis of the functioning of the production system; statistical modelling may play a role in the investigation. It is easy to see how such an analysis is indispensable to the design of automated systems for control of technological processes (ASUTP), in a chemical factory for example, but we should not be surprised at the difficulties found in applying this approach to a whole enterprise or larger unit.

A classic example of a means of implementing the second approach, based on the existing management system, is the so-called matrix informational model. The model is used for the analysis of the information system of enterprises, but might equally well be applied to any level of the national economy. It may also be used, together with the input–output model of material production, of which it is the informational counterpart, to give a composite account of material and information flows in the unit, though such joint treatment is unusual. Its generality (and ingenuity) justify an account of it in this section.

The originators of the matrix informational model were a research team headed by A. A. Modin, currently a deputy director of TsEMI. The new technique was reported as long ago as 1966; since that time it has been refined and subjected to practical tests. It is intended to form the basis for analysis of the management model, and the following advantages are claimed for it (Integrirovannye (1970), p. 32).

'It reflects in a graphic form the process of formation and the sequence of transmission of indicators and documents.

'It reflects in a uniform, integrated way all data about the activity of a sub-division.

'It makes possible the presentation in an integrated form of all necessary data about the activity of the whole system under discussion.'

Like the matrix model of the annual plan of the enterprise – another application developed by Modin – or the standard Soviet input–output table, the matrix information model consists of four quadrants. There are also, as illustrated in Figure 4, two auxiliary divisions, on left and right. The first quadrant, which as in the input–output table is square, shows the 'input' of one indicator into producing another within a particular section of the enterprise. The designations of the rows and columns are lists of all quantitative indicators used to present the data on which calculations are made. If indicator m is used to calculate another indicator n then the mth row of the nth column is marked with a cross; otherwise it is left blank. Hence reading down the nth column of the first quadrant we will get a list of indicators needed to produce the nth indicator: they will be those indicators whose rows are marked with a cross. Conversely, looking across the mth row we will see which indicators the mth indicator contributes to: they will be those in whose columns there is a cross.

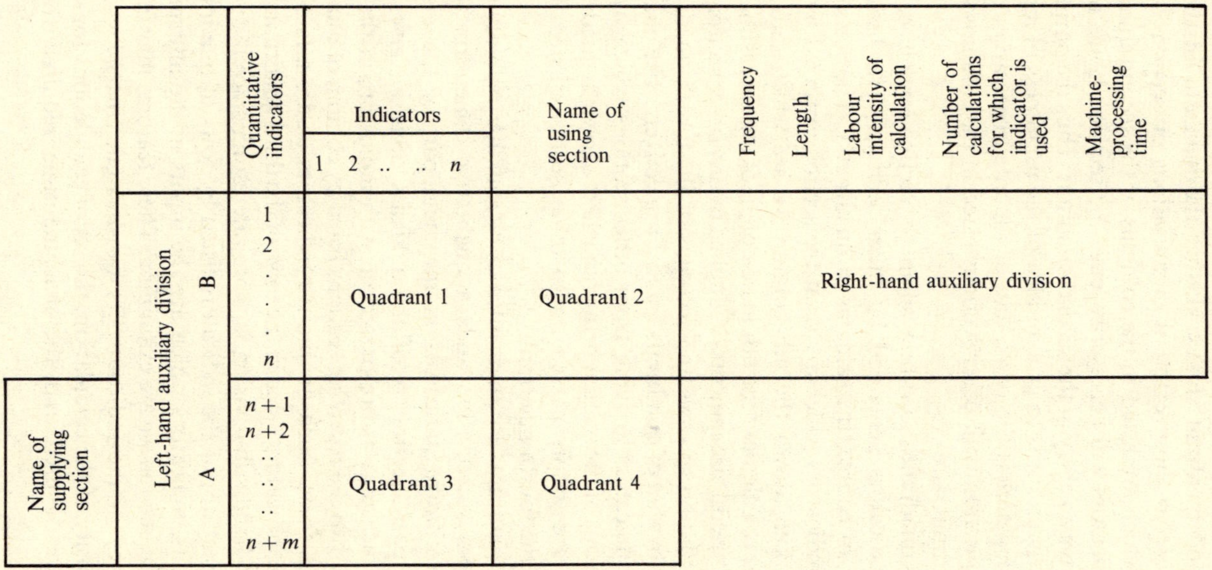

Name of supplying section	Left-hand auxiliary division	Quantitative indicators	Indicators 1 2 .. .. n	Name of using section	Right-hand auxiliary division
	B	1 2 . . . n	Quadrant 1	Quadrant 2	Frequency — Length — Labour intensity of calculation — Number of calculations for which indicator is used — Machine-processing time
	A	$n+1$ $n+2$: : : $n+m$	Quadrant 3	Quadrant 4	

Figure 4   The matrix informational model

The second quadrant shows whether the indicator in the *m*th row is of use to those external organisations or sections of the enterprise which are listed in the columns of the second quadrant. Not all indicators will necessarily leave the section: hence not all rows will have an entry in the second quadrant. Thus the purpose of the second quadrant is to give an idea of the usefulness of an indicator, reading across the rows, and of the interpenetration of the section in question with other sections listed in the columns of the second quadrant.

The third quadrant shows how reliant the section is for its calculations on indicators generated by other sections. The listing of columns is, of course, the same as in quadrant 1. The rows show the list of indicators which arrive at the section arranged by their origin. Looking down the *n*th column we see which indicators were needed to calculate the *n*th indicator; looking across the rows we see how 'useful' are indicators supplied by any other section.

The designation of rows and columns of the fourth quadrant is determined by that of quadrants 3 and 2 respectively. The quadrant shows the indicators arriving from other sections which by-pass the calculations of the section being modelled, shown in quadrant 1, and which are simply passed on to other sections listed in the columns of the fourth quadrant.

The four quadrants are augmented by two auxiliary sub-divisions. The left-hand sub-division adds a qualitative dimension to the strictly quantitative indicators in the main part of the display. The upper part, Section A of the auxiliary division, gives such qualitative measures as are passed on with indicators in the rows of quadrant 1 to the receiving sections listed by column of quadrant 2. Section B shows such qualitative indicators as are attached to quantitative indicators listed in the rows of the third quadrant.

The right-hand sub-division is more interesting since it displays additional features of the indicators listed by rows of quadrants 1 and 2; that is, indicators which are the inputs in the information process in the section we are examining. These features may include the frequency of the indicator, its word-length (*znachnost'*), the labour intensity of the calculation, the set of calculations for which the indicator is used and the machine time required for the processing.

There are various ways in which the matrix informational model can be used. First of all we note its flexibility. The area of activity covered in the first quadrant may cover any unit from a shop or lower to the highest levels of planning. Sets of lower level models can be aggregated to a single model; the extension of coverage means that quadrants 2,3 and 4 are assimilated to quadrant 1. Another form of aggregation is to consider the transformation of documents into other documents rather than of indicators into indicators. Alternatively, the model may be used for reforming the system of documentation, so that indicators which are used together are transmitted where possible in the same document.

The analogy with matrix production models is clearly seen when we consider the triangulation of the first quadrant. Consider the model for preparing an enterprise production plan. Certain indicators which are needed for the plan construction come from outside the system: that is, they appear in quadrant 3. But the process of plan formation in quadrant 1 is a progressive one, with indicators established in the later stages dependent upon earlier calculations. Hence there must be an ordering of indicators by rows and columns which eliminates any below diagonal elements in quadrant 1. This is analogous to the triangulation of an input–output matrix so that it is possible to calculate gross output needed to produce a given net output by a method akin to that of material balances (see Montias (1963)). Otherwise cycles would be observed with two or more indicators being mutually interdependent. Alternatively, the matrix can be ordered so that ex-post accounting data appear as below diagonal elements, and planning data, which are the outcome of the process, on above-diagonal squares. Inversion of the matrix of quadrant 1 will show 'gross' input needs for any given 'net' output of indicators (Fedorenko (1969a), p. 336).

Building a matrix model for a unit in the economy may be, and has been, used for the purposes of introducing an automated system of management. It has certain inadequacies: for example, it is essentially static, ignoring the deadlines which different indicators have to meet, though this deficiency may be made up in some cases by network models. But it is firmly based on the existing system of management and has the virtue of practicability.

Another important feature of the introduction of computers in the Soviet system is that it is a gradual process. As far as partial coverage between units is concerned the point needs little elaboration. Some enterprises in a branch will have an automated system of management while others may not. This places a restriction on lines of development both of enterprise systems and of the branch automated management system. Progress will tend to be restricted to the pace of the slowest member, and any reorganisation of the branch as a whole will be delayed until coverage is nearly complete. The same problem of incomplete coverage arises within the confines of a single unit, and has a bearing on the discussion reported above about whether the real sphere or the control sphere is the correct starting point for an analysis of the management system.

We noted earlier the opposition of the two approaches *ot zadachi* and *ot fotografii*. Soviet specialists found themselves trying to implement the former more fundamental approach, yet in fact being forced to fall back on a partial and inadequate use of optimising models lacking coherence or generality of application. Modin proposes a solution to this dilemma in which on the basis of a general model of the unit a central core of mathematical models is isolated, covering the basic tasks of planning and management within the unit. This approach has been recommended for both branch and enterprise systems. The stages in the combined approach are as follows, in the formulation for enterprise systems (Fedorenko (1972a), pp. 36–8).

1 A general model of management is prepared for the unit as a production system. This conceptual model describes 'the laws of the productive-economic activity of the enterprise or branch'.
2 On the basis of this model, an estimate is made of losses from the inadequacy of the management system. This isolates areas where improvements will be most effective.
3 Specific parts of the management system are ranked according to their potential improvement; this ensures maximum results from initial expenditures.
4 An expert evaluation is made of ways of carrying out these management functions. Two classes of calculation are considered: simple planning calculations (i.e. routine operations) and optimising planning decisions. The former require 'investigation and formalisation of analogous processes in the existing system of management', the latter 'investigation and formalisation of the selected area of development and functioning of production'.
5 Stage-by-stage development of the management model is carried out on the basis of experience and in the light of technical developments.

This combined approach is intended to give the designers of automated systems of management the maximum room for manoeuvre in changing the management system, subject to the constraint of what is technically feasible. But it is doubtful if it has been generally adopted. The official guidelines for enterprise and branch automated systems stipulate a broad coverage of management functions, rather than concentration, initially at least, on a few key areas (see Chapters 5 and 6). This requirement places an exceptional strain on system designers, who may be effectively disbarred from any fundamental reappraisal of the management system.

To summarise then, the development of computerisation in the USSR is constrained within fairly narrow limits. On the one hand there are technical restrictions: the appropriate methods and techniques for analysis and synthesis of systems are still being developed. On the other hand there are limitations on the changes in the management system which are feasible given the strategy of computerisation adopted and the economic background. We shall see in succeeding chapters what form these limitations have taken at different levels of the management system.

3

COMPUTERS IN GOSPLAN

A crucial role in Soviet plans for the automation of planning and management belongs to the automated system of planning calculations (ASPR), intended to cover the activities of Gosplan USSR and the Union Republican Gosplans. This chapter discusses the development of ASPR. The first section describes the history of the project; it is followed by two sections dealing with the economic models proposed by various economists as being suitable as a basis for ASPR, and with the conception of ASPR which is being accepted and implemented by Gosplan. The fourth section discusses developments in the republics and the fifth section the provision of information for ASPR. There is a final section of conclusions and assessment.

It is however important to make it clear from the outset that this chapter is based upon incomplete information. A veil of secrecy has always surrounded the activities of Gosplan, and this applies as much to new methods of planning as to the old. Hence although there is open discussion and lively debate about alternative possible ways of using computers in Gosplan, the actual extent of their use is shrouded in some mystery. All I am able to do in this chapter is to outline the debates and proposals and discuss the limited evidence available to me on practical applications.

1 THE DEVELOPMENT OF ASPR

Work on ASPR began in Gosplan[1] in 1966, when a small group of specialists was formed from various divisions and research organisations in Gosplan, the Central Economic and Mathematical Institute (TsEMI) and Moscow State University. In the following year a conference was held to discuss the general strategy of development. It heard a report from Rakovskii, deputy President of Gosplan USSR, containing a theme which was frequently to recur on such occasions, that the scale of scientific research on mathematical planning methods was much greater than its impact on planning practice. The conference adopted a series of unpublished recommendations. At this stage the main emphasis seems to have been placed on building up the technical base for ASPR (the computer centres), and on the development of automated systems of Union Republican Gosplans, to which Rakovskii devoted much of his address to the conference (Rakovskii (1967)). A number of speakers contrasted the solution of individual planning problems by mathematical methods unfavourably with an integrated computer-based system, but it is clear that no-one had a very clear idea of how to construct such a system, beyond recognising the need to distinguish sub-systems of ASPR and to apply the 'systems approach' to integrating them. The conference heard reports on particular sub-systems, including that for calculating a balance of income and expenditure on consumer goods (Proskurov (1966)). A final subject of discussion at the conference was the use of network methods to represent and control Gosplan's work in preparing the plan.

In the course of the next two years the membership of the Special group grew to sixty. In 1968 it produced a document entitled 'The Automated System of Planning Calculations (principles for its introduction and functioning)', which was adopted as a preliminary specification (*avanproekt*). The text of this document is not available to me, but it is possible to infer its contents from contemporary published works by the same group of authors (B. A. Volchkov, Yu. R. Leibkind, E. Z. Maiminas and A. A. Modin) and from discussion of the document at two meetings in 1969. The general line of thought behind the preliminary specification can be summarised as follows (Problemy (1969a), pp. 192–211):

1 ASPR is a man–machine system, comprising the calculations which make up the work of drafting the plan, the technical equipment used for those calculations, and the personnel who take decisions and evaluate results, control the process of plan formation, and organise and service the technical equipment.

2 ASPR is not an adjunct to the traditional system, solving particular planning problems by new methods, but an information and computation system covering the whole planning process and using a radically different technology.

3 At the same time, planning calculations are divided into groups of sub-systems, which themselves are further sub-divided. As a result, sub-systems within ASPR have a degree of autonomy which permits local automated calculations.

4 The purpose of ASPR is to produce a plan; its effectiveness will be evaluated by two sets of criteria: (a) external criteria, reflecting the quality of the plan that is produced, (b) internal criteria, bearing upon the process of plan formation.

5 Two distinct approaches to ASPR are possible: (a) the method 'from the problem' (*ot zadachi*) takes as its basis the 'object of planning' (i.e. the economy), (b) the method 'from the photograph' (*ot fotografii*) which takes as its basis the existing process of plan formation. Under the former variant, the problem is formulated as that of finding an extreme value of an objective function (scalar or vectorial) subject to a variety of resource constraints. This forms the external criterion. The internal criterion is reflected through constraints dealing with the functioning of ASPR, which ensure that it does not take too long and is not too costly. If the latter variant is adopted, the existing system of planning is analysed, formalised and, where appropriate, transferred to a computer. The plan thus constructed should be no worse than that formed by traditional methods (external criterion) and the process of preparing it no longer and no costlier than before (internal criterion).

6 An approach intermediate between the two outlined in (5) is recommended: more precisely a progression through a series of intermediate stages which approach the more fundamental approach. This solution speeds up the initial introduction of ASPR and ensures flexibility, particularly in the development of relatively independent sub-systems. Four or five stages are distinguished, ranging from the use of new methods to solve particular planning problems through the progressive integration of automated procedures into planning practice until finally the system forms a complete whole, reflecting a qualitative change in the process of plan construction.

7 The design of the system involves the following stages: (a) outline draft (*eskiznyi proekt*) – an outline in general terms of the future shape of Gosplan's activity – (b) detailed (*tekhnicheskii*) and final (*rabochii*) drafts – the stages of detailed design – (c) introduction of ASPR.

8 The design and development of the system require simultaneous work on a number of fronts: in particular development of the information base of the system and of the hardware and computer programmes required, and reconstruction of the organisational framework of planning.

As we shall see the development of ASPR has followed the general course set out in this initial document although the rate of progress has no doubt been slower than its authors originally expected.

At the Second Conference on ASPR held in 1969 Rakovskii recommended a timetable for the introduction of ASPR as follows (Problemy (1969b)):

1969–70: elaboration on the basis of the preliminary specification of an outline draft of ASPR.

1971–5: preparation of a final draft and gradual transition to using ASPR to prepare the plan.

However at this stage the project ran into delays. A seminar on ASPR held in Riga the following year noted significant steps forward in solving individual problems and that 'the systems approach to establishing ASPR and to its functioning has become the norm of thought both among its developers and also among many planning workers' (Seminar (1970), p. 790). But evidently progress in the mental sphere was not matched by advances on the organisational front. The preliminary specification had not yet been formally approved, nor had the co-ordination plan for setting up the system. An organisation to supervise the design of the system had not been designated. The seminar heard a series of theoretical papers by TsEMI specialists and other more detailed presentations.

Some of these deficiencies were made up in September of the same year (1970) when a special session of Gosplan USSR was devoted to a discussion of organisational measures for creating ASPR. It laid down the basic stages of development and designated the Chief Computer Centre of Gosplan USSR as the head organisation for designing the system (Sozdanie (1972), p. 4). But this decision was followed by another delay. In 1971, Shatalin, a deputy-director of TsEMI wrote: 'Establishing ASPR in Gosplan USSR is going on very slowly: there is no single conception of the system, primarily as a system of optimal perspective planning ... To a certain degree this is connected with the fact that at the moment Gosplan's basic energies are directed towards the elaboration of current plans, and this, of course, should not be its chief function' (Shatalin (1971), p. 20).

Finally, in May 1972, Gosplan USSR approved the technical specification (*zadanie*) for ASPR and adopted a co-ordination plan worked out jointly by the Chief Computer Centre of Gosplan USSR and the division for overall national economic planning. *Planovoe Khozyaistvo* noted in a leading article: 'Hereby an end has been put to the stage of investigating the problems and laying down the specifications for the integrated modernisation of national economic planning on the basis of the widespread use in planning work of mathematical–economic methods and computers' (Sozdanie (1972), p. 4).

The timetable then adopted provided for five subsequent stages:

1 Elaboration of technical specifications of ASPR sub-systems – 6 months
2 Outline (*eskiznyi*) draft – 1 year
3 Detailed (*tekhnicheskii*) draft – 1 year
4 Final (*rabochii*) draft – 1 year 6 months.
5 Introduction – 1 year 6 months.

The same meeting of Gosplan in May 1972 allocated responsibility for designing automated systems for Union Republican Gosplans and recommended the establishment of an Institute of Directors (*Institut rukovoditelei*), formed from the leaders of teams working on particular sub-systems (although in September 1973 this body was still not functioning). The Chief Computer Centre of Gosplan USSR was allocated responsibility for, amongst other sub-systems, that for labour and personnel, and, jointly with the relevant division for overall planning in Gosplan USSR, that for material balances and distribution plans (Mosin (1972), p. 32). The rule was established that all design documents for each sub-system must be approved by the head organisation for drafting ASPR (Gosplan USSR's Chief Computer Centre) and by the division for overall national economic planning (Vazhnyi (1973), p. 5).

But the delays continued. The fourth conference-seminar on ASPR in Kishinev in May 1973 was told that the preparation and approval of the technical specifications was taking an excessive amount of time: Gosplan's Chief Computer Centre was blamed for the delay (ASPR (1973), p. 156). By the beginning of 1974 a deputy President of Gosplan, N. P. Lebedinskii, had been given responsibility for the design of ASPR and a special council formed in the Chief Computer Centre, but the specification was only completed by the end of 1974, and the outline draft of the system as a whole was finally approved only at the end of 1976, after the usual complaints of poor organisation (Lebedinskii (1977), p. 9). By this time work which should have taken eighteen months had taken three times as long, and it was acknowledged that a number of issues were only provisionally resolved in the outline draft.

However while the outline of the overall system was being delayed at least a first section of ASPR came into use at the beginning of 1977. This consists of 51 functional sub-systems, of which 40 are branch sub-systems and the remaining eleven include the sub-system for overall national planning (Pervaya (1977), p. 4). The first section of ASPR is concerned chiefly with routine planning calculations (*pryamye planovye raschety*), but about one quarter of its work is based on use of a mathematical model, though this proportion rises to between one third and one half for five-year and long-term planning (Lebedinskii (1977), p. 15). However as much as 70% of the optimising calculations run in parallel with and duplicate traditional methods (Romanov (1978), p. 55).

Essentially then the first section of ASPR consists of a number of localised sets of calculations, connected with one another in the traditional way. The deficiencies of this situation are widely recognised, and it is intended to correct them with the second section, due for introduction in 1980, which will embody the overall conception of ASPR in the outline draft and integrate the separate calculations in a more comprehensive way. According to Lebedinskii much of the design work for most of the sub-systems in the first section of ASPR was done with the final shape of the whole system in view, and only the later stages of design and introduction were geared specifically to the immediate objective of completing the first section (Lebedinskii (1977), p. 9). However, with so many questions about the overall conception still unanswered, it is hard to see how this aim was achieved; and the past history of delays with ASPR raises doubts about whether the deadline for the second section will be met.

2 SOME MODELS PROPOSED AS A BASIS FOR ASPR

The previous section has given an account of the rather protracted development of ASPR over a twelve-year period since 1966. Throughout this period the designers of the system have not lacked advice, some of it contradictory and confusing, about the sort of models which ASPR should use. In this section I given an outline of various conceptions of the planning system as it might operate when the use of computers had been fully assimilated. I limit the discussion to those proposals which are specifically linked either by their authors or by others to ASPR. The next section discusses how the system has developed in practice.

Academician Fedorenko, as director of TsEMI, has been active

in proposing models for use in ASPR. At the second ASPR conference in 1969 he asserted that the deficiencies of the planning system
could be made up only by adopting some such model as the five-
level system of models for medium-term planning developed in
TsEMI. At the ASPR seminar held in Riga in 1970, Fedorenko
proposed explicitly as the basis of ASPR a second system of models
prepared at TsEMI (Problemy (1969), p. 784; Seminar (1970),
p. 784). Both systems of models, the former developed by the late
B. N. Mikhalevskii (Mikhalevskii (1967) and (1972)), the latter by
Baranov, Danilov-Danil'yan and Zavel'skii (Baranov (1971)),
have been extensively publicised. Both present considerable
problems of exposition, as they are highly developed and extremely
complex. I shall do no more than given an outline of the latter.

The authors of this set of models draw attention to its relevance
to ASPR: 'the set of models and the process of constructing an
optimal, socially-balanced development and location plan for the
economy may be regarded as the basis of the specification for such
a system (ASPR)' (Fedorenko (1972b), p. 294). The models claim
to yield an optimal development plan for the economy over ten
to fifteen years. The period chosen is fixed by the time necessary to
design and commission new capacity. Here I describe only the
first variant proposed: the second gives pride of place to regional
planning.

The chief features of interest in the system are the combined
treatment of regional and branch aspects of planning and the
partial integration of social planning with the economic planning
process. In particular an attempt is made 'in the process of the
calculations to link the composition of the plan and consideration
of such social and economic consequences of its execution as
changes in the location and distribution of population and labour
resources by region, professionally qualified group and economic
sub-division, changes in consumer demand etc.' (ibid., p. 236).
In practice the social balance section concentrates on labour supply
and manpower forecasts; it provides for such equilibrating mechanisms as raising wages to counter labour shortages, with the repercussions of such measures on, say, consumer demand being covered
in other balance relations.

The core of the model is the preparation of the plan in its regional
and branch aspects. It is based on a two-level planning procedure,
with the special feature that the top or Gosplan level problem is
decomposed in two directions into both regional and branch sub-

problems. Hence the double nature of the upper level objective function, and the dual classification (by branch and region) of any product, resource or investment project in the model.

We start off with assumed knowledge of the so-called overhead expenses of the economy: expenditure on defence, management, science, external trade, stocks and reserves and resources to be carried over into the post-plan period. These, in principle, are given from outside and invariable. The upper level works out a first approximation of the plan using input–output models (static and dynamic), based on forecasting techniques and guided by objectives set by the Party and State. Branches receive minimum output targets and regionally differentiated prices for resources. The latter may in the first iteration be actual prices. They select, from a list of possible projects each characterised by dated input–output vectors, a profit-maximising combination. These plans are passed to the upper level and examined for consistency and optimality according to the centre's criterion of maximising the return to labour and natural resources. Resources required for transportation are calculated; targets and allocations are then recalculated and iterations continue until an optimum is reached.

At this stage the regions enter the picture. Each regional authority examines the list of projects selected by branches in its regions, bearing in mind the evaluations of goods and resources set by the upper level, and prepares a balanced regional plan maximising its criterion, the integral over the planning period of the real incomes of the region's population. Regional evaluations of products and resources are made. In the event of a divergence between regional and branch plans, new regionally-differentiated prices are assigned to the latter and the process is repeated. Otherwise a transport plan is prepared and the final plan checked for social balance. The two-dimensional decomposition determines the curious nature of the upper level objective function, the difference between the return to labour and natural resources and the real income of the population. In the first decomposition the latter is taken as given; in the second, the former.

This outline of one variant of the model is enough to alert us to the gulf between existing long-term planning practice and the procedures of the model. The authors attempt to allay these anxieties by pointing out firstly that the optimal plan which is the outcome of the process contains only indicators which in content are close to those used today, and secondly that the model relies primarily on the existing system of accounting and planning information, supplemented by information which can be collected without too much difficulty or expense (ibid., p. 236). The second point is rather questionable and, even if information were available, the computational requirement of the model is enormous, the more so since doubts exist about its convergence. An experimental test of the model required a number of simplifications and a high degree of aggregation (Baranov (1976)).

The model discussed above is seen by its authors as being embedded in a framework of forecasting and planning models, stretching from forecasting development 20–30 years ahead to day-to-day operational control. Such a set of models may incorporate rolling plans with annual recalculation of a new five-year plan and preparation of a new long-term plan every five years.

This feature of rolling plans is present in the more recent set of models proposed by Fedorenko under the title of 'system of integrated planning' (*sistema kompleksnogo planirovaniya* – SKP). It is of special interest inasmuch as unlike the model discussed above which covers a single time period, SKP covers the whole range of chronologically interlocking plans. It can therefore more plausibly than the others be proposed as the methodological basis for ASPR. Its claims have been pressed vigorously at various meetings and discussions since 1972 (see Fedorenko (1972c) and (1974a); Novikov (1976)).

One of the system's distinctive features is its starting point, the elaboration on the basis of the overall aims of society of a tree of goals in which general objectives are broken down into successively smaller sub-divisions. The highest level goal, 'Development and consolidation of Soviet society' is divided in the next tier into (1) Raising the welfare of members of Soviet society, (2) Consolidation and development of the system of social relations, (3) Maintenance of security, and other external objectives and (4) Creating and maintaining potential for the future. Through subsequent disaggregation we reach classifications which are more recognisable as planning targets, such as the provision of food, clothing, housing and cultural amenities (Fedorenko (1974a), pp. 61–86).[2] The degree of attainment of individual goals is represented by goal normatives (*tselevye normativy*). Alternative combinations of such target achievement levels are prepared.

Simultaneously forecasts of various kinds – of demographic processes, of technical progress, of branch development – are prepared and consolidated into alternative integrated and comprehensive forecasts or projections, each of which satisfies alternative goal normatives. Such forecasts make a link between goals and goal normatives on one hand and resources on the other. Alternative forecasts are examined for their requirements in resources, which are not yet taken as being in fixed supply.

The next step involves a second distinctive feature of SKP, the use of programmes as a means of developing and presenting alternative paths of development of an important part of the social–economic system. A programme is 'a planned set of economic, social, technical, organisational and scientific measures' directed towards the achievement of one or more clearly defined goals of social development. The variety of possible programmes is best illustrated by examples: (1) a programme to raise real incomes and equalise living standards; (2) a programme to develop socialist culture; (3) a programme to improve the system of planning and managing the economy; (4) a programme to develop the supply of new material; (5) a programme for the development of Yakutiya (Leibkind (1973), pp. 652–3). A distinction is drawn between goal-oriented (*tselevye*) and resource (*resursnye*) programmes; the former realise final goals directly, the latter indirectly by providing resources. It is recognised that the distinction is rather arbitrary.

Such programmes are prepared at the lower (ministerial and regional) levels, and Gosplan welds selections of these programmes into variants of a general plan for presentation to higher authorities. Such a general plan contains summary indicators charting the course of development of the economy over a 15-year period broken down by periods of 5 years. The plan is represented in such a way that it can be evaluated with respect to higher level tiers of the tree of goals. It also contains details of programmes, balance relations and a statement of reserves.

After the approval by higher authorities of a long-term plan, SKP enters more familiar ground. A perspective plan for the first five years of the general plan is worked out. This gives a year by year breakdown of targets and assigns them to particular executants. A multi-level system of models for medium-term planning is recommended, with participation from both branch and regional authorities. The system of current planning proposed is even closer to the present day realities of ASPR: the authors of the proposal observe that use can be made of branch models, based on mathematical programming methods, of regional input–output models and material balances (for working out the supply plan) and of financial models (for working out the budget). The basic instrument of control over the course of fulfilment of the programmes can be network planning methods (Fedorenko (1972c), p. 338).

One of the ideas on which SKP is based, the formation of inter-branch complexes to formulate and execute programmes, was first advanced in a narrower context by Aganbegyan. He proposed that the economy should be divided into nine complexes, through amalgamation of appropriate ministries (Aganbegyan (1969), pp. 59–60). Two of Aganbegyan's colleagues in the Institute for the Economics and the Organisation of Industrial Production have proposed a set of plans for different time periods which is similar to SKP (Lemeshev (1973)). They content themselves with developing a two-tier tree of goals, the lower tier containing six sub-goals. Each interbranch complex is linked exclusively to the achievement of one of these six goals, whereas in SKP it is recognised that a single programme, covering one complex, may help in the attainment of several goals. Besides providing for a less elaborate analysis of objectives, the Lemeshev–Panchenko proposal differs from SKP in placing more emphasis on the directive character of planning. The practical influence of these proposals is described below.

3 GOSPLAN'S APPROACH TO ASPR

The attitude of Gosplan officials towards the models discussed in the previous section has often been hostile. This is particularly true in the case of the Baranov model, published in a TsEMI monograph edited by Fedorenko. This volume outlined the conception of economic management developed in the 1960s and revived in the 1970s under the title of 'the system of optimal functioning of the economy (SOFE)'. As described above, this is a 'single integrated system including both the elaboration of optimal plans for all links in the economy and optimisation of the very process of implementing these plans'. The proposed relationship of ASPR to SOFE is as follows: 'ASPR must make concrete, link up and realise the principles and methods of the system of optimal functioning of the economy, in application to the system of national economic planning' (Fedorenko (1972a), pp. 3, 542). According to a leading article in *Planovoe Khozyaistvo* (Vazhnyi (1973), p. 4):

As such a [methodological] basis [for uniting mathematical–economic models in a single complex] the so-called system of optimal functioning of the economy (SOFE) cannot be used. In the theoretical foundations of SOFE and the practical conclusions of its authors concerning improvement of planned management and methods of running the economy recognition is not given to the decisive significance of conscious applications of objective economic laws in scientific planning and consequently in economic management. SOFE tries to solve the problem of finding the optimal path of the economy's development without previously fixing a definite length to the planning period. From this stems the rejection, in essence, of the directive character of plans, which are converted into constantly repeated forecasting calculations.

In a companion article Lebedinskii, the official in charge of the design of ASPR, reinforces the attack on the TsEMI monograph. He asserts that the section on medium-term planning is totally taken up with a description of models of medium-term 'plan-forecasts' and 'forecast-plans', and that annual plans are totally ignored (Lebedinskii (1973), p. 9). Even if the attack is overstated by selective quotation it clearly focuses on a crucial area of dispute, whether the greater concentration on long-term planning will lead to a devolution of authority for medium- and short-term planning and management. Such a proposal is unmistakably the intent of the TsEMI volume and explicit in the first proposal for SKP (Fedorenko (1972c), p. 341). It is interesting to note that the April 1973 management changes have altered the situation in some respects. The newly formed production and industrial *ob'edineniya* are designed to operate with expanded powers at the middle level of management, and this new system conforms more closely to the ideas of the proponents of SKP. In a subsequent revision of the system they placed greater emphasis on the potential role of these new units in the proposed new planning system (Fedorenko (1974a), pp. 143–161).

Lebedinskii also criticises the treatment of goals in SKP, alleging that 'the defect in the so-called "tree of goals" consists in the fact that only one aspect of the process is considered: the direct connection between goals and resources necessary for their realisation. In other words, when the tree of goals is under discussion only direct expenditures are considered' (Lebedinskii (1973), p. 10). But this criticism seems invalid because SKP incorporates input–output models at various stages of plan construction and thus takes account of indirect resource costs as well.

Having considered the criticism levelled by Gosplan officials at models proposed by other economists, we must now examine the actual development of ASPR and consider why it has taken the form it has taken. We note that proposals to make a sharp break with the traditional planning system have not been helpful in a situation where the work of the planning bodies must go on even while their structure and functions are being re-examined. This need for continuity has meant that a step-by-step approach to the design and introduction of ASPR has been adopted, with parts of the new system working side-by-side with parts of the old. In other words the part played by formal mathematical models is a partial one, limited by the difficulties of modelling and of getting suitable information. Individual models may be applicable for different parts of the planning process but will normally cover only a fraction of the total process. The implementation strategy for ASPR has thus been one of progressively expanding this coverage and where possible linking up the individual models (Urinson (1978), pp. 63–6).

From available descriptions of the specification for ASPR, it seems that the projected system is based closely upon existing planning practice, with the system as a whole divided into a number of sub-systems, which themselves fall into two categories, functional and service. The latter comprise 'the methodological, informational, technical, mathematical and personnel requirements for solving planning problems' (Vorob'ev (1972), p. 20). A functional sub-system is defined as a relatively isolated or separate block of calculations within the overall planning system.

Functional sub-systems are divided into three categories or levels. The highest level deals with problems of overall (*svodnyi*) planning of the economy as a whole and is responsible for 'on the one hand, defining the social and economic objectives of the plan, the economy-wide rates of growth, proportions and summary indicators of development of the national economy, and, on the other, for the elaboration of the methods and organisation of the process of economic planning as a whole, and for ensuring its unity' (Budavei (1974), p. 22).

The second level includes sub-systems dealing with specific aspects of planning – such as labour, finance, costs, profits or living standards – with material balances and distribution plans, with regional planning and with the planning of foreign trade. The third level of the structure is made up of branch sub-systems. According to the detailed specifications there would be about three hundred branch sub-systems, of which the central core would be forty or so branch sub-systems of Gosplan USSR. These deal with all aspects of branch planning, including production, supply, capital investment, costs and profit, and science and technology (Lebedinskii (1973), pp. 10–11). We first examine the highest level system, that concerned with the overall national economic plan. Since 1974 Gosplan has had two divisions discharging this function, one concerned with current, the other with perspective planning.

The available sources do not permit a detailed account of developments in this area, but the main function of this sub-system is to lay down the main directions of development of the economy, and to establish a feasible plan covering both production and supply within the economy. Inevitably much of the discussion of this sub-system has revolved around the possibility of using input–output models to make multi-variant calculations.

The possibility of applying input–output models in Soviet planning has been the subject of much discussion both in the Soviet Union and outside. As long ago as 1959 the overlap of functions of input–output and the Soviet system of material balances was noted. An accounting input–output table for the same year was the first All-Union table to be prepared in the USSR. However a catalogue of reasons preventing the substitution of the balance system by input–output soon became familiar: the fact that alternative methods of production are not considered; the assumption of constant returns to scale; the lack of correspondence between the pure (commodity-based) branches of input–output models and the administrative (establishment-based) branches in which the plan is elaborated; the incomplete coverage of the plan; the lack of computer capacity to perform the necessary computations; and the inadequacy of the information base.

ASPR is specifically designed to overcome the last two of these difficulties. It is natural that the input–output model has featured prominently in discussions of and plans for ASPR. It has the double advantage of being a new departure which at the same time fits conveniently into the existing framework of planning. Rakovskii told an audience in 1969 that 'the basic structural model must be the input–output model: in long-term planning dynamic models can be used' (Plenum (1969), pp. 472–3). An identical form of words was used in a leading article in *Planovoe Khozyaistvo* discussing the timetable for designing ASPR in 1972 (Sozdanie (1972), p. 5). Finally an article on the introduction of the first section of ASPR asserted that for purposes of overall national planning the models most widely applied in practice had been of the input–output type (Pervaya (1977), p. 5). However a distinction must be drawn between the use of input–output in annual and in long-term planning.

In preparing the long-term plan for 1976–90, Gosplan used an 18-sector dynamic input–output model. For the final year of each five-year plan aggregate value indicators were calculated and then broken down for each year of the first five-year plan using a 260 × 260 interproduct table, prepared in physical and value terms (*natural'no-stoimostnyi balans*). Both of these tables were prepared and used by Gosplan's Chief Computer Centre and the Scientific Research Institute for Economics attached to Gosplan (see Zaitsev (1974), Urinson (1975), Birger (1978)). The larger table is that described by Vorob'ev in an article on the use of input–output in Gosplan in 1973. Vorob'ev noted that the coverage of the model was incomplete (corresponding to that adopted in the plan) and that by 1973 only calculations in physical units had been possible 'owing to the failure to resolve a series of methodological problems of evaluating input–output relations in value terms and difficulties in obtaining information' (Vorob'ev (1973), p. 55). A Gosplan official has recently written that the most likely developments in this field are linking up the small dynamic model with the larger balance in physical and value terms, and integrating the latter with branch models. A longer-term development is the dynamic model incorporating inter-regional as well as inter-branch links under development at the Institute for the Economics and Organisation of Industrial Production at Novosibirsk.

The prospects for using input–output models in annual planning are more restricted. The reason is clearly stated by Vorob'ev: 'the area of application of aggregated models is limited by the fact that they do not include all inter-branch links and do not provide for the solution of concrete problems in the process of working out national economic plans at the level of branch and overall functional divisions of Gosplan USSR' (ibid.). Thus input–output plays a subsidiary role in annual planning, restricted to calculating the effects on the economy of small changes in plan targets. The tables prepared for each of the five years of the ninth five-year plan were used for this purpose; for example, to calculate the consequences of a reduction in the supply of fuel and iron in the 1973 plan, and for similar calculations in 1974 (Oganesyan (1975)). But the division for overall planning would use the results of these calculations only as a preliminary to compiling material balances in the normal way. The data in the input–output models are approximate only; they are worked out before the start of the five-year plan and hence fail to take account of changes in coefficients arising from structural shifts within and between the product groups since that time.

Vorob'ev summarises the position by stating that the models worked out in Gosplan 'do not contradict and do not in any sense replace existing models of economic planning and they do not rule out the construction of either the national economic balance or material balances, but serve only as some sort of supplement to the existing balance methods of planning' (Vorob'ev (1973), p. 56). This attitude has been endorsed in general terms by Baibakov, the President of Gosplan, who has stressed the limitations of mathematical–economic methods and has regretted the decline in theoretical and methodological work on the traditional balance method (Baibakov (1974), pp. 11–12).

Thus opinion is still divided on the desirability as well as on the feasibility of using input–output models within Gosplan, and this ambivalent or even hostile attitude has ensured that the first section of ASPR introduced at the beginning of 1976 does not rely entirely on the input–output model. However a start has been made, and one interesting development is the model developed jointly by Kossov, a Gosplan official, and Pugachev, an economist working at TsEMI, which attempts to integrate the economy-wide and sectoral aspects of ASPR for long-term and five-year planning. This is further discussed below.

The middle level of ASPR consists of sub-systems dealing with aspects of the plan overlapping all or many ministries, such as labour, capital investment and profitability, or with such distinct areas of planning as foreign trade, regulating the demand and supply of consumer goods (known as 'the balance of income and expenditure of the population') and planning the metropolitan areas of Moscow and Leningrad. Here I consider two sub-systems, those dealing with labour and labour resources, and costs and profit.[3]

The traditional method for compiling the labour plan is by means of a labour balance (*balans truda*), which, like a material balance, presents data on the supply of and the demand for the resource in question. Balances are prepared at different levels of aggregation, but the most important is the summary balance of labour resources. In this balance, information is presented on the supply of labour from different quarters, and the allocation of labour is given in a threefold classification, by nature of employment, by branch and sphere of production, and by social group (Kostakov (1970), p. 148).

The evidence suggests that this basic format is retained within the ASPR sub-system for labour and personnel, the principal change introduced by the latter being the use of mathematical models for particular aspects of the calculations, and a system of information flows which achieves better links with both higher- and lower-level (i.e. branch) sub-systems.

Functionally the sub-system consists of four blocks, known respectively as demography, labour resources, labour, and labour expenditure. The demography block provides data on the size of the population by age, sex and territorial distribution, and calculates the availability of labour resources. The labour expenditure block compiles an inter-branch balance in labour units. The labour block calculates rates of growth of productivity in various branches, and also the size of the wage fund and the average wage in different branches and regions, while the final block on labour resources compiles the summary balance of labour resources, and identifies shortages both overall and for particular categories of qualified and specialised personnel (Bezrukov (1976), p. 68).

The use to which these blocks are put varies with the time period of the plan. For long-term planning demographic forecasts are of considerable importance. An outline of methods used is given by Bezrukov, but it is clear that such methods could be – and very probably were – used before the development of ASPR. Long-term requirements for labour are estimated from two sources: first the sub-system receives information on the volume, structure and territorial distribution of output over the next fifteen years from other sub-systems, together with estimates of capital invest-ment and forecasts of new technology. Then estimates of producti-vity growth are prepared, using a variety of methods ranging from regression to production function analysis. Labour input require-ments can be estimated in this way.

For five-year and annual planning the emphasis shifts to the other three blocks in the sub-system. Productivity growth in indus-try is planned by a complicated method which seeks to identify four separate sources of growth – an increase in the technological level of production, improvements in management, changes in the volume or structure of production and special branch factors (in extractive industries for example). This procedure is laid down in

Gosplan's Methodological Instructions (Methodicheskie (1974), pp. 329–40), and may pre-date the introduction of the ASPR sub-system, though 'the application of mathematical–economic methods makes it possible to integrate calculations for the [four] factors into a single system, linking them with calculations of plans for the development and distribution of production by execut-ant branches' (Bezrukov (1976), p. 102).

This stage is the prelude to the chief innovation in labour plan-ning achieved by the sub-system, in Bezrukov's account. This is the use of an input–output model to make calculations measured in labour units. Calculation of a matrix of total (direct and indirect) material inputs per unit of output and subsequent multiplication by the vector of direct labour inputs make it possible to calculate the total labour requirement for producing any final bill of goods. According to Bezrukov alternative variants can then be ranked by comparing the ratio of total labour input to the value of final output (ibid. pp. 102–3). But obviously the results are sensitive to the price system, the vagaries of which would thus determine the plan, and such an eccentric procedure for selecting among alter-natives can scarcely be taken seriously. It is more reasonable to regard the input–output model as a means of checking the overall feasibility in aggregate terms of a particular plan variant. Even here the drawbacks applying to input–output analysis noted earlier still apply, though some effort has been made to perform calculations for pure (commodity-based) branches, with a procedure for convert-ing data from its normal form, by administrative branch (ibid., pp. 105–6).

This leads us to the final block in the sub-system, that entitled 'labour resources' which attempts to calculate imbalances in the supply and demand of labour. This is done in the traditional labour balance way, except that the calculations are done by computers. Where shortages of labour emerge corrections are made to the planned allocation of labour. Some sort of priority system may operate in the case of overall shortages, but it is not described.

The practical impact of the sub-system for labour and personnel seems to be slight. The input–output model plays a peripheral role, though its use for some preliminary calculations was reported in 1973. Apart from this the chief advantages which the sub-system can offer appear to be more sophisticated forecasting methods, the performance on a computer of routine calculations and better and more immediate communication with other sub-systems within

Gosplan, though the last depends upon the successful achievement of uniformity in data-processing. These advantages are not inconsiderable, but do not amount to a substantial change in planning methods.

The second intermediate level sub-system to be considered here is a similar case. This is the sub-system for costs and profit, which is responsible for 'determining the size of necessary, economically justified expenditure on production and of the income obtained from production and sale of output (in the form of profit)' (Kotov (1976), p. 60). The sub-system has close links with other ASPR sub-systems covering finance, labour and personnel, and output and distribution plans. It is recognised that separating the monetary side of the production process is rather artificial: 'having it off into a special sub-system has come about not because the subject matter of the plan is independent, but as a result of the existing organisation and methodology of preparing the plan, chiefly the fact that in the tasks performed by the sub-system there is a broader and fuller reflection of economic relations not included in current methods of production planning' (ibid.). This illustrates the way in which ASPR sub-systems are being designed to fit in with the traditional procedures used in Gosplan.

The sub-system contains branch sub-divisions, which are part of the branch sub-systems of ASPR, and an overall block covering the whole economy, for which the Chief Computer Centre of Gosplan has developed a technical specification and a detailed draft. The same organisation in conjunction with the Division of Finance and Costs has developed and approved methodological materials for the branch sub-systems. As a result of problems with data the implementation of the sub-system is gradual, beginning with mechanisation of certain laborious calculations. One of the aims of the system is to use an input–output model, with units measured in money terms, to operate in conjunction with the model with measurement in physical units which is to be used for production planning. However this development is hampered by the incomplete coverage of input coefficients. The automated system of norms discussed below may solve this problem, but to do so it would have to be adjusted to include more input coefficients in value terms (ibid., pp. 65, 67).

The evidence of these two intermediate level systems suggests that the development of ASPR is not far advanced in the sub-systems dealing with special or functional aspects of planning.

We now consider the lowest level sub-systems within ASPR, those dealing with particular branches.

The branch sub-systems of ASPR operate in conjunction with the appropriate automated systems in the ministries (OASU). A. A. Modin, a deputy director of TsEMI with extensive practical experience in developing both ASPR and OASU, wrote in 1970 that the relationship between Gosplan and Ministry would remain substantially the same, but with a greater emphasis on long-term planning (Modin (1970), pp. 64–6).

As far as the models used in branch sub-systems are concerned, there seems to be considerable overlap with those used in the sub-systems for perspective and current planning in branch management systems.[4] Branch sub-systems of ASPR are responsible for co-ordinating the planning sub-systems of OASU and are said to work closely with them, but some inconsistency and duplication occur. Sometimes ministries and Gosplan use essentially the same planning model, but different objective functions. Sometimes straightforward duplication takes place, as in some calculations for long-term planning (Kisilev (1976), p. 135). The Ministry of Instrument Building and the corresponding division of Gosplan were specifically designated to test the interaction of the two levels, but many branch systems were introduced before the results of these trials became available, and a satisfactory relationship has not been achieved. As well as the issue of allocation of responsibility between the two levels, the major question of where information should be collected and stored is unresolved.

This completes my consideration of the three levels of sub-systems within the first section of ASPR. The reader will have noted that in spite of much emphasis on the need to develop ASPR as an integrated whole, a general conception of its overall operation is lacking, and instead the developers of sub-systems are usually confined to making modest alterations to an individual aspect of plan construction. This restriction applies particularly to short-term planning with its demanding routine of preparing detailed plans for immediate execution.

For the more schematic long-term planning, however, a more integrated approach is practicable and one model linking branch and overall sub-systems of ASPR and requiring the participation of the ministries has found support within Gosplan. This is the model of Kossov and Pugachev, referred to above (Kossov (1974)). A model of this type is envisaged for the second part of ASPR

(Yun (1978), p. 48). It is essentially an iterative model, linking optimal branch plans through a highly aggregated input–output model. The procedure is also designed to satisfy economy-wide constraints of capital and labour by variation in the coefficient of relative effectiveness (the inverse of the recoupment period) in the branch plans.[5] In fact the branches prepare sets of alternative plans at each iteration, corresponding to different output levels and values of the coefficient, and these are then weighted at the centre. As the process advances, the range of these variables contracts and the plan becomes more accurate. Essentially the model links two kinds of calculations which have taken place independently before. A more recent version, in keeping with the trend in Gosplan's thinking noted below, introduces inter-branch complexes as an intermediate link between the branch models and the inter-branch model of the whole economy (Pugachev (1977)). But although this model differs from those described in the previous section in that it is consistent with some of Gosplan's traditional planning work, and although it has undergone some experimental tests, it is clear that it is still a long way from implementation.

The first section of ASPR described here was designed and in use by 1977. As a result it reflects only incompletely a trend in the organisation of planning which has recently come into prominence. The new approach involves the introduction of a level intermediate between the branch and the economy as a whole, known as the interbranch or multi-branch complex. Although the impetus for using this new level of planning does not spring primarily from the increased use of mathematical methods, its emergence does have implications for the general structure of ASPR in the future, and deserves brief consideration here.

Gosplan is now devising means to introduce what is variously known as the integrated (*kompleksnyi*), programme (*programmnyi*) or programme–goal (*programmno-tselevoi*) approach to planning. Officials have spoken in favour of using this approach for some years, but it has come into particular prominence since its strong endorsement at the XXV Party Congress in 1976, where the last of the three formulations above (programme–goal) was adopted (Materialy (1976), pp. 61, 120, 171).

The central idea is the identification of an important long-term objective which can only be achieved by the joint effort of sectors of the economy falling under different conventional subordinations. A programme is then devised for the whole complex, intended to meet the overall objective. A Gosplan official describes the approach thus: 'in application to economic planning it can be characterised as a method of compiling a plan which involves the identification of basic goals of social, economic, scientific and technological development and the elaboration of co-ordinated measures to achieve them in the specified period by comprehensive and balanced provision of resources and effective development of social production' (Budavei (1978), p. 3).

A number of programmes of this kind, many of them of a regional nature, are already in operation (ibid., p. 8) and Soviet authors have wasted no time in tracing a distinguished ancientry for the new approach dating from the Goelro plan of the 1920s. What is new, however, is the intention to extend the approach to a large part of the economy.

Recent discussions of the approach have revealed uncertainty as to how to apply it in practice. Some contributions to the debate have been highly abstract (Danilov-Danil'yan (1977)), and the director of Gosplan's research institute has criticised some writers for employing excessively complex tools and methods, which have hampered practical applications (Kirichenko (1978), p. 42). There are undeniable problems, however, particularly in linking the long-term programme to the system of five-year and annual planning. Some reorganisation of the basic divisions of the plan is envisaged (Budavei (1978), p. 10), but other problems remain. Will the chief executant of a programme, which may be a ministry or independent commission, have powers over other organisations? And will the conventional planning system with its rigid vertical hierarchy stifle the horizontal information flows which the programme approach is intended to nurture?

Although this new approach has features in common with the SKP described above, a more direct influence is probably Western management techniques such as PPBS (Planning, Programming and Budgeting System) which came to be widely used in the United States after being first applied in the early 1960s in the defence sector. In fact the link which some authors, among them Lebedinskii, have identified between mathematical methods and the programme approach is by no means a necessary one. It is rather that ASPR has to be adapted to take account of the changes brought about by the programme approach.

One approach to the formation of inter-branch complexes which minimises the changes in overall planning methods is to see them merely as unions of existing ministries, the union being founded on ministries having either supplier–customer relations, or similarities in output or technology or similar or inter-related objectives.[6] This approach would do little more than introduce an additional level in the planning system rather than reorient it towards the achievement of basic goals. In fact it was claimed in 1974, before the programme approach received official endorsement, that three such complexes had been formed, covering energy, transport and machine-building (Budavei (1974), p. 22), though a more recent source asserts that only the energy complex was in operation by 1977 and that the second part of ASPR, by 1980, would see the operation of no more than three further complexes (Yun (1978), p. 49). Many programmes have been limited to particular regions of the economy rather than to particular groups of ministries, and the new approach can be seen in part as yet another attempt to reconcile the territorial and branch elements in the plan. To date, however, the programme approach has not been worked out in sufficient detail for its overall impact on the future development of ASPR to become clear.

There have been developments in one further area of planning, which is closely related to the design of ASPR. This is the use of network methods. Network methods are used for controlling the fulfilment of a series of operations some of which must be carried out sequentially. For example, in the process of plan construction within Gosplan, certain sets of calculations have to be completed before further calculations can begin: before the material balances can be constructed information must be obtained on supply and demand for the relevant products from all branches in the economy. Network methods can be used to control the process of plan construction. They can be used to control any system of plan construction, automated or traditional, but the connection between network methods and ASPR often made by Soviet authors is not accidental. Complex sequential processes can be represented on a computer, and algorithms exist for establishing the critical path or minimum period in which a series of sequential and parallel operations can be carried out. As more calculations are done with computers it is a natural step to monitor and control their fulfilment by network methods. The outcome should be a lessening of delays in preparing the plan.

Most information is available about the use of network methods in Gosplan of the Russian Federation, which has been selected from among the Union Republican Gosplans to co-ordinate work in this area. A full network model was drawn up (Zenchenko (1972), p. 25), and after some delay the system was scheduled to control the elaboration of the plan beginning in 1973. Each week a computer-prepared questionnaire is distributed to all sections of Gosplan, soliciting information on the progress of work in the previous week, and expected progress in the following two or three weeks. The directors of Gosplan RSFSR, heads of sections and the Chief Computer Centre of Gosplan USSR are informed of progress, and steps are taken to correct deviations from the planned time-table. Attempts are made to reduce the critical path by speeding up particular operations. Where necessary, personnel may be re-allocated to reduce fulfilment times. The system used by Gosplan RSFSR was adopted as a standard design by the Gosplans of all republics and was incorporated within ASPR as a sub-system for controlling the planning process, though it would be introduced before other sub-systems (Chizhikova (1974), p. 692).

It is an important feature of network methods that their use entails no fundamental changes in plan construction, though it is not correct to say that they lead to the production of the same plan; a plan ready on time is not the same thing as a plan with identical indicators and instructions which arrives late. The use of network methods is a modest success for those seeking to en-courage planning officials to persist with more adventurous models. But Zenchenko is quick to point out that network methods by themselves cannot solve the other problems affecting the planning process (Zenchenko (1976), p. 44).

4 ASPR IN THE REPUBLICS

The Union Republics have from the beginning received attention in discussions of ASPR. Rakovskii devoted the greater part of his speech to the first ASPR Conference to their achievements and problems (Rakovskii (1967)), and much emphasis has been placed on the scope for standardisation of the separate republican systems. But their development has been noticeably uneven.

In 1972, two Union Republican Gosplans were chosen to co-ordinate the design of republican systems. The Ukraine and Lith-uania were selected, the former as a republic with numerous *oblasts*, the latter, as a republic without *oblast'* division. The two Gosplans were instructed to co-ordinate specifications for ASPR sub-systems in all Union Republican Gosplans under the direction of Gosplan USSR.

The ASPR of the Lithuanian Gosplan is based on a complex model the core of which is a simulation model consisting of eleven separate blocks. The model, which can be used for either current or long-term planning, has been described in several works of the director of the Lithuanian computer centre (Rayatskas (1972a and b).

There are, however, some puzzling features in the descriptions. It is stated that: 'the model presented can be regarded as the basic nucleus of the (automated) system (of planning calculations of the Lithuanian) Republic's Gosplan' (Rayatskas (1972b), p. 17), yet, despite its large size and complexity, the model does not provide for a regional breakdown within the republic and we know that territorial aspects are a particular weakness of republican planning, where 'a badly organised and unsystematised information base, absence of centralised accounting of resources and low planning discipline characterise the system of plan formation' (Modelirovanie (1972), p. 202). This omission is specially serious when we recall that one of the chief ways in which republican Gosplans impinge on planning decisions taken by Union ministries is with respect to the location of enterprises within the republic. Secondly and most crucially, there seems to be a lack of proportion between the size of the model, which contains 159 variables, and the size of the problem of current planning which the model purports to solve. This comes out most clearly from the dimensions of the republican input–output table which plays an important role. For one set of calculations, the 1966 table of more than 100 sectors was reduced to 33 (Rayatskas (1972a), p. 66). Commodities were divided in 105 groups. This may be adequate or more than adequate for constructing a long-term plan, but it is too small for detailed annual planning and provokes the suspicion that the material balance method is not superseded in Lithuania any more than it is in Gosplan USSR. The most recent discussion of the model confirms that implementation of its different sub-systems is uneven (Rayatskas (1976), pp. 271–6).

The ASPR worked out for the Ukrainian Soviet Socialist Republic has been adopted as a model for union republics which are large enough for division into *oblasts*. The Chief Scientific-Research and Information and Computer Centre (GlavNIIVTs) of the Ukrainian Gosplan has been designated its chief designer, under the scientific direction of the Institute of Cybernetics of the Ukrainian Academy of Sciences (Kirilyuk (1974), p. 10).

In 1974 a detailed draft of the system was in preparation. In structure and content it is similar to that adopted by Gosplan USSR, with three types of sub-system – overall (common to all branches and *oblasts*), branch, and territorial.[7] The input–output and branch optimising models play an important role especially for medium-term planning (Mikhalevich (1974); Shatilov (1974)). As in the case of Lithuanian Gosplan, the decisions of Gosplan USSR are an important linking factor or constraint on the decisions of Ukrainian Gosplan. Accordingly, two modes of operation of the system are envisaged. In one the system functions on the basis of receiving certain key indicators from Gosplan USSR; in the other it operates in a semi-independent mode, using forecast magnitudes or data received at preceding stages.

Relations with branch automated management systems have also received attention, particularly in the case of All-Union ministries which are beyond the control of the Ukrainian Gosplan. Initially information on output plans and other indicators relating to these ministries would reach the republican Gosplan through ASPR of Gosplan USSR, but it was proposed that at a later stage information would be collected on a regional basis within the republic and subsequently be aggregated at the All-Union level. Thus the flow of information would be reversed. This new procedure corresponds to the conception of OGAS, the Statewide Automated System, recently proposed by Glushkov and Zhimerin (see pp. 19–20 above). As a step in that direction the Ukraine is developing an overall Republican automated management system (RASU), uniting all automated systems within the Ukraine. The technical specification was approved in 1974, and the first section, comprising 26 sub-systems, was accepted in 1976. Evidence of similar developments in other republics is sparse and fragmentary.

5 INFORMATION FOR PLANNING: LINKS WITH ASN AND ASGS

A new pattern of activity within Gosplan requires new information flows and new data-processing methods. These have been the subject of much analysis and discussion, some of it theoretical, some of it more practical, dealing for example with the problems of coding and classification. It is difficult to arrive at a clear view of what changes in Gosplan's information system have taken place. Generally speaking some reorganisation of information has occurred within individual sub-systems of ASPR, but there is little evidence that an overall approach embracing all information within Gosplan has been adopted.

However two features of the information system deserve particular attention. The first is the link between Gosplan's automated system and the automated system of state statistics (ASGS), through which the Central Statistical Administration supplies Gosplan with plan fulfilment data. The second is the automated system of normatives (ASN).

The automated system of normatives forms a sub-system of ASPR, but its ramifications extend right down the structure of management to the enterprises where input coefficients or normatives are ultimately formed or verified in production. Thus ASN collects and supplies a specific type of information at all levels of management, and although at each level it is regarded as a sub-system of the appropriate automated management system, it also has an independent existence. Accordingly its development has taken place independently of other automated management systems.

Work on ASN began in 1969 on the basis of a Gosplan decree. The Institute responsible for developing it, the Scientific Research Institute for Planning and Normatives attached to Gosplan USSR (NIIPiN), was instructed to prepare an outline draft by 1971, and a detailed draft over the period 1971–3. The introduction of the system began in 1974 (Nurbagandov (1974), p. 18).

The data processed by ASN are first registered at the production unit on punch cards. As the coefficients move up the management hierarchy they go through a process of successive aggregation, at the ministry and later at Gosplan. Thus the original data are recorded once only, and lower level units at each stage supply higher level units with information. This ensures consistency, although there are obvious problems of choosing appropriate aggregation techniques. The system can also be used for the imposition of progressive norms. Gosplan controls this process as follows: targets are established on the basis of a plan for introducing new techniques, applying cost-saving materials, using substitutes etc.; ministries submit indicators to Gosplan which meet these targets; after emendation and approval by Gosplan they are passed down to the ministries which subsequently allocate differentiated targets to their subordinate production units (Gorshunov (1972), p. 74). Automation of the system makes it possible to rely less and less on crudely averaged norms.

The data provided by ASN are used extensively in the formation of material balances and the compilation of distribution plans, and have made it possible for these plans to be compiled without the need to collect indents (*zayavki*) from users (Lebedinskii (1974), p. 9). It is also obvious that accurate data on input coefficients are needed for input–output models, though aggregation problems may cause difficulties. ASN is designed to serve any system of planning which relies upon the centralised collection of input coefficients, irrespective of how far the rest of the system is automated. Marshalling a mass of input coefficients on automated data-processing equipment relieves planning officials of much low level planning work with or without ASPR. Yet ASN is also an important part of the general programme of management automation, which at Gosplan level includes the introduction of some mathematical models. This circumstance has made it a sensible policy to introduce ASN at the same time as automated management systems, but to a degree independently of them.

The second aspect of information for planning to be considered is the relation between ASPR and the automated system of state statistics (ASGS), which is designed to perform many of the functions carried out by the Central Statistical Administration (TsSU). Chapter 1 has described the competition between Gosplan and TsSU for the role of chief organiser of the overall programme for management automation. We have seen how the issue was resolved after the XXIV Party Congress in 1971 in a way which left Gosplan the dominant role, in the sense that the major information flows would still correspond to the lines of authority in the hierarchy of management and that these basic information flows would not be channelled via an information system controlled by TsSU. This has limited the role of TsSU in the Statewide Automated System to that traditionally performed by the statistical services. Accordingly the automated system of state statistics is given only a brief description here with emphasis on its links with Gosplan's automated system.

ASGS has been developed on the framework of TsSU's regional machine-accounting stations (MSS) which process statistical data for TsSU and also offer a data-processing service for enterprises on a *khozraschet* basis. The first MSS were established in the

1950s and 70 were in use in 1957. By 1971 their number had grown
to 1,200 (Starovskii (1971), p. 11). As they were equipped with
computers the stations were redesignated information and computer
centres. By 1975 there were 2,500 stations in total, of which 1,600
were equipped with computers. There were also about 100 computer
centres serving *oblasts*, autonomous republics etc., computer
centres in every Union republic and a chief computer centre
(Sazonov (1975), p. 5).

ASGS is being established in two sections. The first section,
which was completed in 1975, provides for the automation and
consequent speeding up of data collection on the basis of the
existing system of statistical reporting. Thus the output of ASGS
is broadly similar to the output of the old system, but the process
is faster. The first section covers 40% of the total data at the republican and *oblast'* level, and 54% at the Union level. The labour input
required to process a unit of information has gone down by 60%
(Pervaya (1976), p. 4).

The second section is projected to include the development of
automated data banks, operating at different levels (USSR, republic,
oblast') and storing all statistical data in a retrievable form
(Volodarskii (1978)). This is a long-term project which requires
for its success the solution of a number of major problems of coding
and classification, as well as the obvious technical problems of data
storage and access. It is also necessary to establish the relationship
of ASGS to other automated systems.

There is evidence of a continued attempt by TsSU to serve as
a link for certain types of accounting information between enterprises and ministries and Gosplan. Thus Sazonov, a deputy head
of TsSU, has written (Sazonov (1975), p. 7):

the interaction of ASGS and the automated systems of ministries and departments assumes, in the first place, the elimination of parallelism and duplication
in their work, i.e. the preparation of accounts [*otchet*] to be centralised in
the state statistical organs, solely within the computer centres of TsSU;
secondly, access by ASGS to data of automated management systems of
ministries and departments, enterprises and organisations, control of their
accuracy and receipt of necessary data; and thirdly the transformation of
the technical base of ASGS into the technical base for entire management
systems for enterprises and organisations, where it is inexpedient to set up
departmental computer centres and stations.

In the past other organisations have shown a certain reluctance
to allow flows of information to be mediated by TsSU, so it was

unlikely that this proposal would find favour with Gosplan and the ministries. Moreover, for this expanded role for TsSU to become even technically possible, the network of TsSU computer centres would have to be expanded and the automated data bank established. So there is some doubt whether TsSU's conception of its role will be realised. In the meantime it is largely restricted to supplying Gosplan through ASGS with information which was previously supplied by traditional means.

However in the supply of statistical information from ASGS to ASPR, TsSU and Gosplan can jointly make some improvements. For example, the Chief Computer Centres of TsSU and Gosplan in conjunction with a TsSU research institute have jointly devised a sub-system for Capital Construction, intended to improve the collection of statistics, planning and management in this area. The quantity of data required to keep track of progress on construction sites is enormous, and the sub-system operates by keeping a register of all sites. Any changes are recorded as soon as they happen. The register contains data on the number and location of sites, the source of finance, the size and form of capital investment, the extent to which capital equipment has been commissioned, the duration of construction and so on (Simakova (1975)).

The existence of this bank of data will permit Gosplan and TsSU to use identical indicators to plan, control and analyse the process of construction and to obtain accurate data quickly. Similar advantages of speed and accuracy are claimed for another sub-system of ASGS covering the balance of the national economy, or the preparation of ex-post statistical input–output tables. In 1975 the detailed draft of this system was in preparation. The sub-system is intended to have close links with the branch sub-systems of ASGS, which supply it with basic information. It will prepare tables for the USSR as a whole and for the Union Republics, and experience in Estonia is said to have shown the advantages of processing the data on computers rather than by hand (Figurnov (1975)).

Developments in information for planning naturally mirror any changes in the procedures by which plans are prepared. We have seen in the previous sections that with certain exceptions the methodology of plan preparation within Gosplan has remained the same, although there have been changes in the techniques for calculating the same basic indicators. These changes have made it possible to use more data, and desirable to get it more quickly.

Most of the developments in planning information have been directed to these ends. There are instances where new methods of planning are used, such as input–output models, and these have imposed extra needs. In these cases new information systems, such as the automated system of normatives, are required. But difficulties with the new information system combined with the problem of altering some aspects of planning while leaving others intact have limited the scope of such new developments.

6 ASSESSMENT

One of the main points to emerge in this chapter has been the gulf between the ambitious models proposed by various economists as a basis for ASPR, and the cautious changes introduced into the planning system to date. However I shall begin this section by isolating the areas of common ground among all those involved in the discussion.

The largest area of common ground is on the need to expand the scope of long-term planning, with the implication that Gosplan should spend a greater part of its time on this function. This was recommended by the XXIV Party Congress in 1971, and has found expression in the general plan covering the period 1976–90. There is a broad measure of agreement that an expansion of time horizons is not only desirable but necessary, in view of increasing gestation periods and the pre-eminent role of technical progress.

Rather more controversial is the need to develop a system of rolling planning with annual pushing forward of the plan horizon by one year. The feasibility of such a procedure depends upon the level of automation of plan preparation. At the moment it takes at least three years to prepare a five-year plan, and the resources required to prepare a general plan, though unknown, must be substantial. Annual preparation of the five-year plan would not require three times the work force, as there would be a substantial carry-over from one year to the next, but it would certainly be desirable, if not strictly necessary, to arrange for a substantial number of operations to be carried out automatically, in order to reap the benefit of the same kind of economy as can be achieved by multi-variant calculations on the same data.

However it would be a mistake to ignore the mobilising and propagandistic function of the system of five-year plans as it exists today. It would be possible to obtain that effect by publishing a single plan every five years, but it is unlikely, if the fact of annual recalculation and extension of the period were widely known, that any such document would retain the authority which it has today in spite of target revisions. The case for recalculation of a general plan every five years is a stronger one, which will no doubt be accepted.

On the question of the methodology of long-term planning there is more disagreement. To take an example, the system of integrated planning (SKP) contains a proposal to analyse the objectives of the economy by preparing a tree of goals. Conceptually this is an important advance as the proposed elaboration of the tree of goals from high levels to lower levels breaks down the sharp and clear-cut distinction between objectives of planning and resources. Items at the intermediate level of the tree can both satisfy objectives directly and further the achievement of other goals. The tree of goals is a more flexible instrument than the more familiar conception in economic planning of a single objective function. It permits the consideration of other objectives than quantitative, purely economic ones, and it also recognises that the process of elaborating the plan may cause a reconsideration of the goals to which it is directed. However although the tree of goals may be useful in encouraging orderly thought, it can hardly be seen as a practical instrument of planning. The nearest planning practice has come to this approach is to identify certain major objectives, such as the development of a region of the country, and to devise an overall programme of measures intended to achieve such an objective. These measures are then incorporated within the conventional plan, though administrative reorganisations or special procedures may be needed to ensure their implementation. This is the 'programme' approach, discussed above, which probably draws more on Western management techniques than directly on SKP.

The decomposition proposals such as that of Baranov have attracted even less support within Gosplan. In this context we can recall Kornai's remarks on decomposition methods, that they can be interpreted either as convenient methods of solving large computational problems or as blueprints for a decentralised system of planning (Goreux (1973), pp. 525–30). In the former interpretation, there are grave doubts about their technical feasibility. In the latter they involve in addition changes in the economic system to which Gosplan has frequently expressed objections. In the Baranov proposal, and in SKP, annual planning is something which can by and large be left to the ministries or lower organisations. Gosplan condemns such proposals for breaching the directive character of planning. The two sides have different conceptions of planning and therefore understand different things by ASPR. They disagree not only, or not so much, on how Gosplan should plan but on what Gosplan should plan.

These disagreements are reflected in the different conceptions of ASPR which have been current since the middle 1960s. Initially the system was conceived within Gosplan simply as a means of relieving planning workers of routine arithmetic chores. Investigators concentrated on identifying routine calculations and performing them on computers. In a second stage ASPR was conceived of as an integrated data-processing system, containing individual balancing and optimising calculations. In other words while routine data-processing would be integrated, gaps in the system would be filled by human decision makers operating on roughly traditional lines. This progressive widening continues in the third conception, in which the system is considered not as something built on to the existing planning process, but as something which replaces it. Moreover the new planning system must be organically linked with the implementation process. This is the conception represented by SKP.

The current stage of ASPR corresponds largely to the first concept with some elements of the second. The current plans for ASPR, when implemented, will complete the transfer to the second conception.[8] But theoretical discussion concentrates on the third conception which, although not fully developed, includes elements which are radically different from existing planning practice.

From the description of the new proposals given above, it is clear that Gosplan's opposition is based not so much on bureaucratic inertia or jealousy of power, as on a realistic appreciation of the difficulties involved. The computational requirements of some of the procedures go far beyond those now available, yet when a plan is to be implemented with economic levers and without the safety net of quantitative controls, as some of the proposals recommend, it must be calculated in detail and with accuracy. This objection alone is enough to rule out many proposed procedures, even if the conceptual difficulties associated with them could be overcome.

Thus it is unlikely that the introduction of ASPR will be associated with radical changes in the methodology of planning. The more likely outcome is that computers will be used more and more for data-handling and data-processing with a gradual and limited integration of partial mathematical models into the planning system. This is less than many economists would like to see, but improvements in information flows and planning organisation can still have a beneficial effect on Gosplan's operations, especially when combined with the improvements in planning and management at other levels which are discussed in the following chapters.

4

COMPUTERS IN GOSSNAB

The close interrelationship between the planning of production and the planning of supply has been a feature of the Soviet economy since the period of the early five-year plans. The administrative framework within which the two aspects of national economic planning have co-existed has frequently changed, but the basis of the system has throughout remained remarkably constant.

Since 1965 the supply planning side of this complicated but not ineffective system has been undertaken largely by the USSR State Committee on Material–Technical Supply (Gossnab), which was created when the planning and management system reverted from a regional to a departmental and ministerial basis. This chapter is concerned with the use of computers and mathematical methods in Gossnab, more specifically with the design and introduction of the automated system of supply management, which, since 1969, or loosely speaking since 1966, has been an objective of government policy. First I give a brief outline of the organisational structure of Gossnab and of the tasks it performs, and discuss developments in Gossnab's organisation and functioning which are taking place simultaneously with, yet independently of, the construction of Gossnab's automated management system, ASU MTS, and which may impinge on its operation.

1 GOSSNAB'S ROLE IN THE MANAGEMENT PROCESS

Although it does not control the supply of all commodities,[1] Gossnab comprises more than eight hundred separate organisations and its employees number hundreds of thousands. The overwhelming majority of these organisations are local, performing routine warehousing or shipping functions, but here we shall be concerned chiefly with the central apparatus of Gossnab and the higher-level regional organisations.

The highest tier in the Gossnab hierarchy is the central apparatus, which comprises a number of functional administrations and administrations for the supply and distribution of certain important sectors. (This account is taken from Spravochnik (1974), pp. 14–35.) The functional administrations are concerned with such things as finance and legal or scientific matters, and they include a division for the introduction of the automated system of supply management (ASU MTS). The other kind of administration covers important groups of products such as machine- and instrument-building, metallurgical products, chemicals, fuel and construction materials. The precise function of these administrations is unclear, but it seems likely that they work closely with Gosplan USSR.

Beneath the central apparatus are two sets of organisations based respectively on a product classification and a regional division. The product groups are called Chief Administrations for supply and sale (*Soyuzglavsnabsbyty – SGSS*) and Chief Administrations for supplying new and reconstructed enterprises with equipment (*Soyuzglavkomplekty – SGK*). There are twenty-four SGSS (for example *Soyuzglavtsement*, which deals with cement) and twelve SGK (for example *Soyuzglavkomplektavtomatika*, which supplies enterprises with automation equipment). The arrangements for oil supply are slightly different, and are not discussed here.

The product division is duplicated by a regional division into Chief Administrations for supply (GUMTS) and Administrations for supply (UMTS). Each republic in the USSR has a GUMTS, and three republics also have UMTS. The Ukraine and Kazakhstan each has seven UMTS subordinate to its GUMTS, which is itself responsible, like the other GUMTS, jointly to Gossnab USSR and the Council of Ministers of the Republic. In the RSFSR there are thirty UMTS subordinate only to Gossnab USSR. The regional organisations control a local network of specialised or general-purpose warehouses (*sklady*), depots (*bazy*), offices (*kontory*) and shops (*magaziny*).

Most of Gossnab's efforts are concentrated on the planning and management of supply for periods of a year or less. An overall outline of the Soviet annual planning system has been given above (Chapter 2, pp. 32–5), but it is worth describing in more detail the functions of each of the tiers in the Gossnab hierarchy and the interaction between them and with other organisations, in order to appreciate more clearly the scope for using computers at each level. As the subject is well documented and widely discussed, the treatment is brief. (See Spravochnik (1974), pp. 14–71, Iotkovskii (1974), pp. 101–7 and Kalinin (1977)).

The supply organisations have two main planning functions – the compilation of material balances and the preparation of a distribution plan. When enterprises and *ob'edineniya* receive their production plans for the following year, they calculate their requirements for material inputs and communicate them, usually to a local supply organisation. These statements of requirement or indents (*zayavki*) are aggregated regionally and, when the commodity is distributed by a central organisation, they are aggregated over the USSR as a whole. Then a balance between production of and demand for each commodity or group of commodities is compiled, the identity of the balancing organisation depending on the importance of the commodity and determining whether a national or a regional aggregation of indents is required. There are six classes of commodities each with a different balancing agent. They are:

1 Commodities for which the material balances and distribution plans are approved by the Council of Ministers. In 1977 these numbered 274.
2 Commodities for which the material balances and distribution plans are worked out and approved by Gosplan USSR. These numbered 1,767.[2]
3 Commodities distributed by Gossnab USSR and its subordinate organisations. These numbered 13,200 in 1977.
4 Commodities distributed by central ministries and departments. These represent a small proportion of output but a large number of separate products (about 40,000). Since 1968 Gossnab has played a role in channelling indents for some of these commodities to the appropriate ministry, and in some cases organising their allocation.
5 Decentrally-planned commodities distributed by republican ministries and local Soviets. They are usually produced and used locally and comprise a large and heterogeneous range of products.
6 Products distributed through wholesale trade. In this case wholesale trade organisations transmit the indents to the appropriate organisations. Some commodities in this category are distributed without allocation certificates.

When the balancing organisation has achieved a satisfactory

level of consistency, it then prepares a distribution plan, allocating output to ministries and other bodies whose subordinate organisations use the commodity in question, or to regional supply organisations. In 1977 Gosplan for example made a distribution among 215 allocation holders (*fondoderzhatel'*). The units in which the commodities are distributed are those in which the balance is compiled, which are usually highly aggregated. When enterprises have received their supply allocation they prepare a detailed specification of their requirements and transmit it to the appropriate supply organisation, which in the case of Gossnab-distributed products is the regional UMTS or GUMTS. This information is passed on to the body responsible for preparing the distribution plan. The latter, on the basis of its knowledge of producing enterprises' capacity, specialisation and location, carries out the attachment (*prikreplenie*) of customer to suppliers and the issuing of legally-binding allocation certificates (*zanaryadka*). Thus customers receive their supply plans and suppliers receive detailed production plans through their ministries. Finally contracts are exchanged between customer and supplier. This completes the planning stage, but Gossnab is also responsible for monitoring and controlling plan fulfilment and for allocating certain categories of above-plan output. Material balances are compiled in a similar way for longer-term planning, though in more aggregated form. For the 1976–80 plan, Gosplan compiled 234 balances (154 of them approved by the Council of Ministers) and Gossnab a further 106 (Kalinin (1977), p. 86).

The faults of this system have been widely discussed. Achieving mutual consistency of the balances is a well-nigh impossible task, and the tendency to adopt excessively taut or inconsistent plans leads to failures of supply which have repercussions throughout the rest of the economy. The figure of the *tolkach* or expediter, whose task it is to speed or divert supplies, makes frequent appearances in Soviet newspaper articles.[3] One of the chief objectives of the automated system of supply management is to eliminate these deficiencies. However, the introduction of ASU MTS is not the only measure being taken to achieve this end. A series of other changes are taking place in the supply system which affect and are in turn affected by the plans to use computers and mathematical methods. The most important of these are now briefly described (see Schroeder (1972)).

One of the more widespread changes is the transfer of Gossnab organisations to the new system of management and economic incentives outlined in the 1965 economic reform. This process began in December 1966 and was confirmed both by a decree of the Council of Ministers in 1969 and by the XXIV Party Congress in 1971. By 1972 about half of Gossnab's turnover was accounted for by organisations working on the new system, including five SGSS, twenty-seven UMTS or GUMTS, and over five hundred other supply and sales organisations. The new system for supply organisations closely parallels that introduced for enterprises in the 1965 economic reform; the same three incentives funds are set up, and there is a similar reduction in the number of centrally established plan indicators for the supply organisations. The change has meant that automated management systems are being established in an environment of extended *khozraschet*. Soviet writers are unanimous in commending this development, but some authors have gone further and recommended, as part of the development of ASU MTS, schemes for expanding the independence of supply organisations which go far beyond the provisions of the reform (see Section 3 below).

Another change in the arrangements for supply planning is the increased reliance on direct long-term links between customers and suppliers. The idea was first approved in 1965, and the 1969 decree referred to below instructed Gossnab to transfer enterprises to direct ties in 1969 and 1970. Although the change has not taken place as quickly as planned, there has been substantial progress. In 1966 direct links were formed by 600 suppliers and 1,300 customers; in 1973 the numbers had risen to 5,000 and almost 20,000 respectively. In 1971 the value of shipments by this method amounted to 12 milliard rubles, increasing to 24 milliard rubles in 1974 (Selivanov (1975), p. 12). Kosygin's report to the XXV Party Congress in 1976 spoke of extending the system further; in 1977 37 milliard rubles of supplies were allocated in accordance with direct links, and an increase to 45 milliard is projected by 1980 (Glotov (1978)). The advantage of a direct link is that the supplier is able to cater more effectively for the needs of his customers, and the customer can be sure of a product of standard quality. A Soviet author advocating direct links refers to the case of a chemical factory which in 1968 received a certain input from four different factories. Although the product in each case satisfied the relevant State standards, the variation in quality seriously impeded the work of the customer factory (Lagutkin (1970), p. 261). If the factory had been supplied throughout by a single shipper this difficulty would not have arisen.

The existence of long-term direct links must be taken into account by the automated system of supply management. As we shall see, one of the earlier uses of computers in supply planning was the preparation of optimal attachment plans by the use of linear programming. The solution of a problem of this type will often be in conflict with the principle of long-term direct ties, inasmuch as any change in the production plans may well require a whole new set of attachments, if the original programme is re-run using the new data. In Soyuzglavkhim, the SGSS responsible for chemical products, it was estimated that using the results of the programme unamended would involve assigning a new supplier to each customer every quarter.[4] It is said to be worth increasing transport costs by up to 10–15% to get the benefit of long-term direct links (Lagutkin (1970), pp. 257, 266). However this factor changes the way in which computers are used for attachment rather than eliminates them. Working out a stable long-term link is a problem subject to mathematical formulation and computer solution, but it will often require more sophisticated techniques, including the use of Monte-Carlo methods to evaluate the stability of the proposed links in the face of changing circumstances (Geronimus (1973), p. 62).

Closely related to the establishment of long-term direct links is the development of wholesale trade. There has been a great deal of debate in the USSR about the appropriateness and significance of this form of distribution. The XXIV Party Congress in 1971 approved the extension and development of wholesale trade and it is intended that the value of such trade should double from 1976 to 1980, reaching 12 milliard rubles (Kurotchenko (1978), p. 12), but it has been stressed that wholesale trade is not the same as free or derationed trade. Drogichinskii, the head of Gosplan's section for the introduction of new methods of planning and incentives, defines wholesale trade thus: 'wholesale trade in the means of production is one of the forms of planned distribution of the means of production on the basis of long-term direct links and long-term contracts between supplier and customer organised in a planned way either directly or through an intermediary. As a rule, wholesale trade in large lots is done between suppliers and customers directly, and in smaller lots through an intermediary; small-scale wholesaleing is done through Gossnab shops or through the USSR Ministry of Trade' (Drogichinskii (1974), p. 29).

In practice the change to wholesale trade will mean that the number of plan indicators measured in physical units approved by Gosplan and the USSR Council of Ministers will be substantially reduced. Equally ministries will be less rigid in laying down planning targets for their subordinates and leave more room for negotiation horizontally between supplier and customer. Gossnab's territorial supply organisations will play the role of intermediary in many of these transactions, and will be remunerated accordingly. As noted earlier, some authors have gone further and proposed that the Soyuzglavsnabsbyty should be reorganised as organisations wholesaleing on a *khozraschet* basis, but this proposal has not been approved or implemented.

The general direction of all these changes was determined at the time of, or fairly soon after, the announcement of the Soviet economic reform in 1965, which was made before the official decision to develop automated systems of supply management was taken. But the detailed specification and gradual implementation of the change has taken place since that decision was taken, and, as is the case with other organisations involved in Soviet economic management, simultaneous changes in the manner of operation of the supply system have imposed changing and sometimes even contradictory requirements on the design of the ASU.

2 THE DEVELOPMENT OF ASU MTS

We have already noted the scope for using linear programming techniques to solve the problem of allocating suppliers to consumers, which is the function carried out by Gossnab in preparing the distribution plan. The data for the problem are the size and location of supply and demand, and the distance or cost of transportation from each supplier to each customer. The objective function is the minimisation of transport costs or of total transport distances measured in ton–kilometres. The Soviet author A. N. Tolstoi in 1939 and 1941 outlined this problem, which has become known as the transportation problem, but gave no rigorous mathematical solution. A general method of solution was given by Kantorovich and Gavurin in 1949 (Nemchinov (1964), p. 35). By the early 1960s a number of solution methods were known and used but they made little or no impact on the organisations responsible for arranging transport of goods. The reluctance to use the optimal system of shipments became an often-quoted example of the irrationality of the planning system (Kantorovich (1978), p. 831). If transport organisations receive their plan in terms of ton–kilometres, they are reluctant to use a rational system of shipments which reduces the value of the variable to which their bonuses for plan-fulfilment are attached. Thus the use of computers and mathematical methods in supply, as in other areas of Soviet planning and management, had little initial impact.

This situation began to change in 1966. In August of that year the USSR Council of Ministers adopted a decree entitled 'On immediate measures for establishing a system of management of supply using mathematical methods and computer technology'. The decree provided for the development of automated systems of management in four chief administrations (SGSS) attached to Gossnab USSR, those responsible for ferrous metals, for non-ferrous metals, for chemical products and for bearings; in eight chief or regional supply administrations (GUMTS or UMTS); and in five large warehouses and depots (Lagutkin (1971a), pp. 34–5). No provision was made for using computers and mathematical methods at the highest level of Gossnab USSR, for example in the administration concerned with inter-sectoral flows.

The decision immediately sparked off the publication of a number of articles in Gossnab's journal, *Material'no-tekhnicheskoe Snabzhenie*, none of which betray a clear conception of how the proposed automated systems would operate. One author came out strongly against basing the system on computer centres which would be common for all organisations in economic management, and in favour of a separate system with links with other computer centres (Bystrov (1966), pp. 53–4). To help with the proposed developments two new institutes were set up. The first was a specialised scientific research and design institute for management systems (NIISU), attached to Gossnab USSR and situated in Tula; the second was a branch of TsEMI, attached to Gossnab to help with the use of mathematical methods in supply.

The director of the latter, Geronimus, and TsEMI's director Fedorenko were soon arguing for the elaboration of a set of mathematical–economic models within the framework of which individual local applications would progressively be developed. This was in keeping with TsEMI's general view at that time on the futility of unco-ordinated local applications of mathematical methods. The insistence on the important role of *khozraschet* and material incentives as a complement to the new methods is also characteristic of

TsEMI's thought at the time (Fedorenko (1967), pp. 58, 66).

The specific instruction of the 1966 decree, to develop automated management systems in four SGSS, was carried out by a number of organisations. The system for Soyuzglavmetall, known as ASU Metall, was designed under the direction of the Institute of Control Problems (formerly known as the Institute of Automation and Remote Control). The system for non-ferrous metals, ASU tsvetmet, was designed by NIIMS, Gossnab's scientific research institute for the economics and organisation of supply. TsEMI and NIIMS were involved jointly in the system for the SGSS distributing bearings, and TsEMI was responsible for the ASU in Soyuz-glavkhim, which allocates chemicals. This division of responsibility sowed the seeds for later difficulties, as each organisation tended to go its separate way.

The SGSS not included among the initial batch of four were to concentrate their efforts chiefly on improving their document circulation and information flows, and on mechanising basic supply management operations. However, the use of computers for compiling attachment plans extended beyond the four SGSS. In 1967 TsEMI prepared a *Temporary Standard Method for Calculating Optimal Plans for Attachment of Customers to Suppliers in the Chief Administrations for Supply and Sale of Gossnab USSR*. This was approved by Gossnab, the State Committee on Science and Technology and the Presidium of the USSR Academy of Sciences and came to be widely applied (Khrutskii (1974b), p. 505). One problem was the size of the mathematical programme to be solved. The number of supply and demand points was often between two thousand and ten thousand, while computer programmes in 1967 could usually accommodate a maximum of one thousand locations (Ekonomiko-matematicheskie (1967), p. 54).

There is some evidence that the 1966 decree allowed only the period 1966–8 for carrying out its provisions. This target proved to be over-optimistic, and the introduction of the ASU provided for in the 1966 decree took place only after – in some cases quite a long time after – the publication of a further important decree of the USSR Council of Ministers on supply in April 1969. This decree made more precise many of the developments in supply management discussed in the previous section, but it also widened the scope of application of automated management systems in Gossnab. As well as confirming earlier developments, it instructed the Academy of Sciences to work out in 1969, through the agency of TsEMI, the basic provisions for an automated system of supply management. TsEMI was appointed the head organisation for working out the system (Resheniya (1970), p. 405).

In 1970 a large symposium was held in Moscow, to discuss achievements to date and the problems of developing ASU MTS (Problemy (1970b)). In the same year Gossnab approved a temporary decree on the sequence of working out and introducing the automated system. It laid down the familiar stages of setting specifications, preparing the outline, detailed and final drafts of the system, to be followed by introduction (Lyapin (1970), pp. 75–7). By this time Gossnab's deputy president Lagutkin had worked out a list of functions to be performed by ASU MTS at all levels, including the central apparatus which had not been covered by the 1966 decree. The list is as follows (excluding the functions of depots and warehouses) (Lagutkin (1971a), p. 48):

Gossnab USSR
Planned distribution of products in the classification used by Gossnab USSR.
Supervision of shipment plans of the most important products.
Control of reserves and stocks of the most important products.
Planning and control of the organisations of Gossnab USSR.

Soyuzglavsnabsbyty and Soyuzglavkomplekty
Determination of demand, calculation of product balances and distribution to allocation holders.
Allocation of orders to suppliers.
Attachment of suppliers to customers and issue of allocation certificates (*zanaryadka*) for products.
Formation of direct long-term economic links.
Integrated supply (*komplektovanie*) of construction sites.
Control of sales and shipments of products in the classification used by the SGSS.
Book-keeping and accounting.

Territorial supply administrations
Determination of total demand for products at a detailed level.
Distribution to customers.
Control of trade in means of production.
Choice of the mode of supply to customers (transit or warehouse).
Planning, setting of norms and control of stocks.

Control of shipments and sales.
Strategic use of resources and management of reserves.
Decentralised procurement and mobilisation of internal reserves.
Settling up for commodities, book-keeping and accounting.

By this time work on individual systems was sufficiently far advanced for a number of deficiencies to be noticeable. By the middle of 1971 the outline draft had been completed and the detailed draft begun for each of the four SGSS designated originally in 1966, and ASU were being established in a number of UMTS and GUMTS (Lagutkin (1971b), pp. 8–9). Yet a contribution to the 1970 symposium made the point that each of the systems for the four SGSS had a different coverage of functions and that there was no unified methodological and organisational basis for the product systems (Problemy (1970b), p. 17). The problem arose from the design process, which involved thirty-one research and design organisations of Gossnab and another twenty departmental bodies (Povyshat' (1974), p. 27). There were also doubts expressed about the quality of design work. The director of NIISU acknowledged in 1969 that his institute's resources were too widely scattered and too deficient in qualified personnel to do much more than mechanise the existing supply system (Basnin (1969), p. 20). In 1971 NIIMS was criticised for superficial analysis and for not helping enough to put its research into practice (Lagutkin (1971b), p. 12). Better progress was made in installing hardware. By 1971 Gossnab had built up a network of thirty-six machine-accounting stations, eighteen computer centres, and a chief computer centre equipped with a British ICL 4–50 computer (ibid., p. 9). By 1974 this network had grown to thirty-seven computer centres and sixty machine-accounting stations. In 1973 optimal attachment plans were calculated on this equipment for 340 million tons of goods, permitting an economy of ten thousand railway wagons (Povyshat' (1974), p. 27).

In 1972 TsEMI's division for the automation of the process of supply management prepared a document on ASU MTS which was accepted by Gossnab USSR. In one account the document was an outline draft for ASU MTS (Khrutskii (1974b), p. 519), but this description is at odds with the usual design sequence as it predates the acceptance of technical specifications. It is most probably identical with TsEMI's submissions entitled 'Basic Provisions for Establishing the Automated System of Supply Management of the USSR National Economy'. Whatever its title, the document seems to have been methodological and conceptual in tone and much less than a blueprint for implementation, even in outline form. In any event there took place at about this time a reallocation of responsibilities for the design of ASU MTS. According to Lagutkin, experience had shown the advantage of concentrating design and research work within Gossnab. On this argument, by the beginning of 1973, TsEMI had been replaced as head organisation for the design of ASU MTS by NIIMS, Gossnab's own research institute, though TsEMI remained head organisation for the use of mathematical methods and computers in supply (Khrustkii (1973), p. 68). The director of NIIMS was named chief designer of ASU MTS and NIIMS was made responsible for working out a unified series of documents for use in the supply system. NIISU and the production–technological *ob'edinenie* Ukrglavsnabsistema were allocated the roles of head organisations for design of various levels of the system, and Gossnab's chief computer centre was made responsible for software, hardware and information inputs. A Council attached to the Chief Designer was formed to co-ordinate the work (Basnin (1974), p. 17).

By 1973 the Scientific and Economic Council of Gossnab had examined and approved a technical specification for designing ASU MTS (Kurotchenko (1974), p. 4). Unfortunately little is known of this document, which was said to inaugurate 'a new stage in the planning of supply'. Like Gosplan's automated system the ASU would consist of functional and service parts. It would operate at all levels of the supply system and include functional sub-systems performing the following tasks: supply planning; formation of economic links; stock control; control of shipments; financial and economic activities of supply organisations. Of these the first is concerned chiefly with the formation of balances, the second with the preparation of a distribution plan; the third is self-explanatory, while the sub-system for control of shipments will supervise the implementation of the supply plan. The final sub-system for financial activity will oversee the operation of subordinate organisations (ibid., pp. 11–12).

All the evidence suggests that the completion of ASU MTS as currently envisaged will bring little fundamental change to the organisational structure of Gossnab. Indeed a Gossnab inspection committee in 1975 condemned some of the design work for adhering too closely to the existing structure (Yakobi (1975), p. 27). However the overall system's chief designer has observed that initially it is necessary to exploit in the design of ASU MTS the extensive experience already available of using computers in supply-experience accumulated in what is essentially the traditional regime of supply planning. A dissenting view is discussed in the following section.

One·aspect which has been stressed in discussion of the specification is the need for standardisation of design. This problem was first tackled in 1970–1, when Gossnab began to prepare standard designs for automated systems of management. Among the SGSS, some standardisation has been attempted on the basis of the product systems, ASU Metall and ASU tsvetmet. Among the SGK, Soyuzglavkomplektavtomatika was chosen as a model for all the others in the design of ASU (Zhimerin (1972), p. 46). This approach to standardisation has been described as the 'group method': a representative member of a group is selected, an automated system of management is designed for it, and that system is then adapted for other members of the group. The disadvantage of this approach is that the area of application of any complete standard design is limited and the number of basic variants correspondingly large (Isaev (1974), pp. 72–3). Furthermore it takes a long time to develop a comprehensive standard design and before introduction it may be overtaken by changes in the economic and organisational environment.

To deal with these drawbacks a new method has been developed, the use of standard design solutions. This method, which originated in the Ministry for Instrument Building (see pp. 126–7 below), has been accepted by NIIMS in the specification. The basis of the new method is that 'the algorithm of the supply and sale process is successively divided with respect to functions, tasks, levels and other characteristics into elementary operations which in aggregate are performed by the system as a whole. From this set identical categories of operation are distinguished as standard elements, design documentation is worked out for each of them and rules are made up for combining these standard elements into a system with given parameters' (Basnin (1974), p. 15). A further development is the so-called modular principle according to which the elements or modules are combined for each organisation on some general principles, the combination being effected in some cases on a computer. Although the initial cost of developing these general methods is high, it is recouped by a reduction in the costs of design of the automated system as a whole. It also should ensure a degree of uniformity within the system.

The practical results of the standardisation drive seem to have been slow in coming. The example most frequently referred to is the standard method for determining demand, which has been prepared for a number of SGSS, limited according to some sources to engineering branches, according to others to a wider range of products. Other developments include the preparation of the draft of a standard decree on the computer centre of a (G)UMTS, the standardisation of documents being undertaken by NIIMS in conjunction with the ministries, and a standard design for mechanising accounting work, completed in 1974. By 1980 the preparation of a further 32 standard design solutions should be completed (Kurotchenko (1978), p. 11). The problems of implementing this clearly rational policy of standardisation will become apparent when some existing automated management systems for supply are discussed.

3 A MATHEMATICAL MODEL OF SUPPLY PLANNING

This section describes a model of annual supply planning worked out at TsEMI over several years and also the arguments which have centred around TsEMI's proposals for using the price-system and profit-maximisation as a means of establishing and implementing the supply plan. Exactly what role this model has played in the construction of ASU MTS is not clear, but presumably it underlay TsEMI's documents on ASU MTS submitted in 1972. The authors of the model describe it not as a 'unified mathematical–economic model', the construction of which is, they say, impossible, but as a system of local models (Khrutskii (1974b), p. 514).

The system consists of five stages, involving five levels in the planning system. My account introduces a number of simplifications; the reader is referred to the original for further details (Geronimus (1973), pp. 29–58). Much of the complexity of the model arises from a multi-level system of classification of products. In a descending order of aggregation, these levels are: (1) the classification used by Gosplan; (2) the classification used by Gossnab; (3) the classification in which SGSS prepare their balances; (4) the specified (*spetsifitsirovannaya*) classification used by enterprises and regional supply organisations; and (5) the assortment (*assortmentnaya*) classification used chiefly in detailed negotiations between production units.

The process of annual supply planning recommended in the

model begins with the transmission from Gosplan to Gossnab of a set of targets for net and gross output levels specified in Gosplan's highly aggregated classification. Gossnab disaggregates these targets by solving the following mathematical programme.

Let Y_i and X_i be net and gross output levels of commodity i in Gosplan's classification. Let $Y_{i(j)}$, $X_{i(j)}$ be net and gross output levels of product group j in Gossnab's classification, itself a component of product i in Gosplan's classification.

$a_{i(j)k(l)}$ is the input coefficient of commodity $i(j)$ per unit of output of commodity $k(l)$
$A_{i(j)k(l)}$ is the matrix of such coefficients
$B_{i(j)}$ is the maximum possible output of $i(j)$
$\bar{Y}_{i(j)}$ is the forecast demand for $i(j)$.

The constraints are:
    All output levels are non-negative:

$$Y_{i(j)} > 0 \tag{1}$$

Gossnab's disaggregated categories sum to Gosplan's aggregate targets:

$$\sum_{(j)} Y_{i(j)} = Y_i \tag{2}$$

Gross output in each product in Gossnab's classification provides for final output and intermediate inputs:

$$X_{i(j)} = Y_{i(j)} + \sum_{k(l)} a_{i(j)k(l)} X_{k(l)} \tag{3}$$

Production capacity is not to be exceeded:

$$X_{i(j)} \leq B_{i(j)} \tag{4}$$

Various objectives functions are considered, but preference is given to the following:

$$\sum_{i(j)} \left(\frac{1}{\bar{Y}_{i(j)}} (Y_{i(j)} - \bar{Y}_{i(j)}) \right)^2 \to \min \tag{5}$$

To solve this quadratic programme it is recommended that the constraint (2) be dropped; if it is not satisfied by the solution, then Y_i or $\bar{Y}_{i(j)}$ will be changed.

The formulation of the model has some odd consequences. The forecast levels of demand are obtained in some unspecified way and do not seem to be revised in the light of the solution of the programme unless the constraint (2) is not satisfied. This is at variance with the system of compromise and revision which takes place in Soviet planning offices as new information on the feasibility of plan targets becomes available. But the most questionable element in the model is the objective function. The solution of the model gives a minimum of the unweighted sum of the squares of proportional deviations of supply from forecast demand. This means that a given percentage deviation of an unimportant product counts as much as the same deviation in a vital commodity. This difficulty will be overcome only if each product in Gossnab's classification is of roughly equal importance. Moreover in the quadratic formulation an excess supply counts as much as the same level of excess demand, although the repercussions of the latter are more damaging. At the same time the quadratic function does capture the fact that successive deviations of supply from forecast demand are progressively more damaging, although this feature of the model is purchased at the cost of the extra computations required by a quadratic programme.

The next stage involves the third level in the supply planning process, the SGSS and their equivalent level in the production planning hierarchy, the ministries. Each SGSS receives output levels in Gossnab's classification and disaggregates them into its own classification on the basis of forecasts and other data. Ideally an input–output model covering all products in Gossnab's classification would be required to ensure compatibility between inputs and outputs, but this is made impossible by the size of the problem. So each SGSS works out its own input–output model, treating shipments to other SGSS as final demand (see pp. 115–16 below). The set of equations for an input–output model is one of the constraints in a linear programming problem solved by the SGSS. Other constraints are upper and lower limits for output levels of individual products, and limitations on productive capacity and use of primary resources agreed with the appropriate ministry. The objective function is of particular interest; the SGSS is to maximise the excess of the value of output over the value of inputs, evaluated at prices which in the first iteration are wholesale prices, and in subsequent iterations are recalculated by Gossnab. The preliminary plans of all SGSS are collated, and when demand for a commodity exceeds supply, its price is raised or the level of final demand adjusted. These prices can also be used to evaluate the performance of the supply organs.

Data on prices and quantities are agreed by the SGSS with the producing ministries which transmit them to their subordinate enterprises. Simultaneously SGSS communicate the prices and expected levels of demand to regional supply administrations (UMTS or GUMTS). Enterprises, on receipt of their production plan, prepare a detailed supply plan which they communicate to the UMTS. The UMTS compare actual demand with their provisional allocation, and bring the two into equilibrium by an adjustment of prices within overall limits set by the SGSS or by re-negotiation with the SGSS.

The SGSS then has the problem of assigning the output of each ministry's enterprises to a particular territorial supply administration. This requires the solution of a linear programme known in Soviet literature as a problem of the production and transport type. (Some examples of this problem are given in the following section.)

The final stage of the model is the detailed allocation of supply to individual enterprises by the UMTS. Where long-term direct links exist, this decision is pre-empted, although the model does provide for detailed price decisions to be taken by negotiation between the parties. In other cases the UMTS has to allocate supplies to particular enterprises and at the same time decide whether the supply should be effected by direct shipment from the producer or from a warehouse. This problem can be formulated mathematically, and solved with knowledge of the minimum size for transit shipments established by Gossnab for each commodity (Khrutskii (1974b), pp. 516–18). Finally the UMTS works out the precise routes (*marshrut*) and sequence (*grafik*) of shipments from its subordinate depots, which form the fifth and lowest level in the system.

The most striking feature of the system is its use of prices to equilibrate supply and demand. There are five levels of classification, and prices are used together with direct quantitative allocations to balance supply and demand for all of them, except at the Gosplan level. Usually the prices at a lower level of classification are constrained to average out to a price established at a higher level, and quantitative limits are set within which output levels must remain. As far as I know the mathematical properties of a model of this kind have not been examined rigorously in Western or in Soviet literature. This is hardly surprising as the inspiration of the model clearly is drawn from existing supply practice, and many of the procedures are informal. However the grafting of flexible prices onto this system, an addition very characteristic of models originating in TsEMI, is also designed to fit in with a proposed method of implementing the supply plan, through a radical extension of *khozraschet*.

This is an issue with extensive ramifications concerning the nature of the supply process. Although the supply branch of the Soviet economy is not deemed to employ productive labour, as we have seen this has not prevented the introduction of the new planning and incentive system. It is argued at TsEMI that the supply branch is providing a service, for which there should be a system of remuneration leading to an optimal allocation of resources.[5] Thus plan implementation in the TsEMI proposal is brought about by a combination of three factors: a system for setting prices for commodities which is implicit in the planning model outlined above, a system for setting prices for supply services, and an objective function or maximand for organisations in supply.

The last aspect was the subject of a series of discussion articles in the journal *Material'no-tekhnichesko Snabzhenie*, published over a number of years (Kilin (1972), pp. 74–7). At the 1970 symposium Kurotchenko distinguished three alternative positions. TsEMI favoured maximisation of profits; the Institute of Control Problems favoured the minimisation of losses from supply shortages, while NIIMS, Gossnab's own research organisation, proposed maximisation of turnover. Kurotchenko noted that the profit maximising objective presupposes an optimally functioning economic system, the theory of which he regarded as being based on inadequate foundations (Problemy (1970b), pp. 20–1). Other authors have denied the existence of a single objective (Yakobi (1975), p. 30).

However in TsEMI's view profit maximisation would be combined with a new method of fixing prices for the services of supply organisations. In the present system, the income of supply organisations comes from a mark-up (*natsenka*) on prices of goods shipped through a warehouse and a deduction (*skidka*) from the price received by a producer shipping his output directly by the 'transit' mode to a customer. The precise nature of TsEMI's alternative proposal is unclear, but it appears to be closely based on the dual prices obtained with the solution of a linear programming problem of the transportation type. These prices – christened potentials (*potentsialy*) by Kantorovich in his original work – are the dual prices associated with the constraints in the programme, and can be interpreted as the (competitive) price of the product delivered and at the supplier (Dorfman (1958), pp. 122–7). In the TsEMI proposal these prices will be adjusted by a proportionate mark-up of transport costs to cover the expenses incurred by the supply organisations in finding the optimal solution. Although the details are obscure, this mark-up will require a readjustment of suppliers and customers. Some such procedure underlies the suggestion that SGSS be converted into state wholesale trade organisations, operating on full *khozraschet* principles within the guidance of the economic plan (Fedorenko (1972b), p. 206).

This conception of the supply system is at variance with those of the Gosplan official Drogichinskii and of Kurotchenko, the designer of ASU MTS, whose views are reported above. Nor is there any evidence that flexible prices will be used systematically, even in conjunction with physical allocation, to prepare the plan. However some of the individual components which the TsEMI model has tried to weld into a coherent whole have been put to use, as we shall see in the next section which discusses the use of computers in the SGSS and SGK.

4 AUTOMATED MANAGEMENT SYSTEMS IN THE SGSS

ASU Metall

We have seen that the 1966 decree on the development of automated management systems in supply provided for the design of ASU in four SGSS, of which one was Soyuzglavmetall. Work on this system, which became known as ASU Metall, began at once under the direction of the Institute of Control Problems (IPU), which was designated head organisation by Gossnab and the State Committee on Science and Technology. Other institutes involved were the Institute of Cybernetics of the Ukrainian Academy of Sciences, the Institute of Mathematics of the Siberian Division of the USSR Academy of Sciences and a research institute of the Ministry of Ferrous Metals (VNIIOchermet). The project attracted a number of distinguished scientists, the head of the design process being V. A. Trapeznikov, and the chief mathematician L. V. Kantorovich. However the arrangement under which the design was directed from outside Gossnab was not satisfactory to all parties. In November 1970 a conference held in Tula recommended that IPU be replaced as co-ordinator of the project by NIISU, Gossnab's own institute (Kazz (1971), pp. 87–8).

By 1971 the outline draft for ASU Metall had been submitted and work on the detailed draft had begun. By this time as many as forty organisations were involved, though their work was hampered by the absence of an overall framework for the automation of supply (Mamikonov (1972), p. 6). The decision was made to adopt a stage-by-stage method of designing and introducing the system. A general outline of the system as a whole would be drawn up, and then concurrently with the preparation of the detailed draft particular planning and accounting functions would be taken over by the computer. This policy has been carried out, and individual problems have been solved before the complete introduction of the system.

ASU Metall comprises three levels: Soyuzglavmetall, territorial organisations for metal supply, and local metal depots (*metallobazy*). The intermediate level is intended to concentrate all the metal supply of a region within unified structural sub-divisions of territorial supply organisations known as Metallosnabsbyty. Much attention has been given to this level. By 1974 NIISU had completed the detailed draft for the first section of ASU Metall for GUMTS and UMTS, for introduction by the end of 1975 (Povyshat' (1974), p. 28).

Great emphasis has been also placed on the need to develop *khozraschet* relations within the metal supply system. Soyuzglavmetall was selected for the introduction of *khozraschet* in the 1969 decree on supply, and in the same year it was reported that NIIMS had worked out the appropriate measures (Belkin, N. (1969), p. 4). Yet in 1973 the subject seemed still open to debate. It was proposed that each of the three levels of the metal supply system should operate on *khozraschet* principles, and that the computer centres serving the management system should operate in the same way (Odess (1973), p. 19). Exactly how this last arrangement would work is not clear.

Within ASU Metall four functional sub-systems are distinguished: for planning demand for and allocations of metal products; for determining detailed requirements and issuing allocation orders for metal products; for operational regulation of shipments and stock control; and an information and reference system. The first section of ASU Metall was planned to include the final sub-system –

the information system. The second stage would include the determination of detailed requirements and optimal attachment plans, while the third stage would extend ASU Metall to include the other sub-systems (Laptev (1972), p. 5).

The need to develop an alternative forecasting system arose because of the inadequacy of the earlier method, which was based upon collection of preliminary indents (*zayavki*). The problem was that when the indents were collected in the April or May preceding the planned year enterprises lacked not merely a detailed production programme, but even the overall outline of their production plans. As a result the quantities stipulated in the indents did not correspond to actual needs.

This system was replaced by one which relies upon direct forecasting of demand for metal products, using input–output data, except that the indent system is retained when the demand is new, when the commodity is in short supply, or when for some reason requirements cannot readily be forecast (Protsenko (1973)).

Forecasts are compiled at three levels – at Soyuzglavmetall, at the GUMTS, and at supply and sale depots. First, 6–8 months before the planned period, Soyuzglavmetall makes a forecast of demand for metal products on the basis of the overall targets of the annual plan. The forecast is made at an aggregate level for the economy as a whole, but it is also broken down by major allocation-holders and by regions. This latter breakdown is co-ordinated with forecasts prepared by local supply administrations. The forecasts are communicated to the production ministry, the Ministry of Ferrous Metals, which on the basis of the forecast and the five-year plan of the branch prepares a detailed preliminary production plan.

The local supply organisations receive their allocation within the forecast totals, and compare them with the detailed information they collect from each enterprise. Any divergences of supply and demand are taken up with Soyuzglavmetall by the allocation-holders. The effect of this is to spare Soyuzglavmetall examination of all preliminary indents, and to confine its attention to cases where allocations do not correspond to the levels implied by the production plans of the using enterprises. When these problems are sorted out Soyuzglavmetall comes to a second agreement with the ministry and forms a final version of the supply plan in the aggregated classification.

More detail is added at the stage of estimating demand for the shorter time period, usually six months, for which the allocation orders are issued. This process begins three or four months before each period and comprises forecasts in a detailed classification prepared by local organisations for different forms of supply (direct, warehouse, wholesale trade). These data are used by Soyuzglavmetall for the allocation of orders, the function carried out by the second ASU Metall sub-system. As well as short-term and annual forecasting of demand, some effort is made at medium-term (two to five years) and long-term forecasting (five years or more).

The significance of the demand-forecasting sub-system is that it is a partial way out of the awkward situation which arises from separating production and supply planning: without the supply plan the production plan cannot be prepared, and equally the supply plan presupposes knowledge of output targets. As for how the forecasts are made, the methods used appear to include use of input–output models and multiple regression analysis. These methods are described below.

The most important sub-system of ASU Metall is that which solves jointly the task of production scheduling at metal-cutting factories and the assignment of customers' orders to individual enterprises. A number of mathematical models have been worked out to perform this function by scientists at Gossnab, at the Institute of Cybernetics of the Ukrainian Academy of Sciences and at the Institute of Mathematics of the Siberian Division of the USSR Academy of Sciences. The most commonly used model, developed under the leadership of Kantorovich, combines both the production and the transport aspects of the problem (Kantorovich (1972)).

The programme calculates the levels of output of different products at steel mills and shipment plans from the mills to customers, which are grouped together in regions. The maximand is the difference between the value of free time of mills (available for above-plan output) and transport costs.[6]

A mathematical formulation is as follows. The data are:

T_j = available cutting time of the jth mill, in hours

f_{ij} = hourly rate of the jth mill in producing the ith output

b_{ik} = demand for the ith output in the kth region

d_{jk} = cost of transporting one ton of output from the jth mill to the kth region

c_j = value of one hour's free time on the jth mill

λ = coefficient for comparing transport costs with the value of free mill time.

The programme is required to find:

x_{ijk} = planned production level of the ith output shipped to the kth region from the jth mill

Y_j = free time of the jth mill for above plan output, in hours

The problem is:

$$\text{Max} \sum_j c_j y_j - \lambda \sum_k \sum_j \sum_i d_{jk} x_{ijk} \qquad (6)$$

subject to

$$\sum_i \frac{1}{f_{ij}} (\sum_k x_{ijk}) + y_j = T_j \qquad (7)$$

$$\sum_j x_{ijk} = b_{ik} \qquad (8)$$

$$x_{ijk}, y_j \geq 0 \qquad (9)$$

Slight variations of this basic model have been used to allocate orders for the output of plate-mills (Bryukharenko (1973)), rolling mills (Kolosov (1973)), and tube mills (Spivakovskii (1973)). In the last case the new method of allocation made possible an increase in output of 2% over plans compiled in the traditional way. However, since the model does not take all factors into account its solution cannot be accepted automatically. It may require alterations in the light of minimum shipment norms, long-term links and developing patterns of specialisation, though some models try to take account of these factors (see for example Kolosov (1973) and Mikhno (1971); the latter describes a multi-level model incorporating heuristic procedures). The problem of establishing priorities in cases where demand exceeds supply is particularly intractable. The accuracy of the solution is also limited by the need to aggregate. For example, the number of varieties of rolled and calibrated steel is a quarter of a million, and the customers for it number forty thousand. Even after aggregation the model for plate-mills includes 6,978 variables, and 2,055 equations.

    A notable feature of all the models discussed is that they substitute mill time for tons of output or some other physical or value aggregate as the basic unit in which the balance of supply and demand is calculated. The new measure has the advantage of greater precision, especially when there are substantial changes in the structure of output. However, it does clash with the units of measurement used by other organisations. Kantorovich has suggested that Gosplan should adopt the new system of measurement for its balances, and that it should make allocations to Gossnab measured not in tons or rubles but in hours of machine time (Kantorovich (1969), p. 70). More controversially he has proposed that the system of dual prices emerging with the solution of his linear programming model be used as differentiated prices for metal products, to stimulate plan fulfilment (Kantorovich (1972), p. 9). However linear programming models which provide good (i.e. stable) primal solutions often have an unsatisfactory dual solution. Thus one might expect the model to be formulated differently if prices are of interest.

Another interesting aspect of the models is that they require a considerable encroachment by Soyuzglavmetall on the functions of the Ministry of Ferrous Metals, *Minchermet*. Essentially, the production plans of all the ministry's mills would, if the models were fully implemented and their results accepted, be worked out by the supply organisations. This a source of potential difficulty and conflict.

The third sub-system of ASU Metall is concerned with stock control and with operational management within the planning period, usually in response to a failure by one party to fulfil the plan. The basic difficulty of specifying the latter problem in a way suscept-ible to a mathematical programming solution is discussed in a later chapter on branch automated management systems (see pp. 142–3 below). Essentially it is a problem of information: the management organisation must know the losses to the economy resulting from any supply failure and should allocate stocks or reallocate supplies to minimise these losses. The Institute of Control Problems has formulated a number of models to deal with particular cases, but there seem to be no practical applications (Burkov (1973)). The part of the sub-system dealing with stock control illustrates the same difficulty (Lototskii (1973)).

The functions of the final sub-system, the information and re-ference system for ASU Metall, are largely determined by the other sub-systems. The information collected includes: input coefficients for particular types of machinery, data on specialisation, transport networks and transport costs, the current state of plan fulfilment, stock levels, and accounting information used for such purposes as forecasting. In all this amounts to more than 200 million symbols, kept on the magnetic tapes and discs which form the basis of ASU Metall's automated information and reference system. The information output of Soyuzglavmetall is enormous. For 1973, 800,000 allocation orders were prepared, and the quantity of information needed grows at the rate of 11% per annum (Trapeznikov (1972), p. 4).

On the hardware side the organisers of ASU Metall have tried as far as possible to use computational facilities already in existence in preference to constructing special computer centres. The latter course is followed only where the computers would be fully utilised by calculations required by ASU Metall. Thus at the local level the system relies largely on territorial computer centres; at the higher level it initially used a combination of punch-card equipment and computers at Gossnab's chief computer centre. Since 1973 all work in connection with the information and reference system of ASU Metall has been done on computers, chiefly on Gossnab's ICL System 4–50. Other calculations have been done on a Minsk 22 (Belkin, N. (1973), p. 1).

There is conflicting evidence on the question of how effective ASU Metall has been. On the one hand some of the sub-systems – notably that for production scheduling – have been developed fairly extensively, and a number of practical applications have been claimed which exhibit substantial savings. On the other hand some of the sub-systems have eluded precise formulation and have not gone beyond the stage of experimental calculations. Furthermore there is some evidence that even when ASU Metall has been in a position to produce results capable of practical application, either it has not done so or the results once calculated have been ignored. Spivakovskii, the deputy head of Gossnab's Administration for ASU, who earlier played a part in the design of ASU Metall, criticised Soyuzglavmetall on the ground that in 1973 it had not prepared the necessary information for computer calculations and he also noted that 'it is intolerable that the results obtained from the computer should go into the archive and work continue in the old way; this practice has come to light in some divisions of Soyuzglavmetall' (Povyshat' (1974), pp. 27, 32). Unfortunately no explanation is given for these failings and we can only speculate as to their cause. It may be the case that personnel in the supply organisations have received insufficient training in the use of new methods, or that an initial barrier of resistance has to be overcome. An alternative and more fundamental explanation is that frequent changes in both production and supply plans disturb the fine balance of the calculations worked out within ASU Metall, nullify the results computed, and force supply officials to revert to traditional methods. Another possibility is that inconsistencies between the objectives and methods of work of the SGSS and those organisations with which it deals prevent the use of ASU Metall results. There is no evidence which discriminates between these explanations, and they are not, of course, mutually incompatible. I return to the last of them in Section 5.

ASU tsvetmet

The problems faced in allocating supplies of non-ferrous metals are naturally very similar to those discussed in the previous section. The automated management system for supply of non-ferrous metals, ASU tsvetmet, has been prepared under the direction of NIIMS. The first section was due for introduction in 1975. It includes: calculation of and control over allocations, allocation of jobs to suppliers, and optimal attachment of customers to suppliers for copper, aluminium, zinc etc. There is some ground for believing that the allocation of jobs to suppliers and the allocation of suppliers to customers are initially treated separately; the model of the former problem does not include transport costs and regionally-differentiated requirements among the data or variables (Spravochnik (1974), pp. 611–14). Transport costs are introduced only at the stage of preparing the production and supply plan for detailed sub-groups of output, subject to the result of the earlier more aggregated calculations. This system has been used since 1972. The transport model alone had been used since 1970, though its initial introduction was hampered by the fact that NIIMS did not prepare the detailed design of the system as a whole until 1971. Generally, the design of the system has been criticised for not making adequate provision for later developments of the system or for its integration in the structure of ASU MTS (Yakobi (1975), p. 24).

It was proposed that at a later stage a link be formed between ASU tsvetmet and OASU tsvetmet, the automated management system of the Ministry of Non-Ferrous Metals. Already an overall structural scheme has been prepared, and agreement reached on hardware for information transfers. This is a very interesting development which could eventually lead to the amalgamation of supply and production planning not merely within one organisation, but as a fully integrated process.

ASU Soyuzglavkhima

Like the two SGSS above, the organisation responsible for allocating chemical and rubber products was included in the 1966 decree on automation in supply. In 1967 work began on the construction of mathematical models to control the production and distribution of some chemical industry products, starting initially with paints and laquers. The project was undertaken jointly by Soyuzglavkhim and Soyuzkraska, an industrial *ob'edinenie* of the USSR Ministry of the Chemical Industry (Selivanov (1971), p. 28). It was natural that TsEMI, which had undertaken a large amount of work on planning the chemical industry, should be involved. In 1969 a preliminary draft of ASU Soyuzglavkhima was approved by Gossnab USSR. The co-ordinator of the design was TsEMI. A four stage process of transition was envisaged, beginning with the application of computers for forecasting and optimal loading of capacity, with a gradual extension of the list of functions to include other activities and integration of all functions into a single system. In 1969 the first stage was in progress. Although information has been published concerning this first stage, there is little to suggest that the second and subsequent stages have been reached. In 1974 Kurotchenko observed that ASU Soyuzglavkhima illustrated the fact that 'use of institutes of other departments to direct work on automated systems of supply management has not justified itself' (Kurotchenko (1974), p. 15).

TsEMI has investigated a number of methods for forecasting demand, and many of them have been tested on data drawn from Soyuzglavkhim. The chief methods used are regression analysis and analysis of time series. Although in other branches multiple regression analysis has been considered,[7] in the case of chemical products the research has been limited to estimation of a time trend, though a variety of functional forms have been used, all of them susceptible to transformation into a linear equation. But the whole exercise is hampered by a lack of data as documentation is kept for only three years, after which it is destroyed. TsEMI has developed a heuristic method which uses very short runs of time series data, analysing different cases according to rules of thumb. The results showed an improvement over formal mathematical statistics methods and although they were slightly worse than the results obtained by Soyuzglavkhim using the traditional methods they saved a substantial amount of labour. In preparing the forecasts for 1972 Soyuzglavkhim used the results of an improved version of the heuristic algorithm for forecasting demand for 366 products.

Another application pioneered within Soyuzglavkhim is the interproduct balance or branch input–output model. The need for a special model for the chemical industry arises chiefly because of the very high degree of interdependence within the industry. For example to know the required output of sulphuric acid, output targets must be known for the more than 200 chemicals which use it. Its direct and indirect inputs include more than 600 chemicals. For some products more than threequarters of total output is used up within the branch (Korobkov (1976), pp. 6–7). An input–output model enables all these interrelations to be taken account of simultaneously.

The model is compiled using the usual system of equations:

$$X = AX + Y \tag{10}$$

where X is a vector of gross outputs
A is a matrix of direct input coefficients
Y is a vector of final demand
Solving for X,

$$X = (I - A)^{-1} Y \tag{11}$$

The difference from the economy-wide model is that in this case final output includes all demand coming from outside the branch, even when it is an input into another sector. This demand can no longer properly be treated as exogenous, as part of it may arise in a branch which itself produces an input into the chemical industry. An iterative procedure might satisfactorily take account of these feedbacks, but it has not been tried.

Experimental calculations within Soyuzglavkhim were carried out over the period 1968–74. In the traditional system of individual material balances, Soyuzglavkhim compiled about 1,000 balances and Gosplan compiled balances for about 80 of the most important products. Ideally both Gosplan-distributed and SGSS-distributed products would be treated together within a single interproduct balance, but hitherto only products distributed by Soyuzglavkhim have been included, though there are plans to incorporate Gosplan-distributed products as well. Even so the balance includes about 1,500 outputs and 250 inputs.[8] Around 2,000 input coefficients are already required; extension of the system would double this number.

The model is used in the planning process in the following way. At the beginning of the planning year, preliminary estimates of final demand are made by the method of forecasting described above, and fed into the input–output model to derive gross output targets. When this calculation was made for the first time in 1974 it revealed that capacity limits were breached for 150 products. This information was passed on to Gosplan and the Ministry of the Chemical Industry. When production plans are corrected as part of the regular planning cycle from June onwards, the model comes into play again to evaluate the effects of the corrections. At this stage further inconsistencies should be revealed, which would have gone unnoticed under the old system because there would have been no time to process the data; shortages would have become apparent only at the stage of plan execution. The deficiencies are eliminated by a method incorporating some elements of optimi-sation (presumably some kind of priority system or incorporation of substitution possibilities, although details are not given).

As in other cases the practical impact of the system seems slight. The most claimed for the 1975 calculations is that, 'although the results did not find direct expression in the plan for 1976 they played a definite role as analytical material for correcting supply plans and further improvement of the method and sequence of performing optimal calculations with interproduct balances' (Korobkov (1976), p. 12). In any case the final decision on questions of production lies with the producing ministry rather than the supply organisation, and the division of responsibility for supply between Gosplan and the SGSS is an additional handicap which some economists want to resolve by leaving short-run decisions to the supply organisations and letting them negotiate contracts with industrial *ob'edineniya* of the producing ministry. These agreements would be made within the framework of long-term plans laid down by Gosplan. Whether this will come to pass is doubtful, but the interproduct balance is an interesting potential application of input–output for annual planning of a particular sector, the size of which is practicable given the present limitations of Soviet computers. There are plans to extend its use to other sectors (Kurotchenko (1978), p. 11).

The other principal application of computers and mathematical methods in the supply of chemical products is a production and transport model of the kind described above (Khrutskii (1974b), pp. 506–9). An important role is played by the limitations on supplies of raw materials which form an additional set of constraints in the model.

5   ASU MTS IN THE ECONOMIC MANAGEMENT SYSTEM

One point to emerge very clearly from the previous outline of ASU MTS is that it has involved small changes in the actual functions performed by the supply organisations, and has altered only the manner in which they are carried out. This is true not only of the practical applications but even of the proposed overall model of the supply system described in Section 3. Gossnab organisations will therefore retain their links with virtually every other organisation in the hierarchy of economic management. This has two consequences. First it makes it quite fruitless to attempt an independent evaluation of the overall economic effect of the introduction of ASU MTS. The benefits of improving the supply system will usually devolve not upon Gossnab but upon the suppliers and customers whose exchanges of commodities Gossnab arranges. This makes the extensive literature on the recoupment period of ASU MTS virtually valueless, as Soviet authors are increasingly coming to recognise (Novikov (1974), pp. 70–1).

The second consequence is that the question of the compatibility of ASU MTS with other automated planning and management systems looms very large. Planning and controlling the supply system involves Gossnab in dealings with Gosplan, with all producing and consuming ministries and their enterprises, with transport organisations, with the Ministry of Foreign Trade, with Gosbank and TsSU, and with a number of other state organisations. The most important links are those with Gosplan and with the ministries and their enterprises.

The chief means of connecting ASU MTS and Gosplan's automated system of planning calculations is the automated system of norms (ASN). This system, described in the previous chapter, is a hierarchically-organised network of input–output coefficients, based upon data collected at enterprise level. As the data move up the management pyramid, they are aggregated to suit the requirements of the particular level at which they are used. The intention is that both Gossnab and Gosplan should use a consistent set of data, but with different aggregation (Lebedinskii (1974), pp. 7–9). But as we have seen, there is no evidence that this ambitious system is in full operation. As regards relations between Gossnab and Gosplan the current position seems to be that each organisation is still at a fairly early stage of developing its automated system, and they naturally tend to concentrate on their internal operations rather than on the interface between the two systems.

The relation between Gossnab and the ministries is easier to assess, as more developments have occurred at this level and there are several instances where an ASU has been installed in an SGSS distributing products produced chiefly by a ministry which has a branch automated management system (OASU). This creates some conflicts of jurisdiction and of interest.

The conflict of interest between ministry and SGSS arises because whereas the ministry is chiefly concerned to increase output (or lower costs) the SGSS is often more interested in reducing transport expenditure. The two objectives are often contradictory. Minimising production costs usually entails specialisation and concentration of production, whereas dispersion of production lowers transport costs. In cases where transport costs are a significant proportion of the delivered price of output, the problem must be solved by preparing a plan for production and for delivery with the same mathematical model. This approach – formulation of a production and transport problem – was used for ASU Metall and in some branch automated management systems, but not in all. Two authors concerned with ASU MTS note that 'many designers, particularly of OASU, ignore this requirement [of a minimum of total costs] and in the sets of models in their respective designs they look at the problem from a departmental position' (Khmel'nitskii (1974), pp. 68–9). The authors hope that the development of *khozraschet* in the SGSS and in the industrial *ob'edineniya* of the ministries will overcome this problem, but their proposals are rather vague. One requirement for the optimal solution is that the calculation be centralised either within the ministry or the SGSS. As well as raising questions of jurisdiction, this resolution of the difficulty comes up against the problem that the same commodity is often produced in several ministries, and that Gossnab's organisations do not organise all supply in the economy. For this reason no completely centralised solution may be possible.

Gossnab also comes into conflict with the supplier enterprise when it prepares a sales plan which is not advantageous from the enterprise's point of view or which is inconsistent with the indicators it has received from its superior organisation. Several examples of this have been cited, some of them involving substantial losses to the economy. One group of authors has even concluded that the model allocating orders should include a constraint that the funds for material incentives and for social and cultural measures of the producing enterprise should not fall below a certain level. But this solution is clearly sub-optimal, and inferior to the authors' alternative proposal that centralised incentive funds held by the industrial *ob'edineniya* be used to eliminate any unfairness (Khmel'nitskii (1974), p. 67).

Reluctance to reconsider the whole economic planning and management system in the light of the new possibilities created by computer technology is, of course, a general problem affecting the development of ASU, but particularly serious in supply, which has interfaces with virtually all other economic organisations. Gossnab cannot on its own introduce a system of flexible prices on the lines proposed in the TsEMI model described above, nor can it decree that the shadow prices obtained as solutions for a transportation model be used to implement the plan, as Kantorovich has recommended. These are changes which must be made at the highest level, and at present there is no evidence of any will to make them. Until these problems are tackled as a whole, the economic problem of establishing the right relationship between ASU MTS and neighbouring systems will go by default.

Another set of problems, scarcely less intractable, springs from the need to ensure basic technical compatibility between ASU MTS and its neighbours. Compatibility of hardware and software is being progressively assured by developments within the computer industry, but in the field of coding and classification the situation is less satisfactory. The problem stems chiefly from the delays and inadequacies of the Union-Wide Product Classifier (OKP). Although this is a general problem, its effect on the supply system is particularly severe. Appendix I gives a brief account of the difficulties and discusses the prospects for improvement.

5
MINISTRY-LEVEL AUTOMATED MANAGEMENT SYSTEMS

Use of computers for planning and management in Soviet ministries has received a priority commensurate with the central role which ministries play in the management system. The ministry not only acts as an information filter between the basic production units and the highest level management and planning authorities such as Gosplan USSR, but also has itself areas of authority which are substantial and, as a result of the April 1973 management changes, expanding. Thus ministries need the capacity to make soundly-based decisions on large and complex questions as well as the information gathering and processing capacity to superintend the flow of information between production units and higher authorities.

Soviet specialists have repeatedly disclaimed any intention or ambition to ensure full automation at ministry level in the sense of reducing the ministry official's role merely to that of a technician, supervising the activity of computers which have already been programmed to take all the necessary decisions. Soviet computer technology is not up to sustaining such a system, and furthermore the mathematical models for optimal decision taking in such complex matters are often not formulated even at a conceptual level. The connotation of a branch automated management system (OASU) is a system of management in which the information system serving the decision takers is reorganised on the basis of central data collection and storage, and a branch computer centre is available to provide optimal solutions to planning and management problems (when they can be so formulated), solutions which are then analysed and modified by ministry officials in the normal way. In particular the fundamental nature of the relations between Gosplan and ministry does not seem to have been affected by the introduction of ASPR in the one and OASU in the other.[1]

The changes which follow from the introduction of an OASU

in present conditions are more in the manner in which management functions are performed than in the nature of the functions
themselves, or even in the administrative structure of the ministry.
This is chiefly the result of the fact that the ministry's rights and
duties are determined by the allocation of responsibility to different
levels in the economy as a whole, and that automation has hitherto
brought little change in this respect. Of course not everyone concerned with designing OASU is satisfied with this state of affairs, and
there is the now familiar dispute between those wishing to reorganise
the ministry management system root and branch and those determined to stick close to the existing system. It will become clear
that the balance of advantage is with the latter group.

In this chapter I first give an account of the development of
OASU and of the procedures adopted in their design and introduction. This is followed by two sections of which the first discusses
the information and computer systems on which an OASU is
based, and the second the management functions it performs.[2]
Finally, the method for calculating the economic return of an
OASU is examined, and an assessment made of the effectiveness
of the systems.

1   THE DEVELOPMENT OF OASU

The first branch automated management system in the USSR
was designed for the Ministry of Instrument Building, Means of
Automation and Control Systems (Minpribor). The Ministry was
chosen as one of the fastest developing and technically most advanced sectors of industry producing, amongst other things, computers and peripheral equipment. The development of the branch
automated management system, known as ASU-pribor, began in
1966 and was undertaken by a group of ministry research institutes.
Its installation began in 1969 and was completed by November
1970; the following month the system was approved by an Interdepartmental Commission headed by Academician Kirillin (Rudnev
(1972), p. 4).

ASU-pribor, though the first and most developed system, was
one of several OASU to be introduced in the course of the eighth
five-year plan. In 1967–8 a research team at TsEMI under the
direction of its deputy-director A. A. Modin, began an analysis
of the Ministry of Machine Tools and Instrumentation Industry.
The result of these investigations was a preliminary specification

of the OASU-Stankinprom (Modin (1970), p. 6). The number of OASU developed and installed before the end of 1970 is given as nineteen although, according to Rudnev, the plan for 1968–70 provided for 28 installations (Zhimerin (1972), p. 28).

The total number of branches in Soviet industry is estimated to be about three hundred, including All-Union, Union Republican and Republican Ministries, and ministry-level government departments (*vedomstva*). The ninth five-year plan called for the installation of over two hundred OASU by the end of 1975. In the first four years of the plan, only sixty-six ministries were so equipped, including at least twenty-six All-Union Ministries, but over the whole period of the plan 168 OASU were installed. By the end of 1977, 198 systems were in operation.

There are doubts about the quality of some of the systems installed in the early period. Rudnev, the Minister of Instrument Building, spoke of 'unequal fulfilment of the plan for OASU in 1968–70' (Zhimerin (1972), p. 28). In 1971 another author wrote that in practice establishing a branch automated management system had been reduced merely to mechanising work previously done by hand, instead of installing systems for optimal management (Dudkin (1971), p. 65). Complaints centred upon the tendency to exclude perspective planning in the branch from the list of functions covered by an OASU, a tendency still evident in 1974, in spite of the great economies alleged to be made from optimal decisions in this area (Zhimerin (1974a); Sinyak (1973b)). Such a management function was lacking in, for example, the automated system of management of the Ministry of the Radio Industry (Zhimerin (1972), p. 39).

In 1971 an effort was made to impose uniformity in the design of OASU through the publication of 'Directives for the Elaboration and Introduction of Branch Automated Management Systems', approved by the State Committee on Science and Technology (ibid., pp. 329–46). These are supplemented by a 'Standard Technical Specification for Designing OASU' (not available) and 'Directives for Establishing and Equipping Chief Computer Centres for Branch Automated Management Systems (GVTs OASU)' (ibid., pp. 363–95). The Directives replace a temporary document of the same name prepared some years previously; the procedures they outline are based on those adopted in designing ASU-pribor.

The two principals in the design of an OASU, as laid down in the Directives, are the Ministry (the client – *zakazchik*) and the designer (*razrabotchik*). The latter is designated head organisation for the design of the OASU and is typically a research institute or design bureau. The head organisation appoints other sub-contractors to be responsible for particular aspects of the development of the OASU. In the case of ASU-pribor, for example, the head organisation was a design bureau (SKB BFRM) assisted by several other organisations, including Minpribor's Central Scientific Research and Technical Design Institute for the Organisation and Techniques of Management (TsNIITU), which is situated in Minsk and has developed several OASU for Republican Ministries in Belorussia. Another important organisation active in the field is the All-Union Scientific Research and Design Institute of OASU (VNIPI OASU), situated in Moscow, which is part of Minpribor's industrial *ob'edinenie* 'Soyuzsistemprom'. Other ministries have their own research institutes for designing ASU, which presumably take part in the design of branch as well as enterprise systems.

According to the Directives, the client Ministry appoints a special sub-division to supervise its side of the work and the head organisation appoints a chief designer for the project. For the purpose of day-to-day control the client appoints a committee consisting of the heads of major sections of the ministry and representatives of the head organisation and its sub-contractors. Great importance is attached to the continuous participation of high-level ministry officials in the design of an OASU. If this requirement is ignored, a gulf develops between the design team and the ministry, the design does not fully satisfy the latter and the work is rendered ineffective. Glushkov has called this one of the basic principles for any automated management system (Krushevskii (1973), pp. 10–11).

In outline, the ministry's responsibilities under the Directives are: to improve the existing system of organisation and management of the branch; to work out the technical specification; to prepare forms for the collection of data for use in the OASU; to take part in preparing the detailed and final drafts; to approve the documentation at all stages; to finance the development of the OASU; to see to its installation (liaising with the Ministry of Communications); and to take part in submitting it for approval to an Interdepartmental Commission. The designer's responsibilities are: to study the existing system of management in the ministry and to take part in working out the technical specification for the OASU; to prepare a co-ordination plan and a budget; to prepare the detailed and final drafts; to take part in the introduction of the system and its submission for approval by the Interdepartmental

Commission. The head design organisation also exercises control over the work of the sub-contractors (Zhimerin (1972), pp. 332–3).

The most important stage, for which the ministry bears the chief responsibility, is setting the specification for the OASU on the basis of an examination of the existing management system (see Krushevskii (1973), pp. 15–39). This examination involves an analysis of the activities of all the ministry's sub-divisions and their interconnections with each other and with higher levels in the management structure. Particular attention is paid to the information system in the branch. Flow charts of document circulation are prepared and the source identified within the ministry for each indicator used for planning and management. The outcome of the process is a description of the organisational structure of the ministry, a representation of the information system, including copies of all documents used, and a general evaluation of the quality of planning and management in the system with particular emphasis on the identification of bottlenecks.

Using this information the ministry and the head organisation prepare a draft of the specification for the OASU, which is then discussed at meetings in the ministry and the head organisation, agreed with Minpribor, and finally approved by the ministry. Contractual and financial documents are prepared. The ministry concludes a contract with the head organisation, which also forms legal agreements with sub-contractors. The contract lays down the price agreed for the work and sets deadlines for its completion. The specification is binding; any changes must be embodied in a protocol which has the same legal status.

The specification lists the management functions which are to be automated and lays down requirements for the information system and for the hardware and software to be used in the OASU. It also takes account of the system's interfaces with automated systems at higher and lower levels in the management hierarchy, and determines the order in which the work is to be carried out, although the Directives have been criticised for failing to do this last job adequately, so that the work of specialists on different aspects of the design is poorly co-ordinated (Kandaurov (1974), pp. 27–8). The selection of functional sub-systems is a decision of particular importance. These sub-systems are blocks of calculations which can be distinguished as separable management functions and are usually so regarded under the existing management system. The Directives provide a list of sub-systems which can be taken as a starting point for such a selection within each individual ministry; the list is not mandatory and the circumstances of each ministry must be taken into account. The basic list comprises the following twelve sub-systems:

perspective development of the branch

technical–economic (i.e. annual) planning

operational management

control of sales

financial management

planning, accounting and analysis of labour and wages

supply management

planning, accounting and analysis of personnel

management of scientific research

control of capital investment

book-keeping

scientific and technical information.

A detailed description of some of these sub-systems, with an account of some local variations, is given below. When the OASU is introduced in stages some sub-systems may come into operation before others. In these cases it is strongly recommended that the first to be introduced should be those sub-systems which make possible better decision taking in the ministry, rather than those which merely reduce the need for low-level accounting personnel.

The stages following the setting of specifications are more technical in nature and chiefly the responsibility of the head organisation. Important functions performed at the detailed drafting stage include the design and equipment of the branch's chief computer centre and the preparation of software for the system as a whole. The draft typically includes estimates of the costs of the OASU and the expected returns.

The final draft, which, like the specification, must be approved by Minpribor, is the prelude to implementation. The ministry sets up the communications systems on which the OASU will operate. It constructs information points at some enterprises and links up with enterprise-level automated systems in its subordinate units; in some cases group information points are established, serving several enterprises. A detailed statement is made of the functions of all units of the ministry involved in the OASU, in particular the branch computer centre. Finally, a plan and network diagram covering the introduction of the system are prepared.

The introduction of an OASU involves elaborate testing both

with control or artificial data and with actual data acquired in the operation of the management system. In the latter case, the old system and the OASU work side-by-side. When satisfactory results have been achieved the OASU is transferred to regular use and an Interdepartmental Commission is formed to examine it by agreement with the State Committee on Science and Technology. It consists of representatives of the ministry, the head organisation and its ministry, sub-contracting organisations and Minpribor. It is not known whether such a commission has ever rejected an OASU.

The widespread introduction of OASU, particularly the ambitious target of two hundred systems to be installed during the ninth five-year plan, raised the question of how far it is possible to use industrial methods in their design. Sinyak, the director of Minpribor's research institute VNIPI OASU, has been particularly concerned with this issue (Sinyak (1972), pp. 6–7). It has proved impossible to standardise the design of an OASU as a whole, in the face of the variety of circumstances of individual branches. However certain standard elements have been isolated, which it is hoped can be used to build up a system. The elements are known as Standard Design Solutions (*tipovye proektnye resheniya* – TPR). In Sinyak's view they fall into three categories, those relating to algorithms and programs, to the configuration of computing and other equipment, and to procedures adopted by personnel operating the system.

The Standard Designs are incorporated in documentation which, in the case of algorithms and programs, includes a description of the task to be performed, the algorithm to be used, recommended forms for the presentation of data, service routines and a test program. Other sets of documentation contain standard configurations of various computers and data-processing equipment (Kandaurov (1974), pp. 31–4). Some degree of standardisation has already been achieved here by relying on two or three models of computer as the basis for OASU. By the beginning of 1974 the State Committee on Science and Technology had organised the preparation of standard programs for six particular management functions, for use on the second generation Minsk series of computer. It was expected that a set of working programs covering twelve sub-systems would be available by 1975. Similar arrangements exist for third generation computers. Examination of the management system of a number of republican ministries in the

Baltic States and Belorussia yielded an extensive list of typical elements for programming. Co-operation among machine-building branches has resulted in some standard sub-systems and a similar arrangement has been proposed for heavy industry, with a single chief computer centre serving a number of ministries (Barskii (1975), p. 212). Zhimerin estimated in 1974 that the State Committee's action in preparing standard detailed and final designs for OASU and standardising branch computer centres had already reduced costs by one half (Zhimerin (1974a)).

2 THE INFORMATION AND COMPUTING SYSTEMS OF AN OASU

We have already noted the distinction between the service and functional parts of an OASU. The latter are the sub-systems which actually carry out the management functions of the ministry; the former provide the materials and equipment for the functional sub-systems to use. The two parts are closely interrelated, as are the three sub-systems which make up the service part – the information system, computational and peripheral equipment, and software. Consider for example the factors which determine the nature of the information system. These are the methodology of planning and management, the administrative structure of the ministry, and the capacity of the technical equipment on which the information system and the functional sub-systems operate. All aspects of the OASU are mutually determined in the same way.

When work started on the information system for ASU-pribor, the first OASU, the experts involved expected it would be a fairly straightforward process. They were quickly disabused of this belief, and came to recognise both the complexity and the importance of the problem (Rudnev (1972), p. 4). The information system for an OASU must often be developed before the functional sub-systems come into operation, in order to provide the latter with the necessary backlog of data. Moreover the existing information system in a branch is something which has grown up over a long period, as accretions have been tacked on to meet special needs and circumstances. The result is often an improvised system lacking coherence or consistency, and often combining duplication of some kinds of information with a complete lack of other data.

These impressions are confirmed by the findings of a research team at TsEMI engaged in preparing a preliminary study for an

OASU at the Ministry of Machine Tools. Their analysis of document circulation in one of the Ministry's chief production administrations, or *glavki*, revealed that separate organisations within the ministry collected and stored their own normatives, that there was little coordination between the instructions sent down to the enterprise from separate sections of the ministry, and that within the ministry the same indicators were calculated in parallel in different sections and linked and co-ordinated only at the stage of summarising the plan for final approval. Furthermore, the two-stage organisational structure of the ministry, with chief administrations supervised by functional administrations of the ministry, such as the planning and economic division, resulted in the duplication of calculations at different levels, sometimes with a different data base (Fedorenko (1973a), pp. 201–3).

The TsEMI research team favoured a radical overhaul of the existing information system based on the principles of the integrated system of data processing (*integrirovannaya sistema obrabotki dannykh* – ISOD). These principles are quite general in application and have been used largely at enterprise level. In the case of an integrated branch information system all information is channelled through the branch computer centre, where routine processing is carried out by the computer or by unqualified staff. Data are then submitted in processed form to the appropriate divisions of the ministry, which do the necessary calculations and pass them on to other divisions or back to the computer centre. Thus all calculations are done with a common data base, and the branch computer centre builds up a stock of input coefficients and other information.

These principles were applied by the TsEMI research team in reorganising the information system at the Ministry of Machine Tools. The change was restricted to the information system and the existing allocation of functions among ministry divisions was maintained. Modin and his TsEMI colleagues give a description of the sequence of operations based on ISOD in a chief administration. The account corresponds to what we know to be the existing planning procedure. First a production plan is worked out based on control figures sent down from above, and targets are assigned to enterprises. On the basis of these plans, divisions of the administration work out plans for supply, sales and profit, labour and wages, and finance. The only difference is that data for these calculations are provided through the ISOD. The higher level of the ministry operates a similar system (ibid., pp. 203–7).

A means of transferring information from the enterprise to the branch which has been canvassed as a basis for the information system of an OASU is the matrix *tekhpromfinplan* or technical, industrial and financial plan. This is a method of representing the economic activity of the enterprise in a unified way, based on the input–output system. Its major use is for enterprise management, as a balance table of the activity of the enterprise as a whole, formed by the amalgamation of similar tables for subordinate units. However the matrix *tekhpromfinplan* can be used for the purposes of branch-level management as well. It can be used to transfer information from enterprise to ministry in a convenient way and at the ministry the plans of enterprises can be amalgamated by expanding the number of rows and columns of the input–output table to include all inputs and outputs used throughout the chief administration or ministry as a whole. Then if the range of goods produced and inputs used is fairly homogeneous, the resulting summary model can be used to provide coefficients for long-term planning (ibid., p. 129).

The problem of developing the information system for an OASU is made even more difficult by the ministry's situation in the overall management system. We have seen that the developers of ASU-pribor quickly came to appreciate the difficulty of establishing the information system. As well as organising the flow of data within the branch, they also had to reorganise primary data-collection at enterprise level and to take account of the requirements imposed upon them from above, in order to ensure compatibility between the branch and higher-level automated systems.

The extent of rationalisation of data-collection at enterprise level is usually expressed in the reduction of the number of forms and documents used in communication between enterprise and branch. Minpribor reduced the number of forms embodying primary information from 1,174 to 123. For example, only two documents are now required to transmit aggregated input coefficients for materials and components from enterprise to ministry, in place of the original thirty-eight. Such a rationalisation is a time-consuming business, taking two or three years. It also illustrates the difficulty of maintaining compatibility between automated systems at branch and enterprise level. When the enterprise management system is reorganised to accommodate an ASUP, decisions may be taken which are subsequently found to be incompatible with the branch automated management system.

There is a similar requirement of compatibility between the OASU and Gosplan's automated system of planning calculations. Minpribor's system of information on input coefficients was designed to meet the requirements of the automated system of normatives (ASN) at Gosplan level. Enterprises are instructed to compile their normative information in accordance with a single set of instructions and to submit it to the computer centre, which then prepares input coefficients based on weighted averages of the enterprises' figures in accordance with the classification of final products and materials approved by Gosplan. The calculations were found to involve initially the reworking of a vast amount of information (Suprunyuk (1972), p. 15).

The actual quantity of information handled within a branch computer centre is enormous. The official Directives for the Equipment of a Branch Computer Centre estimate that the average quantity of information for the OASU of a machine-building ministry is as shown in Table 2.

Table 2   *Information in a typical branch computer centre*

	Million symbols per year
Information processed by the computer complex	250–750
Total quantity of information arriving at the chief computer centre	100–300
Total amount of outgoing information	350–450

Source: Zhimerin (1972), p. 380.

In Minpribor's experience, the volume of incoming information amounts to 183 million symbols, that of outgoing information to twice as much. The breakdown of information entering and leaving the computer centre is shown in Table 3.

Table 3   *Information categories in ASU-pribor*

Category of information	Incoming %	Outgoing %
Planning	10	51
Operational and relating to production	19	11
Accounting	26	19
Analytical	—	15
Normative	45	4

Source: Rudnev (1972), p. 4.

The amount of processing required for even a single sub-system is enormous. Before the OASU was installed in the Ministry for the Automobile Industry, the quantity of information, incoming and outgoing, used for annual planning amounted to nearly one and a half million indicators, contained in nearly three thousand documents. Rationalisation of the information system reduced both these figures by nearly one half (Tikhonenko (1974), p. 47). The flow of information and the need for data-processing and computation are irregular, with peak requirements twenty or more times the average.

The reorganisation of the branch information system is made considerably more difficult by the lack of an adequate system of classification and coding. The total number of classification systems used in the ASU-pribor is fifty-seven, of which five are All-Union Systems, two are branch systems, the remaining fifty are either local systems or systems used in enterprise-level automated systems (ASUP). The problem of devising such coding systems is an immensely complicated one, not amenable to an easy solution. It is, however, an area in which the delays and incompetence of Gosstandart and of the Ministries have attracted the attention of the Committee for Popular Control (see Appendix I).

The selection of technical equipment for an OASU is made at a fairly early stage in its design. The choice of technical equipment depends on such obvious factors as the size of the ministry and the number of planning and management functions to be undertaken by the automated system. The comparative advantage of different items of equipment – computers or punch-card machines for example – should ideally be examined in each individual case. In practice the standard list of functional sub-systems, contained in the Directives for OASU, has been matched by standard configurations of technical equipment for the branch computer centre. Such configurations have been prepared for one second-generation computer (the Minsk-32) and two third-generation machines.

The first OASU were equipped with second-generation computers. For example, ASU-pribor in its initial phase had two Minsk-32 computers, a BESM-4 and a Ural 14. In 1971, the Directives for the Equipment of the Chief Computer Centre of an OASU laid down that third-generation machines must be installed. But they made a provision (necessary since such computers were not generally available) that up to the end of 1973 the Minsk-32 could be used as an alternative (Zhimerin (1972), p. 381). Many OASU are now equipped with third-generation machines. For example the USSR Ministry of the Automobile Industry and a number of republican ministries in Belorussia have ES series computers. ASU-pribor now has both an ES-1040 and an M-4030 computer, which have made possible the extension of the system under the designation ASU-pribor II. At the beginning of 1976, more than one quarter of ASU of Union industrial ministries had third-generation computers (Pokrovskii (1976), p. 126), and this proportion will have grown sharply since then.

A loose formula has been worked out to calculate the computer power needed in a branch computer centre. The estimated number of computations required in a year is divided by the annual stock of machine time in seconds. The result of this calculation, which expresses the required computer capacity in operations per second, is then augmented by a number of coefficients. First it is multiplied by a factor between 1.5 and 10 to make allowance for calculation failures. This figure is then further multiplied by between 10 and 50 to take account of the reduction in speed of operation caused by inefficiency in the input and form of presentation of data. A computer, or several computers, are then selected to meet this requirement (Krushevskii (1973), p. 50).

The second requirement of the technical equipment of an OASU is that it should be able to transmit information between the branch computer centre and subordinate enterprises. The method of transmission varies with the urgency of the message. For the purpose of regulating production on a day-to-day basis, information must be transmitted with speed and accuracy. The system pioneered by ASU-pribor has been a model for other ministries. Minpribor's branch computer centre receives information from its enterprises in a variety of ways. One group of enterprises can transmit information directly to the branch computer centre by teletype: this group includes enterprises with ASUP; a second group uses the telegraph system, while a third communicates by means of forty or fifty group information points (*kustovye informatsionnye punkty* – KIP), each of which serves a number of enterprises (Adamov (1972), p. 8; (1976), p. 8). By 1973 the total number of enterprises submitting information amounted to over three hundred. The Ministry of the Radio Industry operates a similar system for information transfer.

More recently, the function of the group information points has been expanded to include calculations as well as data transmission. Such centres may carry out some calculations which otherwise would fall on the branch computer centre. Such centres can carry out calculations for the enterprises they service as well as perform those functions which properly belong to branch management. This obviates the need to establish a computer centre in each enterprise and should increase the utilisation rate of computers. When the Ministry for Agricultural Machinery-Building was establishing its OASU it was proposed to set up such computer centres serving a cluster of its enterprises in areas where they were concentrated. In other regions the computer centres would be available for other enterprises outside the ministry as well. The Ministry of Machine Tools set up a number of such centres serving its local enterprises in the course of the ninth five-year plan.

The final shape of the information system of an OASU should, therefore, be that shown in Figure 5.

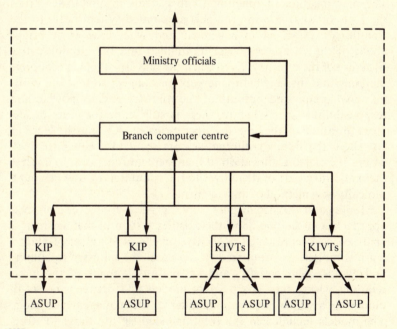

KIP   - group information point

KIVTs - group information and computation centre

ASUP - automated system of enterprise management

Figure 5   The Information system in an OASU

The third and last component of the service part of a branch automated management system is the software. According to one estimate, this makes up 50–60% of the cost of designing and installing an OASU (Kandaurov (1974), p. 95). It is little wonder that attention has been paid to the possibilities of standardising programs and algorithms for use in OASU, through the Standard Design Solutions noted earlier. The requirements of an OASU for software can most clearly be seen in relation to the detailed management operations of the functional sub-systems, which are discussed in the following section. More general discussion has focused on the need to use high-level problem-oriented languages such as Cobol or Fortran.

3   THE FUNCTIONAL SUB-SYSTEMS OF AN OASU

The identification of functional sub-systems in an OASU raises the issue of what relation the new automated system bears to the traditional system of management and what changes it brings about in the nature of functions fulfilled and the administrative structure of the ministry. Even when the ministry's role in economic planning and management is largely unchanged, so that the informational inputs and outputs of the ministry and its powers and responsibilities are as before, there is still scope for more or less reorganisation of the internal operations of the branch. Here as elsewhere the familiar alternatives are available: either to work within the existing allocation of management functions, to analyse them and turn part of them over to the computer, or to work out a radically new method of management.

Modin and his colleagues have argued for a compromise approach. On the one hand the existing system of management is analysed and represented explicitly; on the other, a set of mathematical models is formulated to represent the ministry's planning and management activity, and an analysis is made of the interrelations within the chosen set of models and between the set of models as a whole and the remainder of the management system. The models included in the recommended set are those for forecasting demand and selecting a range of products to meet it, for perspective and current planning and for operational management (Fedorenko (1973a), pp. 76–82).

In fact the distance travelled down the road towards the more fundamental approach is slight. The mathematical models operate not in a vacuum but within the administrative structure of the ministry. The only change is in the techniques by which a decision is made, not in the nature of the decision or the section of the ministry ultimately responsible for making it. The range of sub-systems obtained from using Modin's approach, and from analysis of the operation of a ministry is substantially the same. I now consider the functional sub-systems which appear in ASU-pribor and, with minor modifications, in the Directives for OASU. Most attention is paid to perspective and current planning and to operational management. It is noteworthy that the weighting in OASU of sub-systems concerned with planning has in recent years grown sharply, while the weighting of accounting and statistical sub-systems has declined (Lapshin (1977), p. 195).

The sub-system for perspective planning

This sub-system is responsible for laying down the general lines of development of the ministry for a period of five or ten years ahead. The ministry must be apprised of the level of demand for its output and of the resources at its disposal, and it then selects from a list of possible variants of development that one which satisfies demand in the best way. We noted above the apparent overlap between the sub-system for perspective planning of an OASU and the model used in the branch sub-system of ASPR. It may be the case that although the formal models are identical or similar, the data for the OASU are more disaggregated.

The basic pattern in which the sub-system operates is straightforward enough. The ministry receives output targets for a period of five or more years ahead, in the form of long-term control figures from Gosplan. It will also be notified of the limitations of resources, especially of capital investment, to which it will be subject. To establish a set of ways of meeting these targets the ministry then works out a list of possible development patterns for each of its enterprises, based largely on information provided by the enterprise. The alternatives may include construction of new enterprises, reconstruction of existing plants and even the closing down of some enterprises. Only a few discrete variants are considered for each location (convex combinations are not allowed), and obviously only a single development variant of each enterprise or plant may be included in any given plan. The problem is then to make a selection from the variants which gives an extremal value of some function, for example a maximum of profit or a minimum of cost, while at the same time satisfying the resource constraints and output targets imposed on the ministry from above. This is a programming problem with some integer-valued variables, for which approximate solution methods exist.

Complications to this basic pattern arise in various ways. In the first place, not all of a branch's output is included in the targets the ministry receives from above. Some of it is at the discretion of the ministry itself. Furthermore the branch plays a part in forecasting demand for its products, particularly in breaking down the control figures into a more detailed classification. In a machine-building branch, for example, one of the functions involved is the selection of a range of products to be included in the plan for the following period. Where a branch is planning certain parts of its own output it is often necessary to establish upper limits for the production of certain commodities, based on an estimate of the limit of sales to be achieved in the economy.

The second and major complication arises from the existence of an intervening link between the ministry and the enterprise, viz the chief administration or industrial *ob'edinenie* controlling a sub-branch. Where the intermediate link exists, it is not always clear whether the optimal perspective plan is constructed over the branch as a whole or over a sub-branch only and, if the latter, what linkage there is between the individual sub-branch plans. Some authors propose a two-stage process. For example, Modin and his colleagues suggest a system in which the same model is used in both stages: in the higher stage the chief administration appears as the lower-level unit and the ministry, in the person of its planning and economic division, as the higher; in the lower stage the chief administration acts the role of higher-level unit, the enterprise that of lower-level unit. Apparently the ministry makes an allocation of resources and output targets, based on possible development plans of the administrations, and the latter subsequently make an analogous allocation among their subordinate enterprises, presumably in less highly aggregated terms. The exact nature of the feedback between the two systems is not specified but there are 'frequent linkages of the plans of the chief administrations and of individual enterprises, leading to correction and change in the technical and economic indicators of the plans. Compiling a perspective plan of a branch's development is a complex process done simultaneously at two levels of planning. At the lower level possible variants of perspective development are worked out, at the upper level a choice is made of the best variants' (Fedorenko (1973a), p. 97).

In ASU-pribor, the sub-system for perspective planning provides for solving the programme at the level of the sub-branch or industrial *ob'edinenie*. In the first version, estimates of demand for Minpribor's products were made by research institutes in accordance with the list of products stipulated in the Ministry's output plan (Velikotskii (1972), pp. 5–7; Metodicheskie (1972), pp. 239–54). For five-year planning the 22,000 products produced in the branch were aggregated into 300 groups; the number covered by each of the eleven sub-branches ranged from 12–70. For planning ten years ahead a still more aggregated list of commodities was used. The demand projections took into account imports and exports. On the production side institutes attached to the sub-branch worked out for each enterprise at least three alternative paths for expansion. The variants incorporated different production techniques, different patterns of specialisation and different timings of investment. Each variant was associated with vectors of output and inputs, including capital investment for each year of the plan.

In formulating the programming problem the sub-branches were divided into two groups. For the first group, the objective function was the minimisation of costs, including capital cost (*privedennie zatraty*), subject to a lower bound for output. In the second case, where demand for output was effectively unlimited, the objective function was the maximum of output in a fixed assortment subject to resource constraints. The model incorporated constraints for each year of the period. Transport costs were ignored as they form a small proportion of total value. Each problem took 20–45 minutes to solve on a BESM-4 computer. Sensitivity analysis of the solution was carried out, and it is suggested that some reshuffling of capital investment among the sub-branches may have taken place:[3] 'economic and mathematical analysis [of the results] consists, in the first place, in searching for ways to improve the plan and in analysis of its stability as conditions are varied (changing the level at which demand is satisfied or changing production costs, determining the quantity of capital investment more precisely)' (Velikotskii (1972), p. 6).

In the second stage of ASU-pribor, for which the technical specification was approved in 1971 and which was introduced in October 1975, the sub-system for perspective planning relies on a formal iterative procedure for allocating capital investment among the industrial *ob'edineniya* (Velikotskii (1976); Marshak (1975)). The objective function is to minimise the difference between actual output and the five-year plan control figures, but a priority system is used to weight the deviations of different goods in accordance with their importance. Compared with the earlier version, the new system is credited with more flexibility and a higher degree of conformity in documentary output with Gosplan. It also produces a more comprehensive set of indicators. The new system was used to prepare the tenth five-year plan for instrument building, and for doing some calculations for 1981–90. In the case of the period from 1976–80, the plan formed by the sub-system is claimed to be 6–13% more effective than plans formed by traditional methods. The fact that this comparison was possible indicates that the new system has not wholly superseded traditional methods.

The perspective planning sub-system in ASU-pribor was developed jointly by a Ministry research institute and the Institute for the Economics and Organisation of Industrial Production at Novosibirsk. Minpribor's experience formed the basis of the 'Methodological Regulations for Optimal Branch Planning in Industry' (Metodicheskie (1972)), which give an exhaustive account of variations in the basic model of perspective planning which may be required to meet particular conditions of production. For example, where a ministry produces goods with a high transport cost per unit value, the cost-minimising objective function should include transport as well as production costs, and the location of enterprises will be determined accordingly. In practice, such models have been used extensively in branches of industry before the installation of OASU, and in 1977 a Standard Methodology was approved by the Academy of Sciences (Tipovaya (1977)); this is of particular interest as it proposes the use of the dual variables corresponding to the optimal solution as a way of analysing marginal changes in the plan (ibid., p. 114). Information requirements for models of this type are relatively light, and since immediate solution of the model is not usually required, the calculations can be done by a research institute where the ministry lacks a computer centre. Of course when an OASU has been adopted as a means of integrating all planning and management activity it is easier to link up the branch level calculations of an optimal perspective plan with data sent down from Gosplan and up from the enterprises, but perspective planning is a relatively isolated sub-system. In the case of ASU-pribor it has interconnections only with the sub-systems for current planning and for financial management. It can therefore either be used separately or ignored completely. We have already noted the tendency to choose the latter option. Zhimerin complained in 1974 that only 3–4% of calculations done in an OASU are concerned with the compilation of optimal plans, despite the fact that the greatest benefits are to be found there (Zhimerin (1974a)). Kantorovich reported the same proportion in 1978 (Kantorovich (1978), p. 825).

The sub-system for current or annual planning

Under the traditional system current planning is done in the ministry by the Planning and Economic Division and by the corresponding division of the chief administration (or industrial *ob'edinenie*). The ministry divides its output targets or control figures received from Gosplan among the chief administrations, which transmit them to subordinate enterprises. Enterprises prepare draft plans which are aggregated at sub-branch level, transmitted to the ministry, corrected and sent back down to enterprises. The latter then form final, corrected versions of their plans. The number of feasible or acceptable plans is enormous and as only a few of them can be considered the resulting plan is selected on the basis of individual planners' experience or intuition, or even by arbitrary methods.

The sub-system for current planning of an OASU alters the basis on which the ministry or industrial *ob'edinenie* allocates output targets among subordinate units. In ASU-pribor enterprises transfer onto punch-cards information on their input coefficients and data on the limited resources at their disposal. This information is collected from various divisions in the enterprise, put in systematic form and punched. An average enterprise producing thirty types of product and using two hundred pieces of equipment uses five thousand cards (Burtseva (1972), p. 13). The data are stored at the branch computer centre where they may be used for other sub-systems.

Optimal enterprise plans are found by an iterative procedure. Each enterprise is assigned a notional output target and allocation of shiftable resources. These serve as constraints in a linear programming model, which uses the input coefficients previously transmitted by the enterprise. The maximand is taken as total profit. In this model, unlike the perspective planning model, there are no integer-value restrictions; for current planning the capacity constraint is taken as fixed or subject to small, continuous variation. In 1973 a program existed for solving problems of this nature including as many as four hundred products and four hundred constraints (Shorin (1973), p. 241).

The dual values associated with the constraints are used to re-allocate output targets or resources. Where the shadow price of a shiftable resource is positive the plan would be improved by assigning more of that resource to the enterprise. Where the shadow price is zero, increasing the allocation will not improve the plan, and reducing it will not usually lower the value of the objective function. (The resource constraints are inequalities; hence negative values are ruled out.) The shadow prices associated with output constraints, by contrast, may be positive, zero or negative. All three values are possible because output levels may be constrained from below by the control figures and from above by the limit of demand in the economy. When the value is zero, neither constraint is binding; a positive valuation indicates that demand is the limiting factor while a negative valuation indicates that the limit from below in terms of a minimum output constraint is binding. It is unusual to find the use of the dual mentioned explicitly in Soviet literature dealing with practical calculations as it is in this case. Unfortunately it is not made clear how the reallocation of both resources and targets is done,[4] but elsewhere it is said to be an iterative process (Telegin (1976), pp. 6–8).

When the plan for each enterprise is finally completed it is handed down to the enterprise together with a list of other summary indi-cators dealing with profits, the cost of materials and wages. Enter-prises prepare detailed plans which are transmitted to and stored in the branch computer centre. It may happen that enterprises receive plans which afford them a low level of profit but which nonetheless raise profits for the branch as a whole. In these cases Modin recommends that the plan be made more attractive to its executants by increasing unit payments into the bonus funds (Fedorenko (1973a), p. 111).

The sub-system for current planning has ramified connections with virtually every other sub-system in an OASU. The targets for output and the value of the capital resource constraint are derived in part from the sub-system for perspective planning. The sub-system passes on optimal production plans to the sub-systems for operational management, for supply, for management of sales, for planning labour and wages and for financial management. It

receives from these sub-systems information on material requirements, export demand and sales, the labour plan, the financial
plan and the past performance of the ministry. The current
planning sub-system is included in all OASU for which descriptions
are available.

It is difficult to evaluate the practical impact of the sub-system
for current planning. The solution method described above is a
complicated and unusual one, yet the basic specification of the
model is extremely simple. In particular the linearity assumption
is unsatisfactory as it implies constant returns to scale and no scope
for the substitution of inputs. It is reasonable to assume that the
solutions of the programme are critically evaluated by ministry
officials before they emerge as plan targets, and that the model
serves as a starting point for rather than an ending of the process
of current planning. However no precise information is available
on this point. In any case the annual and quarterly plans received
by enterprises are often amended in the course of execution. Within
ASU-pribor this is the function of the next sub-system.

Sub-system for operational management

The sub-system for operational management (*operativnoe
upravlenie*) is concerned with the regulation of production for short
periods, ranging from a day up to three months. It is the only sub-
system to be described as operating in real time (*v real'nom masshtabe
vremeni*): that is to say, information on the course of production
is transmitted quickly enough for decisions to be reached which
react back on production. Hence the need for the system of
immediate transfer of operational information described above.

The necessity for the sub-system arises from mistakes and inconsistencies at the stage of preparing the plan or from unforeseen
eventualities in executing it. If the plan were perfect and the conditions in which it would be carried out were exactly foreseen, then
the sub-system would be redundant. However neither of these
conditions is fulfilled and the sub-system is used to correct or stabil-
ise the production process. It is therefore involved in the whole
range of management activities at branch level – supply, production,
finance, labour – but the material resource flows set in motion by
the operation of the system are marginal alterations to those
forecast by the corresponding sub-system of OASU chiefly concerned with the activity or resource in question.

The following illustrations give an indication of typical activities of the sub-system. The normal shipment of material supply is interrupted and an enterprise's production plan put in jeopardy: the information is transmitted to the branch computer centre and thence to the appropriate division of the chief administration or the ministry, which takes the necessary steps. Or the enterprise is in financial difficulties over the payment of a supplier; the ministry may be able to assist it. Or the enterprise is in technical difficulties over the use of new equipment; the sub-system is the channel through which information reaches the ministry, which may then assign personnel to give technical assistance (ibid., pp. 151–2).

The disruption of supply of raw materials or components is a specially important case, responsible for many failures to fulfil the enterprise production plan. In this case the sub-system has at its disposal the following information: the enterprise's production plan, the plan for supply and shipment and data on the location of stocks (some of this information may come from other OASU sub-systems). It also knows the enterprise's processing or production cycle and the time necessary to make additional shipments from various destinations. This enables the sub-system to calculate the limits within which it must intervene to ensure continuity in production. This knowledge, which is stored centrally at the branch computer centre, makes it possible to intervene in the supply process and reallocate resources where appropriate. The administrative arrangements whereby this action is taken are determined by the authority of the different organisations involved. For example, if resources are to be transferred between enterprises in the *glavk*, then the matter need not be taken to the functional administration of the ministry. If the agreement of another *glavk* or of the ministry's chief administration for supply (Glavsnab) is required, then the decision is a ministry-level one. If the ministry itself has no resources available, then the annual production plan may need to be corrected or additional allocations made to the branch. This requires the agreement of Gosplan and Gossnab, and the approval of the Council of Ministers, and the decision must subsequently be carried out by lower-level supply organisations. In this last case the information flows are more extensive and the time taken to resolve the problem will be longer even when the Gosplan and Gossnab automated systems (ASPR and ASU MTS) are in operation.

Some authors have tried to formalise the decision processes of the sub-system for operational management on the basis of a mathematical programming model. Finkel'shtein and Lagosha have attempted this with respect to failures in the supply system (ibid., pp. 159–70). The knowns in their model are the initial location and size of surplus stocks of various resources held in the branch, and the needs of each enterprise, taking substitution possibilities into account, for resources in addition to those provided for in the annual plan and actually received by the enterprise. The unknowns are the quantities of resources shipped from one location to another. The objective function is minimisation of the total costs of making the shipments, including both the transport costs and the opportunities forgone in using the resources elsewhere. In a static variant the formulation is a straightforward transport problem, with the coefficients of the objective function known in advance. A feasible solution is guaranteed by the rather unrealistic assumption that all enterprise needs can be met by a limitless supply of the deficit resource held by a higher authority. However, to make the problem meaningful, time has to enter into it. The shipment of resources takes a certain amount of time; there are limitations on the sum of shipments from any source in any period. This opens the door to all sorts of complications. Since future events are not known, the costs associated with using a particular resource now rather than later are not known; hence the coefficients of the objective function are in doubt (curiously, this point is ignored by the authors). The solution must take account of complicated linkages from one period to the next, which require dynamic programming techniques. Moreover, the authors' formulation, complex as it is, fails to take account of other possible means of countering supply disruptions within the framework of operational management, such as the reallocation of output targets among subordinate enterprises.

Where we have information on the working of the sub-system for operational management in a particular ministry, no such complex algorithms are in use. The function of the branch computer centre is simply to carry out arithmetic calculations such as aggregation or averaging of indicators and to pass on the results quickly to the appropriate divisions of the ministry, where decisions are taken in what is basically the traditional, intuitive way. ASU-pribor will again serve as an example (Adamov (1972)).

A total of sixteen separate sets of calculations are performed by the sub-system, each based on information sent to the branch computer centre by the enterprise with a pre-arranged frequency. Bonuses are offered to the enterprise director for the accurate and timely dispatch of information. The computer centre processes the data according to standard programs and procedures and passes it on, using specially prepared forms, to the appropriate sections of the Ministry. The identity of these sections varies with the nature of the information, but the Ministry's Production Administration and the appropriate industrial *ob'edinenie* receive virtually all types of information, the former for the Ministry as a whole, the latter for its subordinate units only. Otherwise, Ministry Administrations receive information relevant to the activities they superintend: the Financial Administration is sent data on the fulfilment of the sales plan; the Accounting Administration data on fulfilment of the plan for the past month; the Administration for Supply data on fulfilment of the supply plan and so on. In ASU-pribor II some minor modifications are made to these procedures (Adamov (1976)).

In the case of some of the information, it is difficult to see what actions the results of the calculations are likely to evince from the Ministry and how they go beyond the book-keeping and accounting activities performed by other sub-systems within ASU-pribor. For example, once a month data on the number of personnel employed in each enterprise are transmitted to the branch computer centre and aggregated; the results are compared with the plan. In this case the sub-system seems to do little more than act as a conduit for the fast transmission of ex-post accounting information.

Some types of information are transmitted daily. Each day the enterprise sends data on its fulfilment of the sales plan.

The information is sent in coded form in the manner of the example below.

Report code	*Ob'edinenie* code	Enterprise code	Plan for the month	Actual plan fulfilment since start of month	Day — Code of reason for under-fulfilment	Month — Control sum 1 + 2 + 3 + 4 + 5 + 6
1	2	3	4	5	6	7
0101	05	02	78,250	77,700	01	156,059

Codes have been given to a total of forty habitual reasons for under-fulfilment of the plan. For example, 01 indicates the lack of necessary materials, 02 a shortage of components. After aggregation and processing the degree of plan fulfilment for each industrial *ob'edinenie* is automatically calculated and submitted to both the *ob'edinenie* and the Production Administration of the Ministry.

Another important set of messages in the sub-system relays information on the supply situation. Between the 7th and 10th days of each month the enterprise supplies the chief computer centre with information on inputs which are in deficit for the current month. The information is presented according to a form which stipulates the material, the supplier, the degree of shortfall and the reference number of the contract covering the shipment. Between the 24th and 27th days of each month a similar form is sent in by the enterprise, giving an account of the situation anticipated in the following month. When the computer centre has received this information, the functional administrations of the Ministry and the industrial *ob'edineniya* take appropriate decisions within a maximum of five days and communicate them by letter and telegram to the supplying enterprise, to the supply organisation and to other ministries. The enterprise in difficulties is informed of the decision through the chief computer centre. In all cases enterprises have the right of appeal to the deputy-minister or even, in the case of a particularly vital resource, to the Minister himself.

Of course, the kind of decisions taken in the sub-system for operational management were taken in the Ministry before the OASU came into operation. The change lies almost entirely in the way in which information is transmitted and presented. Under the old system the enterprise would be supplied with extra financial resources by the Financial Administration; book-keeping information would go to the Accounting Administration. The system was flexible but it led to inconsistencies, both in the data supplied and in the decisions taken in response to them. With the OASU, information is self consistent and processing is automatic and quick. Furthermore, within the information system of the OASU, the sub-system for operational management can use the data base compiled for all sub-systems. This is especially important since operational management is largely concerned with altering plans compiled by other sub-systems.

These changes are sufficient to make operational management more efficient in an OASU, even when the manner in which decisions are taken remains substantially the same, based on planners' judgement rather than the solution of a mathematical model.

Rudnev, who is in charge of the Instrument Building Ministry in which ASU-pribor operates, has argued that the success of the operational management sub-system is shown in a dramatic reduction in the number of enterprises failing to fulfil their plan (Rudnev (1972), p. 3). But this may tell us as much about the plans and the way of compiling them as about the sub-system for controlling their execution. A ministry cannot operate competing methods of implementing plans even in the attenuated sense in which it can have competing methods of devising them. We can only try to evaluate the impact of the sub-system for operational management in terms of the influence of an OASU as a whole. This is attempted in the final section of this chapter.

Other sub-systems in ASU-pribor

The three sub-systems described above form the core of an OASU. The function of the remaining sub-systems is to supplement the basic system by paying detailed attention to particular aspects of planning and management, for example to the labour plan or the financial plan, and to provide a detailed accounting of plan fulfilment. My information about these sub-systems is based on ASU-pribor (Fedorenko (1972a), pp. 224–43). There are certain differences between the list of sub-systems in ASU-pribor and that laid down in the Directives for OASU, but the similarities are large enough for us to take ASU-pribor as a model.

The sub-system for management of material–technical supply in ASU-pribor is concerned with collecting information on material inputs. Using data submitted by the enterprises it calculates weighted norms of expenditure of materials per million rubles of output, and evaluates the potential saving from lowering the material input coefficients. Compiling the supply plan also requires information on those activities in the branch not connected with basic production, such as research work, servicing etc. Particular attention is paid to evaluating the Ministry's needs in precious metals. Finally the sub-system is responsible for compiling a statistical report on supply activities for the Supply Administration of the Ministry. Many of these functions involve co-operation with Gossnab and responsibility must be shared by the OASU and Gossnab's automated system. The supply function is organised centrally in the ministry, by-passing the industrial *ob'edineniya* (Nikulin (1976), p. 48).

The sub-system for the management of sales in ASU-pribor is engaged partly on very detailed control of exports. An export plan is compiled on a quarterly basis, broken down by industrial *ob'edinenie* and by enterprise. The *ob'edinenie* receives monthly reports on possible failures in fulfilling the plan. The sub-system also furnishes a detailed analysis of exports by product and country of destination. In addition the shipment of goods for domestic use is controlled; information is regularly submitted to the transport division of the Ministry and to the industrial *ob'edineniya*.

The sub-system for financial management is responsible for establishing norms of working capital at enterprise level and for calculating certain financial magnitudes. The former task has been performed by constructing a simulation model for the supply and production process. It is claimed that the model made it possible to choose a level of stocks which minimised the sum of storage and interest costs on stocks and losses from the breakdown of production. The sub-system also carries out analyses of the sales and profit plan and makes an evaluation of the financial position of each enterprise. During the 10th five-year plan the sub-system will be extended to cover calculations for the financial plan, and for dealing with bank credit (Polyak (1976), p. 52).

The sub-system for book-keeping (*bukhgalterskii uchet*) is intended to improve the organisation of book-keeping at enterprise level; to reduce the number of primary accounting documents; to speed up the compilation of summary accounting returns for the industrial *ob'edineniya* and for the Ministry as a whole; and to let book-keeping personnel devote more time to analysis of returns by freeing them from routine data-processing.

The first stage of ASU-pribor was completed by two sub-systems concerned with planning and analysis of labour and wages (Pashkevich (1972)), and with personnel management, and a third which deals with the supply of batches of equipment (the sub-system for *komplektatsiya*) (Krasavin (1976)). The inclusion of the last is determined by the special circumstances of the Ministry; no other OASU appears to have such a system. The second stage of the system, ASU-pribor II, introduced in October 1975, includes nine further sub-systems, of which that for the control of product quality has received the most attention. Work is now in progress on ASU-pribor III, which is intended both to ensure closer links between the ministry system and automated systems above and below it in the management hierarchy and to integrate the many sub-systems into four major blocks, for planning, accounting, analysis and operational control (Sinyak (1978a and b)).

4 THE IMPACT OF AN OASU

There are considerable difficulties in calculating the economic return from a branch automated management system. The installation of an OASU is associated with initial investment costs and recurrent costs, and with a return in the form of increased efficiency of production and savings in the costs of management. In 1969 Gosplan's official instructions for compiling the national plan laid down that the method used to evaluate the return from an automated management system should be based on the method for determining the economic effectiveness of introducing new technology and mechanising and automating production processes in industry (Metodicheskie (1969), p. 17), but no details or modifications of the procedure were given. Some writers went into the matter in some detail, but in 1972 Sinyak wrote that strictly speaking there was no method available for evaluating the economic effect of an OASU (Sinyak (1972), p. 7). This deficiency was made up by the publication in 1973 of a method of evaluation approved by the State Committee on Science and Technology as part of the Standard Detailed Design for an OASU (Otsenka (1973)).

The methodology notes at the outset that evaluation of the impact of an OASU is based on the one hand on the general principles of calculating the effectiveness of an investment and on the other on consideration of the special sources of economic effect peculiar to an OASU. The latter fall into five categories:

(a) Production: the quantity and quality of output are increased through better planning; labour productivity is raised and overhead costs reduced;

(b) Capital investment: costs are lowered by optimisation of planning;

(c) Supply and sales: stocks and losses in storage are reduced by a rational redistribution of resources;

(d) Research and development: product quality is raised;

(e) Management: time spent in data processing is reduced, productivity is raised and the number of management personnel is stabilised.

The economic effect is calculated in the standard way. The annual economic effect or return from the OASU is taken as the change in the excess of sales revenue over costs, including capital costs, before and after the installation of an OASU:

$$R_1 = (A_2 - (C_2 + E_n K_2)) - (A_1 - (C_1 + E_n K_1)) \tag{1}$$

where

R_1 is the annual return on the OASU
A_1, A_2 are the values of sales before and after installation of the OASU
C_1, C_2 are the corresponding values of current costs (*sebestoimost'*)
K_1, K_2 are the corresponding values of capital installed
E_n is the coefficient of relative effectiveness for investment in that particular branch.

Alternatively, the recoupment period for the OASU is calculated:

$$T = \Delta K / R_2 \tag{2}$$

where

T is the recoupment period in years
R_2 is the saving in *current cost alone* attributes to the OASU, given by the expression:

$$R_2 = (C_1/A_1 - C_2/A_2)A_2 \tag{3}$$

ΔK is additional capital invested in establishing the OASU.

The two calculations are generally related in the following way: where $E_n < 1/T$, R_1 is positive. This is obviously true where $A_1 = A_2$, that is, when the value of output is unchanged. Complications may arise from a substantial increase in the level of output, when the stated relationship may not apply.

The direct capital expenditure on an OASU can be calculated quite easily. It consists of the cost of designing and installing the system and equipping the branch computer centre and group information points used for transferring data from enterprises to the ministry. Indirect capital costs include such extra information as may be necessary to sustain a higher production level made possible by the OASU; there may also be indirect savings in capital, arising for example from a lower level of stocks. A certain part of the change in current expenditure arising from the OASU is made up by the cost of using the branch computer centre. The most difficult problem is how to estimate the recurrent benefits of the OASU. The methodology lists the benefits in the shape of increased output and lowered costs, and indicates which sub-systems of the

OASU will be responsible for savings. For example, the subsystem for current planning is said to be responsible for increasing output, by calculating optimal production plans, and for saving costs by lowering input coefficients. (This seems to represent a double-counting of the gains.) But the methodology gives no guidance on how to separate the gain due to the OASU from that attributable to other causes. Typically, a large number of changes are occurring in a ministry at the same time. New capacity may come into operation; the management structure may alter; a new incentive scheme may modify enterprise or ministry behaviour; automated systems of enterprise management may be installed. If an OASU comes into operation in a ministry at the same time as one or more of these changes is taking place, then all we can calculate is the average efficiency of investment over a whole range of outlays and there is a danger, moreover, that some of the output gains or cost savings may take place independently of any investment.

Thus the evidence cited here on the economic effect of an OASU must be interpreted with some caution. Some of it relates to the particular impact of a single sub-system, some to the OASU as a whole. We can assume that in most cases the calculations are based on some approximation to the methodology described above, though in some cases curious short-cuts in the method have been used. For example, in one ministry the benefit from the OASU was set equal to one per cent of the branch's output. This figure was apparently chosen at random (Dudkin (1971), p. 71).

The greatest return is usually ascribed to the sub-system for perspective planning. The cost of achieving a given level and structure of branch output in five or ten years' time is calculated for competing plans, one compiled by traditional means, the other on the basis of a programming model. As a rule the latter gives a saving in costs of 10–15% (Mosin (1972), p. 31). In the case of ASU-pribor the saving fell initially in the lower range of 5–6% (Velikotskii (1972), p. 7), though greater savings are now claimed. In making this estimate it is assumed that both plans are feasible (or equally infeasible) and, particularly, that the model used for perspective planning in an OASU fully reflects all the constraints recognised by planners using traditional methods. Suppose, for example, that in the traditional planning process a constraint on closing down even an inefficient enterprise is recognised. It will clearly undermine the basis of the comparison of the two methods if, in the programming model used in the OASU, this limitation is not observed.

The same problems arise in current planning where in 1970 the use of mathematical models for current planning was said to be responsible for increases in output of the order of 7–10% (Khorinzhii (1970), p. 116), and in the case of ASU-pribor a gain of 10% was claimed at an early stage of operation of the current planning sub-system (Burtseva (1972), p. 14). Yet in 1972 this sub-system is said to have increased output by 82 million rubles (about 3% of production in that year) and profits by 36 million rubles, and even these figures are in conflict with another source which puts the total saving from the whole of ASU-pribor as 12 million rubles in 1971 and 24 million rubles in 1976 (Zhimerin (1978)). The impact on production of sub-systems other than that for current planning either cannot be calculated, as is the case for the sub-system for operational management, or is non-existent, as in the case of the sub-system for accounting. For these sub-systems savings in time of managerial personnel are sometimes estimated.

Information on the economic return to an OASU as a whole is inconsistent and confusing. According to Zhimerin, the cost of installing an OASU is about three or four million rubles, and the recoupment period is three or four years (Zhimerin (1974a), while another source cites an average recoupment period of $1-1\frac{1}{2}$ years (Pokrovskii (1976), p. 125). According to Sinyak 'the recoupment period can equal one to one and a half years', but he noted that the method of calculating the economic effect is not the same in all cases (Sinyak (1973b), p. 8).

However this is only part of the story. The Methodology for calculating the economic effectiveness of an OASU notes that the results of installing an OASU are felt outside the confines of the branch (Otsenka (1973)):

The effect from the introduction of an OASU is seen also in neighbouring branches, departments, state organisations (Gosplan USSR, Gosbank USSR, TsSU USSR, etc.) – the so-called diffusion effect. It is achieved on the basis of receiving high-quality and timely information from the OASU, the timely conclusion of contracts and payment of accounts, a better organisation of sales, and other factors.

Thus the methodology recognises but makes no attempt to quantify external benefits from the introduction of an OASU. The influence of these factors can only be considered in the course of an evaluation of the management automation programme as a whole, which is attempted in the final chapter. In the meantime, I can only supplement the partial calculations given above with some general observations.

In the early stages of discussion of OASU, two points were frequently made. Firstly, that the installation of an automated management system must be accompanied by a determined effort to raise the general level of management efficiency in the ministry; otherwise the potential benefits of the OASU would be lost. Secondly, that an OASU must be accompanied by profound changes in the method of work at all levels in the management apparatus.

On the first point, it is clear that the gains from OASU have not all been frittered away by poor organisation. Though there is no direct evidence on this point, it is likely that the clear delineation of functions and the need for quick decisions which are characteristic of computer-based systems of management impose new disciplines on management at the ministry. The second point too has been largely met, at least in the case of some systems for which information is available. I have stressed before that the place of the ministries in the overall system for planning and management has remained largely unchanged, and that the administrative structure of the ministries themselves has changed little as a direct result of the installation of OASU. But even so the method of work of a substantial number of ministry personnel has changed substantially. In the more advanced OASU the information systems have been completely reorganised and scientific methods of decision taking introduced. If the experience of these branches can be extended to cover all the branches in which OASU have been installed, then the quality of management will be raised substantially, and this improvement should take place whether or not the OASU are integrated into a single automated system covering all levels of management.

6

AUTOMATED SYSTEMS OF ENTERPRISE MANAGEMENT

In 1972 more than 40,000 research workers in more than 500 institutes were involved in designing automated systems of enterprise management (ASUP). Both the size of the development effort and the number of institutes making it are a reflection of the immense number and variety of enterprises, which throughout the ninth five-year plan were still the basic production unit in the USSR. There were some fifty thousand enterprises in total, producing an enormous range of goods. The sheer variety of enterprises makes it impossible to identify a representative automated system of enterprise management. Whereas at branch level the functions of planning and management are fairly similar from one ministry to another, at enterprise level differences in size, in type and range of products and in technology of production inevitably impose varying demands on management and create varying possibilities for the use of computers in management. This remains true in spite of the relatively high degree of uniformity imposed by standardised planning, control and accounting procedures.

In the face of the variety of ASUP, this chapter can only present a summary of developments to date in the design and installation of the systems. This is used as a basis for drawing conclusions not about the technical properties of the systems, but about the organisation problems which have arisen and the adequacy of the attempt to overcome them.

1 THE GROWTH OF ASUP

The Soviet economist and deputy director of TsEMI, A. A. Modin, identifies three stages in the use of computers to control production (Fedorenko (1973a), pp. 11–17):
1 solving individual problems of production management;

2 constructing electronic data-processing systems for solving management problems;

3 constructing automated systems of production management.

The dating of the different periods which he proposes – 1954–8 for the first stage,[1] 1959–64 for the second, and post-1963 for the third – is surely overoptimistic. In reality the use of computers at enterprise level as elsewhere was very restricted indeed until the middle 1960s, and there is no evidence of the construction and use of an electronic system of data-processing in 1959. The third period, which covers the construction of automated systems of enterprise management, was indeed inaugurated in 1963, when work started on an ASUP for the L'vov television factory under the direction of the Institute of Cybernetics at Kiev, but this system was not completed until several years later and was in any case probably the most sophisticated of any system introduced in the 1960s.

In fact 1966, the first year of the eighth five-year plan, was the first year in which attention was concentrated on the use of computers to manage enterprises. This was a consequence of the 1966 decree on computer use in the USSR. As Makhrov writes: 'Thus 1966 was the first year when the national economic plan included indicators and integrated targets for ministries and departments of the USSR and councils of ministers of union republics for the introduction of automated management systems, construction of computer centres and use of individual computers. Establishing targets in the national economic plans increased the importance of this most significant aspect of technological progress' (Makhrov (1974), p. 15). Ministries responded by establishing special divisions to control the introduction of computers. In all around 150 ASUP were established in the course of the eighth five-year plan, but according to Soviet authors the main achievement of the period lay not so much in the number of systems introduced but in laying the basis for further developments by accustoming ministries to successful fulfilment of plans for introducing computers, by overcoming the 'psychological barrier' of resistance to integrated ASUP, and by extending the network of research organisations designing the systems.

After the XXIV Party Congress the tempo of work on ASUP speeded up. By 1972 there were 344 ASUP in operation: their number grew to 757 in 1974, and 1,164 by 1977. The overall target for new installations during the ninth five-year plan had been 1,800, including one fifth of the large enterprises in the USSR. In fact only 821 new systems were installed between 1971 and 1975.

In current practice control of the design and installation of ASUP is exercised by a number of organisations – Gosplan, the State Committee on Science and Technology, Minpribor, TsSU and the different ministries and departments. Overall control of planning is exercised by Gosplan's Division for overall planning and introduction of computers into the national economy, which is also responsible for planning the production and allocation of computers. The State Committee for Science and Technology is responsible for approving co-ordination plans for research on ASUP and for supervising their fulfilment, in conjunction with the Academy of Sciences. The Ministry of Instrument-Building exercises a supervisory role over ASUP installed in all ministries, as well as being responsible for the design of at least one third of ASUP which were to be installed during the ninth five-year plan. The functions of designing ASUP and providing enterprises with necessary equipment are carried out by industrial *ob'edineniya* in Minpribor, such as Soyuzpromavtomatika and Soyuzsistemprom.[2] TsSU is concerned with the distribution of certain types of equipment used in ASUP and with organising aspects of information flow within them. Ministries and departments are, of course, involved in the construction of ASUP in enterprises within their jurisdiction.

Planning the introduction of computers is done both over a five-year period and annually. The mechanics of the process are similar to any other aspect of the plan. Ministries and departments submit proposals and Gosplan chooses amongst them, in the light of overall resource availabilities (Lapshin (1977), pp. 90–142). The process of selecting enterprises for the installation of ASUP has itself in one account been taken over by a sub-system of Gosplan's automated planning system (ASPR) (Makhrov (1974), pp. 30–8).

A number of surveys of existing ASUP have been carried out over the past eight years. In 1971, TsEMI made an analysis of systems installed in the eighth five-year plan, and in 1972 a larger sample of two hundred ASUP in twenty-one ministries was examined (Makhrov (1974), pp. 190–9). A more recent survey of nearly 300 ASUP, chiefly in machine-building, yielded the information given in Table 4.

Although the two earlier surveys reveal substantial variations between ministries, there is evidence that ASUP are installed

Table 4

Branch	No. of enterprises	No. of tasks performed	Capital investment (000 rubles)	Annual cost reduction (000 rubles)	Annual economic effect (000 rubles)	Recoupment period (years)
Industry, of which machine-building	287	29	910	252	303	1.8
	186	31	1,024	273	331	1.8

Source: Kruchinin (1977), p. 4.

normally in large enterprises employing on average more than ten thousand persons. There is also evidence that the number of functions discharged by the computer has grown since the 1960s. This change stemmed from a belief that the management functions covered by early ASUP were too isolated and dispersed to benefit from possible economies of scale in information storage and processing. Indeed this increase in coverage has not generally been accompanied by an equivalent increase in costs.

One reason why installation costs of ASUP have not risen is the drive to standardise designs. There are naturally strong pressures towards standardisation, both to reduce costs and to establish consistency. According to one estimate standardisation of design for the ASUP of a machine-building enterprise cuts design costs by two thirds (Brudnik (1972), p. 13). Initially attention was concentrated on the 'group' method of standardisation, by which a representative enterprise is selected to have an ASUP installed and the designs are subsequently used for other enterprises. Glushkov considered that the requirements of the whole economy could be satisfied by thirty or forty standard ASUP (Kirilyuk (1972), p. 3). Either because this estimate proved to be optimistic, or for other reasons, recent work in this area has been directed towards the formation of standard design solutions (*tipovye proektnye resheniya* – TPR), which are intended to cover not the whole system but individual parts of it – the software for one functional subsystem for example, or a standard set of hardware to solve problems of a particular type.

Some progress has been made in welding individual standard elements into an ASUP, particularly in the area of software which makes up a large and increasing proportion of the design costs of an ASUP. In 1972 standard design solutions covered on average about 60% of the content of an ASUP, but with wide fluctuations on either side (Karibskii (1972), p. 4). By 1974, 130 standard design solutions had been approved (Myasnikov (1974), p. 92).

Although the approach has been used in other ministries, the concept of the standard design solution originated in and found immediate application in Minpribor (Karibskii (1970)). In 1966, the ministry selected 13 enterprises in which ASUP would be installed during the eighth five-year plan. Four groups of enterprises were distinguished: (i) those with continuous mass production; (ii) those with a mixed output; (iii) those with varying degrees of serial production; and (iv) those with a small series type of output.

Research institutes, under the leadership of TsNIITU, Minpribor's Central Scientific Research and Technological Design Institute for the Organisation and Techniques of Management, set to work developing these systems. In spite of the differing character of the enterprises studied, the institute came down in favour of establishing in each of the four groups a single variant of ASUP consisting of six sub-systems. They were therefore able to prepare unified designs for individual sub-systems or parts of sub-systems. By 1977, Minpribor had ASUP in 80 enterprises (Rudnev (1977), p. 1).

The standardisation of designs greatly simplified communications between the enterprise systems and the ministry automated management system ASU-pribor: 'Communication between branch and factory automated systems is achieved through indicators used in their respective sub-systems. Thus ASU-pribor's sub-system for planning, accounting and analysis of labour, costs and wages receives from the factory management systems data on the fulfilment of the labour plan. ... Moreover at pre-arranged intervals planning indicators of identical content arrive from the enterprises. In ASU-pribor the information is aggregated and reprocessed in solving problems of accounting and analysis of the activity of the enterprises. The chief and functional administrations use the results of solving these problems for operational control and decision-taking' (Karibskii (1970), pp. 133, 136).

Many of the information exchanges which an enterprise undertakes are with organisations outside its ministry, for example with Gossnab or with enterprises in other ministries. There is therefore a return to standardising ASUP on a national basis. Some attempts have been made to do this by the publication of Methodological Materials for Establishing ASUP. In 1967 a temporary document of this nature covering enterprises with discontinuous production was published by TsEMI and approved by the State Committee on Science and Technology, Minpribor and the Academy of Sciences. In 1971 this was superseded by Branch-Wide Directing Methodological Materials for Establishing ASUP (Zhimerin (1972), pp. 295–328). The materials are in two parts, the first obligatory, the second advisory. A second edition was published in 1977 (Obshcheotraslevye (1977)).

In character the first edition of the Materials is similar to the equivalent document prepared for branch automated management systems. In other words more attention is paid to laying down the legal responsibilities of the parties concerned with designing the ASUP and establishing the sequence of drafts to be gone through, than to outlining a general approach to the problems of design or giving detailed practical instruction. Interesting points in the Materials are the emphasis on the duties and rights of the enterprise management, especially at the stage of setting guidelines – a point much stressed in Soviet literature; the need to take account of the requirements placed on the ASUP by the branch-level system; and the obligation imposed upon the Inspection Commission, which as in the case of OASU examines the system, to consider the possibility of using the design in other similar enterprises. A recommendation to this effect was made by the inter-departmental commission which accepted the ASUP at the Barnaul Radio Factory, and the design was used in over 100 enterprises (Bobko (1976), p. 141). Minpribor plays an important role in exercising general methodological guidance over the organisations which it designates as head organisations for the design of ASUP in individual branches.

The Materials lay down a list of eleven functional sub-systems to be included in an ASUP, covering all major aspects of enterprise activity, including planning and accounting. It has been laid down that design institutes and other bodies can count for the fulfilment of their plan and draw bonuses for only those ASUP which contain all the sub-systems enumerated in the materials. This may have led to a thoughtless extension of ASUP to include areas of enterprise activity where they are not profitable.

Criticisms of the Materials take different and even contradictory lines. Vainshtein criticises them for their lack of any reference to economic incentives, and their exclusive concentration on technical and procedural questions (Vainshtein (1974), pp. 121–3). Yu. Oleinik-Ovod, a deputy director of TsEMI, observes that the results of introducing ASU have not come up to expectations, and attributes this to the absence of a 'systems approach': 'the directing methodological materials, RMM, while claiming it [a systems approach] do not in fact contain any systems principles, but are a list of organisational forms for carrying out the work, confirmed by a "table of contents" of the corresponding sections of the ASU draft'. Again: 'in the RMM there is not a single fundamental proposition which designers might use. In particular there are no clear principles for improving internal *khozraschet* and no observations, even heuristic ones, on ways of rationalising structures.' He goes on to argue for a complete revision of the materials (Problemy (1975), pp. 179–80).[3] A final consideration is noted by Modin. He writes that many ministries inadequately control the introduction of ASUP, citing as evidence the fact that 'less than a third of enterprises installing ASUP have the Branch-Wide Directing Methodological Materials for establishing ASUP and other methodological materials. As a result the designers have to seek their own ways and forms of organising the work and to formulate the design documentation themselves' (Modin (1974), pp. 103–4). In short, the majority of designs are done without the benefit of even the inadequate advice and direction of the official materials.

The overall picture is then very patchy. A ministry like Minpribor has developed and used its own procedures for standardising ASUP design. Other ministries have developed specific branch instructions to supplement the economy-wide materials. But we can infer from the criticisms that in other sectors the situation is much worse and the quality of ASUP correspondingly variable. I return to this point in the final section.

One complicating factor in the development of ASUP has been the March 1973 management changes, which require *inter alia* the formation of production *ob'edineniya* by the amalgamation of enterprises (see pp. 15–18 above). Where an enterprise which already has an ASUP is made part of a production *ob'edinenie*, important changes will have to be made to the system. But since ASUP have typically been installed in large and technologically advanced enterprises, these enterprises will often be the dominant member of the newly-formed production *ob'edinenie*. Thus one would not normally expect the situation to arise in which a newly formed production *ob'edinenie* will consist of enterprises, several of which already have ASUP. This is confirmed in a survey of *ob'edineniya* carried out in the first half of 1974, which revealed that only 7.5% of the sample had an ASU (though 40% had plans to introduce one in the immediate future), and that as a rule the system only covered the chief enterprise (Maksimenko (1977), p. 67).

Even before the announcement of the 1973 changes, specialists on ASU, following the line of the XXIV Party Congress, laid emphasis on the progressive nature of *ob'edineniya*. O. V. Kozlova, in her two-volume compilation on the theory and method of ASU, makes this point clearly (Kozlova (1972), pp. 34–5), and Modin advances the same argument, though he uses the term 'production complex' instead of *ob'edinenie*. Such complexes can be created in three ways, by designing new factories, by amalgamating small or medium-size enterprises, or by clustering a number of small dependent enterprises around a single large one (Modin (1972), pp. 232–3). Another author observed that it was 'entirely clear theoretically and confirmed by domestic and foreign practice that setting up a computer-based management system for a large complex like a firm was enormously more effective than establishing ASUP for enterprises joining the complex' (Grenbek (1972), pp. 30–1). At the same time he complained that in designing ASUP no thought was given to the prospect of switching to an *ob'edinenie* system.

Unfortunately, the implementation of the 1973 management changes is too recent and incomplete for any information to emerge on how in general it has affected automation of management at the lower level, although details are available on a few systems of exceptional merit. As we shall see this is a general problem in the assessment of ASUP.

2 HOW EFFECTIVE ARE ASUP?

In a limited sense the effectiveness of an ASUP can be judged on the basis of the recoupment period for the capital invested in designing and installing the system. However special features of investment in automated management systems led to the use of a number of confused and contradictory methods for this calculation. Each ministry tended to adopt its own method. Some included in the return to the system only savings in management resulting from a reduction in personnel; others included only the return in the form of increased output; while others still counted both effects. According to one source, there were thirty different methods for calculating the economic effect (Samborskii (1974), p. 29). To eliminate these confusions the State Committee on Science and Technology established by decree in 1971 a Temporary Commission to prepare a method of calculating the economic impact of computers and ASU. Its first task was to prepare a document outlining a temporary method for determining the economic effect of an ASUP. The document was approved by the State Committee, by Gosplan and by the Academy of Sciences in November 1972,

and published in 1973 (Vremennaya (1973); Effektivnost' (1973));
a revised edition was approved in 1975.

The Method is based upon the standard Soviet technique for
assessing the effectiveness of capital investment, and similar to the
method for calculating the economic effect of a branch automated
management system described above. Two forms of making the
calculation are envisaged, one yielding a value for the recoupment
period. First the annual increase in profit is calculated:

$$\Delta P = \left(\frac{A_2 - A_1}{A_1}\right)\pi_1 + \left(\frac{C_1 - C_2}{100}\right)A_2 \tag{1}$$

where

ΔP is the increase in profit per year resulting from the ASUP.
π_1 is the annual profit before the installation of the ASUP.
A_1, A_2 are the value of sales, in rubles, before and after the introduction of the ASUP.
C_1, C_2 are the costs in kopeks per ruble of sales before and after
the installation of the ASUP.

From this the annual economic effect (net) of the ASUP can be
calculated:

$$R = \left(\frac{A_2 - A_1}{A_1}\right)\pi_1 + \left(\frac{C_1 - C_2}{100}\right)A_2 - E_n K_n \tag{2}$$

where

R is the annual economic return (net) of the ASUP.
E_n is the standard coefficient of relative effectiveness of investment
for the particular branch.
K_n is the capital cost of installing the ASUP.

Alternatively the recoupment period can be calculated:

$$T = K_n/\Delta P \tag{3}$$

where T is the recoupment period in years.
The relationship between the two criteria is that where $T < 1/E_n$
then R is positive.

Until recently if a proposed ASUP was to be accepted it had to
satisfy not only Gosplan's general requirement for automated
management systems that the coefficient of relative effectiveness
(E_n) should be greater than 0.3, but also special sectoral requirements worked out by ministries in conjunction with Gosplan.

For industry these ranged from 0.3 to 0.4, though a coefficient of 0.25 was apparently used in agriculture (Lapshin (1975), p. 126). However a recent decree from Gosplan seems to envisage use of a standard coefficient of 0.15, the value adopted in the general methodology for evaluating new technology published in 1977 (V Gosplane (1978), pp. 157–8).

Of course, the main problem is how to calculate the magnitudes of the variables involved. This difficulty is particularly hard to overcome in the cases of the costs per ruble of sales and of the increase in output resulting from the installation of an ASUP. Even ex-post calculations of these variables are complicated by the inevitable circumstance that other changes are taking place in the enterprise at the same time, the effects of which intermingle with those of the ASUP. Ex-ante estimates of the return to an ASUP are particularly suspect: one writer has noted that 'some of the people designing ASUP say that without infringing the compulsory method, they can calculate the effectiveness to be of any desired or required size. There is much truth in this bitter jest' (Yakovlev (1972), p. 40). A speaker at an important conference on the economic effectiveness of ASU stated that calculations based upon fifteen machine-building enterprises showed that the actual saving from introducing ASUP was only one half to two thirds of the estimated saving, and a recent survey of 40 ASUP revealed that the recoupment period for investment in the systems was underestimated in 26 cases. The actual average recoupment period was 2.9 years; the projected period was only 1.8 years (Nauchno-tekhnicheskii (1977), pp. 29–31). These grounds for scepticism should be remembered while considering the return to ASUP claimed in Table 4 above, or the results of other surveys, such as that of 208 ASUP made in 1973, which showed an average recoupment period of two years (Lapshin (1977), p. 79).

However much faith is placed in these calculations, they are not the only way of considering the effectiveness of ASUP. We must also consider whether the possibilities inherent in automated management systems at enterprise level have been fully exploited, or whether mere satisfaction of the recoupment period criterion has been considered adequate. The problem in making such an assessment is that Soviet publications tend to concentrate on the extremes of good and bad performance, and the average system is ignored. On the one hand details are given of the most advanced systems; on the other hand particularly ill-conceived and badly designed systems are held up for censure. When articles of the latter sort also describe general deficiencies in the process of design and installation of ASUP, there are grounds for believing that the weaknesses are not merely isolated instances of individual incompetence.

Glushkov has been particularly outspoken in condemning some aspects of the ASUP programme. In a number of articles published in the first half of 1975, he identified a series of important weaknesses. The chief shortcoming in most automated management systems, he notes, is 'their lack of a truly comprehensive systems approach. Yet world practice and the practice of the best automated management systems in our own country have convincingly shown that the automation of existing traditional methods of management does not and indeed cannot have a basic impact in the sense of marshalling all the hidden reserves for increasing the effectiveness and improving the qualitative indices of production. The creation of automated management systems must of necessity include the development of new economic mechanisms and new forms of accounting, and a thoroughgoing re-organisation of paper work, of basic norms, of incentive systems etc. The creation of a genuine automated management system, in other words, implies the transition to a basically new technology of management making full use of the enormous possibilities latent in modern computational equipment' (Glushkov) (1975c).

These genuine systems are contrasted with pseudo-systems which are orientated only towards the use of computers to carry out routine functions in exactly the same way as before. A pseudo-ASU is likely to be installed by managers who 'interpret the automation of management as nothing more than a run-of-the-mill campaign and who report the completion of an ASU once they have one or several of the simplest traditional managerial tasks (bookkeeping, wages, dispatcher control etc.) on a computer'. He cites the example of the Krengolm Textile combine which reported the completion of the first section of an ASU: 'A check-up conducted jointly by the State Committee on Science and Technology and the Committee of Popular Control found that the "first section" was nothing more than an extremely simple system of dispatcher control for one of the combine's three finishing factories – a system moreover that had been poorly-designed and was in fact inoperative' (ibid.).

In another article Glushkov lays the blame for the appearance

of pseudo-systems on three factors – the weakness of Soviet computer technology, the shortage of qualified designers and the
'formalistic–bureaucratic attitude of the directors of a number of
enterprises and ministries to the problems of constructing and
installing ASUP' (Glushkov (1975b), pp. 4–5). The danger the
author sees in the existence of pseudo-ASU is the growth of a second
wave of scepticism. The first wave of scepticism in the 1960s was
based on a total ignorance of the possibilities of computers; the
second is based upon some degree of knowledge and experience
of pseudo-ASU. The gravest form of this scepticism, he asserts
in an interview, is shown by some people who 'are not sure whether
it is necessary, possible or the proper time to go on to the next step
in developing a state-wide automated management system. Would
it not be better to wait, they say, for a while and work in the meantime to perfect the separate, unconnected automated management
systems? This is a real delusion' (Glushkov (1975a).

Unfortunately, when asked what percentage of ASU were real
and what proportion exaggerated and existing merely on paper,
Glushkov did not give an exact reply. He stated that 'one should
not assume that they are all of sub-standard quality. Every specialist,
myself included, can cite a number of systems that have been
properly built and are highly effective – for instance those at the
Leningrad optical-mechanical *ob'edinenie*, the Svetlana *ob'edinenie*
and others'.

Glushkov's remarks are confirmed by a more thoroughgoing
study of the technical level of ASUP, published in 1977. The authors
of this study collected data on a number of characteristics of ASUP,
and subsequently combined their information to derive an overall
index of technical level of more than 300 systems. The results showed
a lot of bunching at the middle. Ten levels were identified, ranging
from the worst (level 1) to the best (level 10). 80% of systems fell in
categories 4–7; only 14% were in the three best categories. The
ASUP examined fell down worst in the proportion of optimising
calculations in their total activity. In over three quarters of enterprises, optimising calculations amounted to less than 5% of activity,
with many enterprises doing no such calculations (Nauchno-
tekhnicheskii (1977), pp. 151, 190–1).

Making a reasonable assessment of the quality of ASUP on
the evidence presented in this chapter is a difficult task. Clearly
the systems are neither uniformly good nor uniformly bad. In
view of the absence of a widely-observed standardisation policy,

the differences between any two systems are probably more notice-able than the similarities. We can however divide the ASUP into three categories. The first category includes those systems, most of them developed by prestigious research institutes, which within the limits of the equipment available have systematically incorporat-ed computers into the management process. This category includes the systems frequently mentioned in Soviet literature, such as the ASU of the Donetsk Machine-Building Factory, the Barnaul Radio Factory system (the latter developed by the Institute for the Economics and Organisation of Industrial Production (IEOPP) at Novosibirsk), the L'vov Television Factory system (designed by Glushkov's institute) etc. The original membership of this cate-gory is small, but it is expanding through the replication of these systems in other enterprises. For example, as noted above, the Barnaul system is now installed in over 100 enterprises.

The second category of ASUP, probably much larger than the first, includes those systems where the designers and the enterprise management have attempted to introduce a genuine ASU, but have failed either from a lack of technical competence or because they have not been prepared to adapt the traditional practices of management to the computer. These systems probably yield an adequate economic return but do not exploit the possibilities of ASU to the full. The third category is Glushkov's pseudo-ASU, where no serious attempt has been made to establish a genuine automated system. These are ineffective. According to Glushkov, who argues that there is no such thing as an ineffective ASU, they are not ASU (Glushkov (1975a), p. 10). The relative sizes of these two categories are hard to judge, and the dividing line between them is impossible to establish with precision. But the number of pseudo-ASU is clearly large and of great concern to the Soviet leaders of the ASU programme.

The guidelines of future policy for ASUP are now clearly laid out. The objective is to standardise new systems on the model of the best existing systems. The new systems will embody in increasing numbers the technology of third generation computers, and should therefore be more effective. Moreover the policy of establishing multi-user computer centres, now preferred to the alternative of setting up a computer centre in each enterprise or *ob'edinenie*, will foster standardisation, as all the users of one centre will rely on a single set of hardware and, increasingly, the same software. This development should make it easier to model new systems on the best of the old. But, as this section has shown, there are serious difficulties to overcome.

3 A NOTE ON COMPUTERS IN THE CONTROL OF TECHNOLOGICAL PROCESSES[4]

Automated systems for the control of technological processes (ASUTP) form part of the overall strategy of OGAS, and data on their numbers are included with those on automated management systems dealing with economic planning and management functions. On this reckoning ASUTP account for 31 per cent of automated systems installed in the period 1966–77. However ASUTP are special inasmuch as control of a technological process presents problems quite different from those of economic management – problems which fall more naturally within the scope of an engineer rather than an economist. Accordingly this note deals only with certain general aspects of ASUTP, ignoring technical issues.

According to Dr Siemaszko, within the Soviet Union the use of computers to control industrial processes has passed through three distinct phases (Siemaszko (1976), Sec. 2.3.2, pp. 1–3). Initially, in about 1960, digital computers were installed as loggers and processors of data generated by conventional (analog) controllers. This stage was succeeded by an attempt to achieve closed-loop control of major industrial processes, by a method known in the West as ddc (direct digital control). It was intended that ddc would replace conventional analog controllers, offering the possibility of using more sophisticated control algorithms and of replacing several analog controllers by a single digital computer. In fact these results were not generally achieved, and concentration on ddc gave way to a third phase in which the use of computers to control technological processes was subsumed within the overall management automation programme under the designation of ASUTP.

The first use of the term recorded by Dr Siemaszko is in the second half of 1971, but serious problems of definition have been noted by Soviet writers. It was intended that ASUTP should refer to supervisory computer control of a process, in which a digital computer uses a model of a production process to provide set points for a number of subordinate analog (or other) controllers. According to this definition ASUTP would form a hierarchical process control system, which could itself be embedded within the hierarchy of an enterprise or *ob'edinenie* and ultimately within the hierarchy of national economic management. However one Soviet commentator, writing in 1973, noted that 'according to some specialists and economists control equipment directly interacting with technological machinery should be included in ASUTP'. This definition would include data loggers and control schemes with and without computers. According to this source only 14% of ASUTP in 1973 conformed to the proper definition (Maksarev (1973)).

This casts some doubt on the data on numbers of ASUTP recorded in the statistical handbook. It also brings into relief the claim made by a number of authors that ASUTP are the most favourable ground for investment, offering the shortest recoupment period. There are a number of difficulties here. First, as Dr Siemaszko observes, 'it is not clear whether in the case of computerised control the comparison is being made with analog automated control (as the obvious first alternative) or with manual control, which would really be an illogical and unfair basis of comparison' (Siemaszko (1976), p. 4). Secondly, the simple replacement of analog controllers by digital computers has often been found in the West to be accompanied by higher costs, and may not improve the quality of control (Smith (1972), p. 8). This conclusion applies *a fortiori* to the USSR where doubts about the reliability of equipment in at least one case led to provision of analog standby equipment offering a 100% standby capacity, in place of the 20/25% capacity usually found in the West. Thirdly, in the case of supervisory computer control, the familiar problem arises of separating the influence of computer control from that of other changes.[5]

The last difficulty arises in particularly acute form when the process control system is itself a part of a larger, hierarchical system operating within the enterprise and beyond. This is a step in keeping with the logic of OGAS, but there is no evidence of a deliberate policy of linking ASUTP with the development of systems at the enterprise or *ob'edinenie* level; although there must be individual instances of the two occurring together, development is usually quite separate (Bobko (1976), p. 144). Complete integration of ASUTP with higher level systems would require the construction of a model of the technological processes operating within a plant, and the selection of an optimal regime of operation on the basis of some economic criterion. This presents very severe modelling problems, and there is no evidence of such applications in the USSR.

In short the development of ASUTP has been conducted separately from that of higher level systems, and, like higher level systems, the ASUTP are of varying quality. But this conclusion can only be stated tentatively. As Dr Siemaszko concludes, 'the unreliability of the sources makes it impossible to say to what degree process control is computerised within ASU, what is the technological level of these computer applications, and what degree of success these applications have achieved' (Siemaszko (1976), Sec. 2.3.2, p. 5). It remains true however that a great deal of attention is paid to these systems by Soviet officials. The number of ASUTP to be installed in the tenth five-year plan is more than twice the number installed in the ninth (Zhimerin (1978), p. 7); and mass production methods are now being developed for them (Stefani (1978)).

7

CONCLUSION

The preceding chapters have outlined the history of Soviet work in the field of management automation and the progress made at different levels in the management hierarchy. This concluding chapter considers three aspects of the management automation programme taken as a whole: the economic effect of the systems and the adequacy of the methods used to measure it; the quality and efficiency of the programme management; and the changes which the use of computers has brought and is likely to bring to the pattern of Soviet economic management.

1 THE ECONOMIC RETURN TO COMPUTERS IN MANAGEMENT

The methods of calculating the economic return to investment in automated management systems have been described in two earlier chapters dealing with branch automated management systems and with automated systems of enterprise management. In each case the method is based upon standard Soviet practice for assessing the effectiveness of capital investment, through calculation of the recoupment period or its inverse (Abouchar (1972/3)).

Quite apart from the difficulty of applying the Soviet method of investment appraisal in the case of automated management systems, the basic method is open to a number of objections. These are well known. For example, a simple rather than a compound method of discounting is used; there is no means of taking account of the varying length of life of projects; the methods for dealing with capital investments which take place over an extended period are crude and contradictory.

Even more seriously, criticism can be made of the way in which the required recoupment period and its inverse, the coefficient of relative effectiveness (CRE), are determined. Several writers have observed that the CRE should be set in such a way that the number of investment projects which satisfy it should just exhaust the investment funds available (Nove (1972), pp. 373–4).[1] If the price system in operation truly reflected social opportunity cost, then the CRE should be the same for all branches of production.

In practice, it seems that in spite of the arguments of many economists for a uniform CRE across all branches the Soviet Union persists in using differentiated coefficients. In general, investment projects in heavy industry are assigned a lower CRE than investment projects in light industry. Moreover the general level of coefficients is kept low. The standard CRE has been 0.12, representing a recoupment period of a little more than eight years. Crude comparisons with other countries and the results of some econometric calculations suggest that a higher discount rate should be used (Fedorenko (1975), pp. 267–8). If this argument is correct then, even ignoring the other drawbacks, Soviet procedures would not if used uniformly select the most advantageous investment projects. Too many projects would satisfy the minimum requirement. Some additional criterion would be required and the good projects would be the enemy of the best.

These considerations give some support to the high coefficient of effectiveness required of investment in most automated management systems installed in recent years. In 1973 Gosplan promulgated a decree, approved by the State Committee on Science and Technology, the Academy of Sciences and Minpribor, stating that the required coefficient of effectiveness of capital investment in ASU should be at least 0.3; the recoupment period, in other words, has been a maximum of $3\frac{1}{3}$ years.[2] As well as corresponding to the levels of recoupment period calculated for systems in use, this unusually high coefficient can be seen as an informal rationing device. The resources used in designing and installing automated management systems, particularly computer hardware and the skilled labour of systems analysts and designers, are in short supply. Their prices do not reflect opportunity costs. The use of a high coefficient compensates in some degree and very crudely for this mispricing of resources, and thereby tends to direct the scarce resources to factories and ministries where the return will be more immediate.

This attempted justification of the low recoupment period required of investment in ASU would be more significant if greater confidence could be placed in the procedures by which the economic return is estimated. We have already noted the thirty different ways of estimating the economic return to an automated system of enterprise management, and the alarming tendency for the actual economic return to fall short of that estimated (see p. 163 above). And we have already discussed the key difficulty in this area, which is to isolate the effects of an automated management system which is introduced simultaneously with other changes in the factory or ministry. This difficulty is not, of course, peculiar to the USSR. Inspection of Western literature on assessing the economic impact of management information systems suggests that no satisfactory method is used in the West (McRae (1971), pp. 213–31). The stumbling-block is the same. It is relatively easy to calculate the savings in management costs which result from the system, but most analysts feel that the greatest benefits are derived from improved decision taking. The outputs of the manual and computer information system are different and therefore a simple comparison of the cost of operation is not enough.

However the management automation programme in the USSR has a feature which creates additional difficulties. The whole hierarchy of management is subject to computerisation, at enterprises, ministries and higher state organisations such as Gosplan and Gossnab. This creates the problem of allocating benefits to particular systems. For example, an enterprise may achieve higher output after having an automated system of management installed. Ignoring other factors, this may be the result not only of better plan formulation and execution at enterprise level, but also of a better allocation of output targets to enterprises by a ministry which has installed a branch automated management system. In addition supply may have improved as a result of Gossnab's automated management system. Clearly the whole benefit cannot be attributed to each system in turn, for that would involve double – or triple – counting. Yet no satisfactory way of dividing the benefits can be found.

The problems is particularly acute at the highest level of the management pyramid, for example at Gosplan and Gossnab, which are separated from the production process by several layers. One group of authors asserts that at Gossnab the bulk of savings and benefits accrue outside the system. 'The basic saving from introducing ASU in Gossnab USSR occurs to the extent of 75–80% outside the boundaries of the supply system; approximately 15% accrues in management units within the system and only 6–10% in the management organisations and computer centres which have .

borne overwhelmingly the greatest part of expenditure on establishing the ASU. In these circumstances the recoupment period on setting up the ASU is stretched out for many years' (Grebnev (1974), p. 36). Although the basis for this division is not described, and the estimate is of doubtful value, the problem underlying it is an important one.

The same authors have considered solving the problem by attributing to high-level ASU covering many branches of industry those increases in output which cannot be 'explained' by other factors. But they recognise that the residual is the combined effect of a complex range of factors, not all of them economic, and that the procedure they outline will give a disproportionate return to the automation of planning and management (Khrutskii (1974c)).

To make matters worse the problem of the indirect nature of the return to a high-level ASU is a growing one. McRae notes that when computers are used merely for generating data which were previously prepared manually their impact can be measured quite easily. But when long-term decisions are made on the basis of information provided by the system it becomes exceedingly difficult. (He notes, writing in 1970, that this stage has not yet been reached in the West) (McRae (1971), p. 225). Grebnev makes a similar point with respect to the Soviet Union. As Gosplan's system develops, for example, the weighting of indirect benefit in the overall impact of the system will increase (Grebnev (1974), p. 36). The problems are recognised, but not overcome, in the methodology prepared within Gosplan to evaluate the effect of ASPR (Silin (1977)).

However, it is worth giving data on the overall economic return to the Soviet management automation programme both because it may give some indication of the order of magnitude of savings achieved and because data on savings, to the extent that they are believed in the USSR, may act as an influence on policy. The ninth five-year plan provided for an investment of 4.5 milliard rubles on 1,200 automated management systems (Zhimerin (1974b)). In fact, although the target for automated systems was not achieved, expenditure on computers and ASU amounted to about 6 milliard rubles, or slightly more than one per cent of total investment in the plan for 1971–5 (Dyagalets (1976), p. 123). In compiling the ninth five-year plan Gosplan estimated an economic return of 1.85 milliard rubles over the five years. In the first three years actual benefits amounted to 700 million rubles, with 500 million rubles projected for 1974 (Myasnikov (1974), p. 89). Since then the number of ASU has grown substantially, and Zhimerin estimated that the systems installed in the ninth five-year plan would, when completed, yield an economic return of 1.2 milliard rubles per year, or about one third of one per cent of Soviet national income in 1976 (Zhimerin (1974b)). However in compiling the tenth five-year plan, Gosplan estimated a total saving from the use of computers of 3.8 milliard rubles over the whole period from 1976–80 (Rakovskii (1978)).

However accurate these figures are, evidence on the economic return to investment is only one way of assessing the impact and effectiveness of the Soviet automation programme. Other approaches are possible, and these are attempted in the next two sections.

2 HOW WELL HAS THE PROGRAMME BEEN PLANNED AND IMPLEMENTED?

According to the handbook on the design of automated systems of enterprise management, establishing an ASUP (and the same applies to a system at any level) is a process similar to designing a new and complex product. 'For this reason it is characterised by all the properties which apply to the process of designing models of new technology. But in view of the continuous dynamic process of development and improvement of an ASUP as a man–machine system, it differs from the process of preparing models of new technology' (Fedorenko (1974b), p. 18). The complexity and size of the Soviet plan for management automation separate it from any but the most wide-ranging projects of technological development, and not merely for the reason mentioned in the handbook, that the design of ASU is a continuous process. Preparing a single automated management system is a process which requires the application of resources and equipment drawn from many quarters. Designing a network of computer-based management systems covering all levels of management, as well as multiplying the problem many times over, raises additional difficulties of co-ordination and compatibility.

To assess the way in which a project of this breadth and diversity has been managed, it is necessary to specify which factors should be regarded as coming within the scope of the project, and which are constraints as far as the project management is concerned. The issue is of special importance in this case in as much as the development of computers is a vital ingredient in an automated management system. The inadequacy of Soviet computer technology has been a constant theme of many Soviet writers concerned with the development of automated management systems. The decision to build the State Network of Computer Centres and to develop the Statewide Automated System is one of the factors which led to the concentration on design and acceleration of production of computers, but, as the frequent complaints of the system designers testify, the level of computer technology is not a factor wholly within their control. Although the highest-level governmental authorities can justly be blamed for setting targets for automation of planning and management which were infeasible at the existing level of Soviet computer technology, lower-level organisations implementing the plan had to accept the quality and number of computers as a constraint. However the same exoneration does not apply to software design, where the development of programmes suitable for use in automated management systems should be a joint responsibility of computer manufacturers and users.

This section will therefore attempt two levels of assessment. At one level the realism of the targets set by the highest party and government authorities will be considered. At the same time we shall assess the way in which those chiefly concerned with implementing the plan have discharged their functions.

One of the most conspicuous and general features of the whole history of the project since 1963 has been the failure to meet deadlines. A prominent example of this is supplied by the Automated System of Planning Calculations (ASPR), developed at Gosplan. The completion of this system has been pushed back to successively later dates. Other examples are the systems developed at four organisations in Gossnab. In 1966, they were scheduled for completion in two years. Yet nearly ten years later they were still not complete. The targets set by the ninth five-year plan for the more numerous branch and enterprise level automated systems were largely but not wholly achieved, but we have noted serious doubts about the quality of these systems, especially at enterprise level. As a general rule infeasible targets have been set, which can only be achieved by compromise or deception. Although the circumstances in which these targets were set cannot be discovered, there is no ground for believing that completion dates were invariably fixed on the basis of an analysis of the nature of the work undertaken, using such techniques as critical-path analysis.[3] It seems more probable that they were chosen on no firm basis, except possibly a desire to set targets which could not easily be achieved.

This practice was a symptom of a more widespread deficiency in the planning of the early stages of the automation programme. For many years there was no firm and coherent conception of how the use of computers would affect or fit in with the existing procedures of planning and management. This issue was essentially resolved at the time of the XXIV Party Congress in 1971, when the Party approved the basic outline of the system which has been put into operation over the last eight years. But before that time there was confusion. The first chapter of this book describes this period in greater detail, but the work on developing automated management systems can be characterised as unco-ordinated, based upon a series of contradictory decrees, and carried out against a background of controversy over the fundamental nature of the economic mechanism in the USSR.

However, as I have argued above, this period did give time for experiment, which was put to good use. As the ambitious targets set by the government and party decrees were not feasible, the harmful consequences of fulfilling them did not materialise. And it can scarcely be argued that the period of economic debate between 1962 and 1969 should not have taken place, in order to secure a consistent attitude towards the automation of planning and management. These arguments may reflect little credit on the decisions taken at the higher levels of governments, but they do suggest that the overall effect of them was less than disastrous.

At a more detailed level, however, the decrees contained unsatisfactory features which did have an impact. The chief of these was the failure to set up a clear structure of authority to implement the plans and the tendency to diffuse authority and responsibility widely among several organisations. After 1971, when TsSU was largely eliminated as a contributor to the overall project, the chief participants were, on the one hand, Gosplan, the Academy of Sciences, the Ministry of Instrument Building (Minpribor), and the State Committee on Science and Technology, and on the other the organisations – State Committees, ministries, enterprises – for which the systems were designed. Relations between these groups were not always stable,[4] though the Directing Materials for enterprise and branch level systems seem to have established a reasonable framework for co-operation of customer and system designer.

But within the first group some duplication of function was bound to develop. The Academy of Sciences is responsible chiefly for research into ASU, through institutes such as TsEMI and the Institute of Cybernetics at Kiev. But it also develops some individual systems. Minpribor produces hardware and also designs individual systems, through its specialist *ob'edineniya*. Gosplan approves the selection of enterprises in which systems will be installed, and plans the production of computers by Minpribor and the Ministry of the Radio Industry. Finally, the State Committee on Science and Technology is intended to form a link between the research and planning side, undertaken by Gosplan and the Academy, and the design of specific systems, which is undertaken or supervised by Minpribor. The State Committee's Institute on Problems of Organisation and Management, directed by Zhimerin, is also responsible for *research* on ways of ensuring compatibility of all systems, with respect to hardware, software and information. Popov, the Soviet management specialist, has regretted that Zhimerin's institute is not in control of all aspects of management, but it is clear from the foregoing that it is not really in overall control even of the management automation programme (Popov (1974), pp. 93–9).

The chief casualty of this diffusion of authority has been the compatibility of various parts of the grand design for automation of planning and management. The examples most frequently cited in the foregoing chapters concern incompatibility of coding systems, of document forms and of computer hardware. But these probably reflect a more fundamental incompatibility between systems at the same or different levels. If two enterprise-level systems produce different information expressed on different document forms, they probably are performing different functions. The variety of sub-systems making up individual ASUP suggests that this is so. If both enterprises are in a ministry with a branch automated management system, the latter may require information which is available at only one or at neither of the enterprise systems.

In spite of a general awareness of this issue and a determined effort to overcome it, the problem of compatibility remains unresolved. The delay in developing the Union-Wide Product Classifier has prevented the use of a uniform coding system. The obligatory Methodological Materials have not taken effect in the case of enterprise level systems, though branch automated management systems seem to be more uniform in scope and function. There are however occasional references to situations in which the operation of adjoining systems is co-ordinated. For example, Gosplan's system, ASPR, may interact with that of TsSU or a branch automated management system (Bezrukov (1975), p. 108). These instances are clearly seen as a foundation for the operation of the system as a whole in the future.

Reverting to the analogy discussed at the beginning of this section, between developing automated management systems and the development of a new product, we can distinguish three phases in the design of automated management systems: the phase of research and development, the phase of prototype production, and diffusion of the systems. It is in the area of diffusion where Soviet performance is least satisfactory. Several of the systems described in the chapters on branch and enterprise level systems seem to operate well in the Soviet context, as measured however imperfectly by their economic return. But, unfortunately, models of automated management systems of poor or variable quality can be diffused throughout the economy at least as easily as can systems of a high quality. The same discovery can be made at numerous different enterprises. Glushkov argued that this is what is happening in Soviet industry, and proposed a new organisational form to deal with the problem, a large research and production *ob'edinenie* to develop standardised and compatible high-quality systems and to install them (Glushkov (1975c)). Whether such an organisation could be created, cutting across the jurisdictional frontiers of Soviet management, remains to be seen. But some such innovation is necessary to impose a high uniform standard on the systems being developed.

In his speech to the XXIV Party Congress, Kosygin argued that 'thanks to the advantages of the socialist economic system, which makes it possible to manage economic and social processes at the level of the country as a whole, the broad application of computer technology as a whole will help us to give our plans a stronger foundation and to make the optimal decision on them' (Materialy (1971), p. 174). This promise has not been realised. The opportunity to establish an automated planning and management system on a uniform basis throughout the entire economy has not yet been taken up. However it must be remembered that the implementation of the overall plan is by no means complete and it is not yet clear what its impact will ultimately be. This issue is taken up in the next section.

3 THE IMPACT OF AUTOMATED MANAGEMENT SYSTEMS ON
SOVIET PLANNING AND MANAGEMENT

In the previous section we discussed the compatibility and degree of unity of automated management systems established in the USSR, and gave provisionally a rather unfavourable assessment, as judged by Soviet aspirations. There is, however, a question of compatibility in a wider sense: is the programme for automation appropriate for an economy at the stage of development and with the overall management system of the USSR? The answer to this question is of course tentative, but it seems desirable to conclude with some observations on this issue.

One of the chief difficulties in making such an assessment is that we are observing a network of automated systems at a very early stage of construction. The long time scale of the project is recognised in the Soviet Union. Kozlov, an official at the State Committee on Science and Technology, spoke of 1985 as the earliest date when the Statewide Automated System would make possible optimal planning at the level of the economy; after another five years the system would be converted from an 'information-advising' system to an 'information-controlling' system (Kozlov (1973)). These dates are speculative, but they do show an appreciation of the extended time-scale in which the management automation system operates.

At the end of 1977 automated management systems were installed in about twelve hundred production *ob'edineniya* and enterprises and in around two hundred ministries, including most All-Union Ministries. The first stage of Gosplan's system had been introduced while at Gossnab, although a few commodity groups were distributed on the basis of plans worked out by computers, the remainder used traditional methods. Other systems which made up the State-wide Automated System (OGAS) were, with the exception of that for TsSU, little developed, either because work on them started late, or because of the fundamental difficulty of the problems encountered.

It was argued in Chapter 2 that the gradual and uneven implementation of the programme was one of the factors which prevented a transfer to one of the computer-based algorithms developed in the 1950s and 1960s for economic planning and made it necessary to adopt a more modest and practical approach to the problem of adapting management procedures to the computer. In fact if we ignore procedures internal to each unit in the different levels in the management hierarchy at which automated management systems are installed, it is hard to cite a single case where the relationship between different units has undergone any significant change.[5] An outline of these relationships was given in Chapter 2 above. There is no evidence in the subsequent chapters of any substantial or fundamental change in the nature of the flows of information and instructions between the bodies identified there, except within an advanced branch system such as ASU-pribor where the pattern of communication between ministry and enterprise has been slightly altered.

This does not mean of course that the installation of computers has changed nothing. Within a ministry such as Minpribor, or within an enterprise with an advanced system, there have been substantial changes in the nature of information collected, the way it is collected, and the way it is used. But if we regard each unit as a 'black box', and observe only the inputs and output of the unit, then we see little change.

If the incomplete coverage of automated management systems were the only factor preventing a significant change in the Soviet economic mechanism, then the eventual date of that change could readily be forecast. But, as argued in the last section, there are other difficulties to be overcome. One of these, the problem of ensuring compatibility, must be overcome before the Statewide system can operate as an integrated whole using radically new procedures. This problem has not been overcome, and I have argued that without some new system of organising and controlling the programme as a whole it will not be overcome. Essentially the change wrought by the programme will be a speeding up of the old system of information flows.

What impact then is management automation likely to have on the overall system of management, if it does not and cannot by itself revolutionise Soviet economic management, and what relation does it bear to other changes in the economic management system? In my view the increasing use of computers has played a role in enabling the Soviet authorities to move towards a new organisational framework for managing the economy along lines indicated by the 1973 management changes. These changes were described in Chapter 1, where I noted that they seemed to be in no way inconsistent with the programme for management automation. Here I want to argue that they can be seen as part of a coherent approach to the problems of management.

Western observers of the Soviet economy both before and after the announcement of the management changes have offered an interpretation of the move towards amalgamation of enterprises into *ob'edineniya* in terms of tendencies discerned in Eastern Europe and in advanced capitalist countries. The descriptions of the new or projected systems are various – the socialist corporation (Smolinski (1974)), a socialist New Industrial State (Treml (1972), pp. 40–2), or the East German model (a term used by Dr P. Hanson) – but the essence of the new system is the same in all accounts: power is concentrated at the middle level of the hierarchy in large associations or 'corporations', which control a substantial part of the output of a group of commodities. In socialist countries this redistribution of power takes place at the expense of the central ministries and lower level units.

In the Soviet Union a particularly vigorous advocate of expanding the powers of the middle level is Bachurin, the deputy president of Gosplan (Bachurin (1974; 1975a and b)). However it appears that Bachurin is in favour of pushing to the limits, or even slightly extending, the powers of the industrial and production *ob'edineniya* under the 1973 decree, while in practice the ministries which would be the principal losers from the redefinition of functions are delaying or limiting the reorganisation.

Some discussions have exaggerated or anticipated the concentration of authority at the middle level. To recapitulate, the 1973 management changes extended in certain directions the powers and responsibilities of both industrial *ob'edineniya* (the successors to the chief administrations or *glavki*) and production *ob'edineniya* (formed by amalgamation of enterprises), but did little to undermine the twin foundations of Soviet central planning, the system of compulsory plan targets, to which managerial bonuses are tied, and the supply system, which acts as an intermediary between producer and customer. In particular there is no question of creating a market for producer goods, with prices free to fluctuate to balance supply and demand. In the new system the degree of central control over prices and of supervision of quantity allocations is left virtually intact.

Now there is no necessary contradiction between widespread reliance on computers to compile the plan and the use of market methods to implement it. Indeed the theoretical approach developed by TsEMI under the name of the system of optimal functioning of the economy provided for just such a division of responsibility. Roughly speaking, the main outlines of development of the economy would be chosen centrally, using computer-based models possibly of the decomposition type; the market and an appropriate incentive system would harness the energies of producers to execute the plan, and would make automatic adjustments for changes in circumstance not foreseen at the stage of plan compilation. In the latter regard it would act as a *'sui generis* computer' – to return to Oscar Lange's words quoted in the introduction – automatically computing the final adjustments to the plan. This is a logically coherent role for computers in planning, and one which finds great favour with economists in both the USSR and the West.

However the Soviet authorities have not chosen to take this path. For reasons given above it is doubtful whether they could do so, and in any case they have often stated that they would not wish to, even if it were possible. Instead they have concentrated on improving the existing system of planning, taking modest steps towards extending the power of intermediate units but stopping well short of a comprehensive economic reform in the manner of Hungary's new economic mechanism.

In any case, even where the degree of autonomy of the middle levels is expanded, the potential for supervision by the higher levels is simultaneously expanded by the faster and more efficient information system which the Statewide Automated System is intended to provide. Thus one can interpret the combination of the 1973 management changes and the management automation programme in terms of the well-known distinction between decentralisation of authority and decentralisation of information. On the one hand the middle level (the industrial or production *ob'edinenie*) is permitted slightly more freedom of manoeuvre; on the other it is more closely observed by ministry or higher-level organisations which now receive information in time to take remedial action. The objective is thus a small step towards indirect centralisation, a system in which lower levels choose to act as the central authorities wish them to, in response to an appropriate incentive system and in the knowledge that any deviant behaviour will be monitored at higher levels. An interpretation in these terms has been offered both by Moiseev (Moiseev (1974), p. 42) and by Glushkov, the latter writing explicitly that 'centralisation of information-processing increases the possibility for decentralising management' (Shorin (1972), p. 38). The computerised management and information systems play two roles in this process. They permit highest level authorities to supervise middle level organisations, and they increase the effective span of management control at the middle level, thus making possible the amalgamation of enterprises into *ob'edineniya*.[6]

If this is the model to which Soviet economic management is tending, then it is a possible solution to some of the difficulties of Soviet planning, synthesising the tendency in the 1960s towards greater independence of enterprises and the more recent moves to amalgamate lower level units. From the standpoint of the political leadership the new system has the merit of retaining intact many of the valued elements of centralisation in the traditional Soviet planning and management system. Indeed to the extent that computers permit the retention of these elements they can be seen as a conservative influence in Soviet economic management.

Will the Statewide Automated System be able to play the role suggested for it in the management system as outlined above? In the first place, it should be noted that the USSR has now attained the level of overall scientific and technological advance at which computer systems were widely installed in capitalist countries (see Amann (1977)). The general level of technical education in the USSR is acceptable. Shortages of manpower are increasingly encouraging the use of computers for management. The earlier chapters of this book have described many automated management systems, which, though imperfect, have contributed to improving planning and management procedures. There is no reason to believe that the project will be regarded as such a fiasco that it will be scrapped in favour of a decentralisation of authority to smaller units, co-ordinated by the market rather than by a well-informed central authority. Early Western experience of computers in management, which was often unsuccessful, did not wholly discredit the idea of their use.

The more likely future course of events is a continuing development and improvement of the automated management systems. In the Report of the Central Committee of the CPSU to the XXV Party Congress in 1976, Brezhnev referred to mathematical economic methods and automated management systems as suitable for application in a broad field of economic management functions. This was part of his overall characterisation of the tenth five-year plan from 1976–1980 as a five-year plan 'for efficiency and quality' (Materialy (1976), pp. 44, 59). However management automation was much less in the limelight then at the 1971 Congress, and no numerical targets were mentioned in the published five-year plan. This is part of a natural progression of attitudes towards automation, in which initial enthusiasm gives way to a more realistic assessment as the systems are seen as part of a daily routine.

On balance then the Soviet programme for management automation has been a limited and unspectacular success. It has not changed the face of Soviet economic management, but, as I have argued above, it plays a role in the gradual development of the new system of management to which the USSR is tending. The design of an economic mechanism is a continuous process, but there is little reason to suppose that the tenth five-year plan and beyond will not see the continuing steady extension of automated management systems, and an improvement or levelling-up of their quality, without any substantial change in their role as an adjunct to or perpetuator of the existing system of management.

THE UNION-WIDE PRODUCT CLASSIFIER

The Union-Wide Product Classifier (*Obshche-soyuznyi klassifikator produktsii* – OKP) is one of many systems of classification and coding which have been developed in conjunction with the State-wide Automated System (OGAS). Other classification and coding systems cover enterprises, establishments and organisations (the OKPO), units of measurement, and documents used for planning and management. Of these, the OKP has received the earliest and the greatest attention.

The need for a unified system of coding and classification is self-evident in a management system relying increasingly on data exchanges between computer centres. The design of OKP began in 1963 under the guidance of Gosplan's chief computer centre. Three hundred institutes and forty ministries and departments were involved. The framework of the system was laid down by a decision taken by Gosplan in 1963 to use a single decimal system of coding, comprising ten digits. Initial experiments were made on the coding of engineering products. In 1968 the higher classification groups for these products were published, but tests showed them to be unsatisfactory in a number of ways. In 1971 Gosplan approved the higher classification groups for the whole system in spite of complaints from TsSU that the system was unsuitable for statistics (Cheshenko (1973)).

Of the ten digits of the OKP, the first six cover the higher classification groups. Each entry will have the following form:

Higher classification groups					Lower level code
Class	Subclass	Group	Subgroup	Sort	
XX	X	X	X	X	XXXX

For example, the first six digits for alkych varnishes are: 231121, where:

23 – class (paint and varnish materials and intermediates)

1 – subclass (paint and varnish materials)
1 – group (condensation resin varnishes, silicatives and solutions)
2 – subgroup (polyester condensation resin varnishes)
1 – sort (alkych varnishes).

The remaining four digits, sometimes augmented by a number of additional symbols, are used to carry information on technical characteristics of the product (Maiorov (1973), pp. 13–15).

The branch divisions of OKP, developed by the ministries, were to be agreed by Gosplan, Gossnab, the Ministry of Trade and the State Committee on prices, and then examined by a Gosstandart Institute for Coding, VNIIKI. According to the co-ordination plan, the branch sections were to be verified and presented for the approval of Gosstandart during the third quarter of 1972. In fact by the middle of 1973 only thirty-three of the sixty-five classes had been submitted. Of these, two subclasses were approved, three classes were made ready for approval, while the remainder were sent back for reworking. Part of the problem was the lack of a standard for the branch divisions. In 1963 Gosstandart was instructed to work out such a standard; after some delay, it was decided that four separate standards were needed; then this number grew to fourteen. These were completed only by 1970, and had little practical influence. This catalogue of delays and poor organisation drew the attention of the USSR Committee of Popular Control, which censured Gosstandart and Gosplan (Cheshenko (1973)).

Several Soviet specialists have criticised the basic decision to use a ten-digit decimal code. They argue that when computers are used to store information, the two functions of classifying and coding can and should be separated. Classification is the process of dividing a list of products into progressively more detailed groups. Coding is simply the process of assigning each classification a number. The two processes are logically distinct, yet in the OKP they are combined. This extends the number of decimal digits necessary to catch all the information required on a product to excessive lengths, while positions in the code are left vacant. Since the decimal system must be converted to a binary one, for storage in the computers, the resulting load on the computer's memory is very large. Only a fraction (about 5%) of the potential capacity of OKP is actually used and the empty cells cannot be taken up by new products (Maiorov (1973), p. 16; Yasin (1974), pp. 49–50; Khaninev (1974), pp. 108–11; for an opposing view see Zhichkin (1971), p. 24).

This is only one of many criticisms levelled against the OKP:

Maiorov lists ten complaints and proposes changes which amount to a complete revision of the basic design (Maiorov (1973), pp. 16–19). The chief problem is that the system is not designed for the purpose for which it is intended, to facilitate planning and management. It does not take account of the different information requirements of, say, production plans and distribution plans (Khaninev (1974), p. 106). Furthermore some essential logical operations, such as aggregation by branch, are not possible with the present structure of OKP; this is a vital requirement for branch automated management systems.

Some of these complaints are contradictory. The code is too long, it is argued, yet it does not contain enough information. The OKP is being asked to fulfil a number of requirements which no coding system can satisfy, of being universal, short, and detailed. These requirements can only be satisfied by having a number of local codes, with the facility for translation into another code, often via the OKP. Khaninev has suggested this system of internal codes, with translation through an external code, or language-mediator (ibid., p. 109). Such a system has been devised within Gosplan, as part of ASPR (Khaninev (1976), pp. 38–47).

In practice such local codes have been created in large numbers, in ministries, enterprises and supply organisations, often without consideration of the need to translate from one code to another. More recently, however, greater attention has been paid to the OKP. Organisations distributing non-ferrous metals employ the higher classification groups of the OKP, though curiously only the first four digits are used: specialised codes give a more detailed specification of products (Kodya (1973), p. 62). Often an inconsistency arises between an organisation using a code based on the OKP, and another organisation using a different code. The problem is particularly acute in the supply system. The head of a local supply administration complains that the Ministry of Ferrous Metals and Soyuzglavmetall, the Union organisation distributing metal products, use different codes (Mikhlin (1974), p. 35; Novitskii (1977)). For chemical products, the Union-Wide coding system proved unsatisfactory for Soyuzglavkhim, the supply organisation, which had to develop a shorter system for direct use, with facilities for recoding (Geronimus (1972), pp. 4–5). Soyuzglavpribor approved the OKP branch division for instruments, but it soon became clear that the classification scheme was unsuitable for use in the supply system (Povyshat' (1974), p. 31). And so on.

In summary the management automation programme makes

a generally used commodity coding system vitally necessary. This need has not yet been met. The OKP has been developed after substantial delays, and these delays have made the task of establishing a single and universal system even more difficult, as local and often incompatible systems have been developed in the intervening period. Moreover, the design of the OKP is inadequate in a number of respects. At the same time there is evidence that the higher groups of the OKP are serving increasingly as an organising principle around which detailed local codes can be constructed to meet specialised local requirements. This conception of the universal code as mediator between and generaliser of specialised local codes seems to have been reached more as a response to difficulties than as a conscious plan, but it may be a satisfactory outcome.

SOVIET COMPUTER
TECHNOLOGY

This appendix contains a brief summary of a larger comparative study of Soviet computer technology undertaken as part of a wider survey of Soviet technological levels.[1] It first covers the level of best practice computer technology in the USSR, and then discusses the diffusion of computers throughout the economy. A limited amount of comparative information is given, in order to give the reader a yardstick against which to assess the level of the computers available for the Soviet management automation programme. The study draws heavily upon techniques of comparison developed by Richard Judy. The reader is referred to his work for an account of developments up to 1968 (Wasowski (1970)).

Since 1968 the chief development in Soviet computer hardware has been the switch to third generation machines, using integrated circuits instead of transistors. Two ranges of third generation machines have been produced: the M-series, produced by the Ministry of Instrument Building, Means of Automation and Control Systems (Minpribor), and used largely but not entirely for process control, and the more important Ryad or ES (Unified System) series developed in the USSR by the Ministry of the Radio Industry (Minradprom). The latter is the result of a collaborative project within the Council for Mutual Economic Assistance. The Soviet Union was responsible initially for producing two medium-sized computers, the ES1020 and 1030, and the two largest computers, the ES1050 and 1060 (Larionov (1974)). The early models in the ES range appeared in 1972, though production of the ES1060 began only in 1978. The range as a whole is similar to the IBM 360 series which has been available in the West since 1965. As well as the central processing units mentioned above the ES series contains a large range of peripherals capable of performances appropriate to the speeds of the central processing units. More powerful replacements for the models mentioned above, equivalent to the IBM 370 series, are now being developed (Davis (1978)).

In 1968 Judy observed that, compared with the United States, Soviet performance in developing software for computers was worse than their performance in developing hardware. Since 1968 there has been some improvement. Both series of third generation computers have been equipped with disc operating systems, compilers for the major programming languages and application programs. There were delays in preparing the software, but they seem to have been shorter than in the case of second generation computers. However the search for an appropriate organisational basis for the provision of software to computer users has not been entirely successful.

Evidence of the size of the Soviet computer stock is conflicting. Since 1966 the output of the computer industry has grown substantially in value terms, by 480% in the eighth five year plan and by 430% in the ninth. The number of computers in the USSR in 1970 is usually estimated as being in the region of 5,000, or about 20 per million population, but some published data for the Ukraine indicate that the stock in that republic in 1970 was closer to 12 per million. These figures compare with a US stock of 344 per million in 1970, and British and Japanese figures of 91 and 96 respectively. By 1978 the Soviet stock has probably grown to about 18,000 or about 70 per million population. Of course the computing power available in the USSR is much less than these figures on computers per head suggest. In 1970 a very high proportion of the American computer stock consisted of third generation computers, whereas in the USSR there was not a single third generation machine of domestic manufacture, and first generation machines comprised a third of the stock. Even at the end of 1975 the overwhelming majority of Soviet computers (83%) were of the second generation (Lapshin (1977), p. 22).

Thus automation of management in the USSR has been hampered by both the small quantity and low quality of Soviet computers. In 1970 the USSR had probably the same stock of computers per head of population that the United States had about ten years earlier, and the United Kingdom had about six years earlier. At the same time the most powerful computer available in the USSR was about one sixth as powerful as the most advanced machine available in the United States, and of a technological level equivalent to that of the United States eight years earlier, on the basis of maximum number of operations per second. The relative Soviet position has improved little or not at all since that date. This substantial technological gap should be kept in mind by any reader wishing to compare Soviet work on management automation with Western achievements in the same area.

APPENDIX III

SOME NOTES ON COMPARISONS WITH THE UNITED KINGDOM

This appendix is devoted to a discussion of the similarities and dissimilarities in the use of computers for management between the Soviet Union and the United Kingdom. To carry out detailed and systematic comparisons would require substantial resources and different expertise than the writer possesses. It would require, in particular, collection of data on British applications in a form corresponding as far as possible to Soviet definitions and detailed comparisons of individual cases. The observations made here have none of the authority of such an investigation. They are based entirely upon existing Western research, and the comparisons, which are the work of the author, can only be tentative and provisional. The three sections consider in turn general problems of comparing computer-based management systems, the procedures and models which are employed, and the problems of implementation which arise.

1 ON COMPARING SOVIET AND BRITISH COMPUTER APPLICATIONS FOR MANAGEMENT

It is unnecessary to dwell upon the substantial differences between the economic system of the USSR and that of the United Kingdom, from which data and information for the comparisons below are drawn. The system of information flows, the allocation of authority among units and the system of incentives – three major characteristics of an economic system – are quite dissimilar. The differences are seen in the organisational framework of the economy and the management functions discharged within that framework. These have large and obvious implications for the manner in which computers can be employed to perform management functions, which are reflected in differences in terminology used to describe automated systems.

Obviously, in an economy based on private ownership of the means of production, there is no all-embracing overall pyramid of management in which each organisation is subordinate to a superior. There are no organisations with the powers and responsibilities of the highest-level units within the Soviet economy, such as Gosplan. In the field of industrial management, comparisons with the West can only be drawn for units which lie at the middle or the bottom of the Soviet hierarchy.

Even here there are substantial differences between the management functions performed, and hence in the nature of computerised management systems. The differences are smallest at the level of control of technological processes, where the potential uses of a computer to control, say, a chemical process will be independent of the economic system, though the particular form of control used will depend on the technological level and historical background of the economy. When the scope of the process controlled goes beyond the technical, to include commercial and economic considerations, the differences become more apparent. For one thing, it is impossible to establish equivalence between Soviet and Western organisations. For another, even if such equivalence could be established, the differences in commercial environment are very substantial. To cite two obvious examples, in Western commercial organisations there is a great preoccupation with cash flow and less significance is attached to output targets in physical terms: in the Soviet Union the priority is reversed. In the West the level of demand for output is subject to large uncertainties; in the Soviet Union it is known with a high degree of certainty.

The differences between the Soviet Union and the West in economic environment are reflected in differences in terminology used to describe computer-based management systems. The generic term used within the USSR is ASU, or automated system of management or control. At the level of process control a similar term is used in Western literature. But at the higher level of management of a Western firm as a whole, the term management information system (MIS) is frequently used, and some writers have identified the two terms. However, while there is a considerable overlap in broad outline between the two terms, for reasons given in the previous paragraph too close an identification is inappropriate.

The problem of terminology obviously bedevils comparisons of the number of computer-using management systems in the USSR and in Western countries. Rough estimates suggest however that the number of computers used for commercial or administrative purposes in the USSR was something of the order of half the number used in the UK in 1970. Per head of population the figure is roughly one tenth. The calculations do not allow for differences in quality of computers used; incorporating this element would further widen the gap. Thus in 1970 the computing power available in the Soviet Union for management purposes was substantially lower than in the United Kingdom. There is no evidence to suggest that this situation has changed since then.

2   SIMILARITIES BETWEEN PROCEDURES AND MODELS

The preceding chapters have shown how computers came increasingly to be applied at all levels of Soviet industry. It is reasonable to assume that stimulus was given to these efforts by the worries expressed by Soviet officials in the 1960s about the shortage of labour.[1] In these terms the overall programme to automate management practices can be justified as a labour-saving innovation.

Even so the selection of individual units for installation of ASU seems initially to have been fairly haphazard, in many cases the result of local initiative rather than a rational allocation of resources, though the arguments for investment in ASU were usually bolstered by economic calculations which often subsequently proved to be spurious. Later when plans for ASU were worked out more systematically, the usual pressures on design organisations to meet quantitative plan targets came into force, and these did not tend to promote a better allocation of resources (Glushchenko (1976), pp. 505–7). A detailed study of computer installation in the UK similarly suggests that investments in computers were made for a variety of reasons, and its author concludes that the decision to computerise in British firms gives support not to a profit-maximising but to a satisficing or behavioural theory of the firm (Stoneman (1976), pp. 106–9).

What overlap is there in functions discharged by computer in Soviet and British management systems? In her analysis of British experience with computers in the late 1960s, with special emphasis on their impact on managers, Rosemary Stewart identified three areas of applications of particular interest (Stewart (1971)):
(i)   Clerical procedures
(ii)   Planning and control
(iii) Long-term planning and policy decisions.

The author defined a number of potential effects on management arising from these different types of computer application and compared these with actual effects observed in companies analysed in case studies. Inevitably the problems which encouraged computer applications and the potential computer contribution to the problems betray a marked similarity to similar analyses conducted in the USSR. We examine each application in turn.

Clerical procedures can be dealt with most quickly. Obviously, there are substantial differences between, say, the accounting function in the USSR and in the UK, but the essential elements of accounting – collection, storage, simple operations upon data – are the same. Thus it is hardly surprising that computers in the two countries are seen as offering the same kinds of solutions to the same kinds of problems – the slowness, inaccuracy and expense of manual procedures (although, of course, the gains are not always realised). We have seen in earlier chapters that a high proportion of work performed in ASU at all levels falls into this category.

The second category, planning and control, includes short-term production planning and control functions, such as stock control, loading and scheduling, and control of work in progress. In broad terms these are the kinds of functions performed by various sub-systems of automated systems of enterprise management (ASUP), in particular the sub-systems for technical and economic planning and for operational management. But the similarity of models used hides very substantial differences between the USSR and the United Kingdom in the circumstances in which the plan is prepared and in the status of the plan. One obvious difference lies in the predictability of output levels. A Soviet enterprise operates within a framework of known demand, set out in the annual plan. In a market economy, scheduling is done on the basis of orders, which may not be known or predictable in advance. Factors such as these influence the area of application of what may be formally the same mathematical model.

A similar observation applies to the third area of computer application, long-term planning and policy decisions. In the Soviet Union this area falls largely outside the scope of the enterprise, and within that of the ministry or Gosplan. However, the type of model used is often similar – a mathematical programming model in which some variable is maximised (minimised) subject to a number of constraints. Such a model was used, for example, for planning first the Canadian operations, and later the company-wide operations of British Petroleum Ltd (Stewart (1971), pp. 128–72). Another interesting example is the model developed for a division of ICI Ltd (Stephenson (1970)). Here too formal similarities in the model may hide important differences in the way the results are used.

3   PROBLEMS OF DESIGN, IMPLEMENTATION AND OPERATION

The previous chapters have reported a number of general problems encountered within the USSR in the course of the management automation programme. This section considers the extent to which the same or similar problems have been encountered in the United Kingdom. The source for information on British computer applications is a number of surveys carried out by questionnaire and interview, supplemented by detailed examination of particular case studies. Systematic survey information is not available for the USSR, and we have to rely upon articles in newspapers and other sources, which often give an indication of how widespread a problem is, even if they give no detailed quantitative information.

The British surveys referred to include two covering process control computers, one of fifty applications in several industries (Fisher (1973)), another of 32 applications in a single industry (Constable (1972)); a survey carried out by the National Computer Centre of computer use for production control (National (1973)), and a similar survey carried out within a British university (King (1972)); and finally a general survey of computer usage in the United Kingdom in 1971, carried out for the National Computer Centre (National (1972)). None of the studies has the same coverage as another or presents data in comparable form, and I shall cite evidence from them individually.

The NCC study of production control by computer notes a number of problems occurring at the design stage. The firms in its sample cited most frequently the following problems: interdepartmental troubles, lack of computer appreciation by user staff, and problems of data capture.

The study notes that 'the areas where there is a higher frequency of problems are those not within the direct responsibility of the data processing section', and that 'technical problems of systems analysis and programming are of much smaller significance' (National (1973), p. 40). Stewart's analysis of case studies revealed a similar picture. She concludes that 'it is most important that management should not abdicate in the belief that it cannot understand, or that it can safely leave computer developments to the specialists' (Stewart (1971), p. 206).

Similar lessons have been learnt in the Soviet Union where there has been frequent reference in newspaper articles and other sources to the need to involve administrators in the task of developing automated management systems at all levels. The official materials for the design and introduction of ASU, described above, require a high level of participation by senior ministry and enterprise personnel at all stages in the design of branch and enterprise level systems. But a Soviet study notes this objective is not always achieved (Krivtsov (1976), pp. 148–9).

Other similarities emerge from British surveys of problems in implementation and operation. Lists of problems met in this connection have been collected by various authors (National (1973), p. 52; Fisher (1973), pp. 120, 123; Constable (1972), p. 134). They show a slightly different emphasis but in other respects they are very similar. I shall consider some of the more important points in turn.

1 Data problems: Here the similarity with Soviet experience is very marked. In the design of ASU data problems have often been the most serious problem encountered, and a problem often underestimated.
2 Lack of management understanding of the system and communication difficulties between management and computer staff: This matter has been discussed above, and here too similarities between British and Soviet experiences have been noted.
3 Unrealistic targets set for implementing the system: it is unnecessary to rehearse here the Soviet experience of broken deadlines for systems at all levels.
4 Shortage of skilled systems analysts: Here too there is a close parallel with Soviet experience.
5 Hardware problems: Given the lag in technological level between the Soviet Union and the West in computer technology, and bearing in mind the frequent complaints made of the low quality of Soviet hardware, we may conjecture that this problem is more severe in the USSR, and acts both to limit the effectiveness of applications attempted and to constrain designers from making certain applications.
6 Relations with suppliers: The NCC survey reports that 14%

of firms questioned experienced a lack of back-up support by hardware or software suppliers. In Fisher's survey, a problem with computer delivery was reported for one quarter of applications examined. In the Soviet Union the system is substantially worse. Whereas in the United Kingdom computer manufacturers offer application packages as a matter of course, this responsibility has not until recently been discharged by the Ministries manufacturing computers in the USSR, and users have had to develop their own software. Another grave problem is the lack of facilities for repairing equipment, which is aggravated by the low level of reliability of Soviet computers, especially of the second generation. These factors combine to make the relationship between suppliers of equipment and software and their customers quite different in the USSR than in the United Kingdom, and we may conjecture that this problem would come higher up the list in the Soviet Union.

A more general yardstick of the achievement of computer objectives is contained in the NCC survey of computer use in the United Kingdom in 1971. The index was constructed so that if expectations were exceeded it would equal 1.5; if exactly achieved 1.0; if almost met, 0.5; and if not achieved, 0. The average index for all seven objectives considered was less than unity. It ranged from 0.75 for the objective of improving services to customers to 0.45 for improvements in corporate planning and control. Financial planning and departmental planning and control lie roughly in the middle of this range (Stoneman (1976), p. 169). This survey, which, as Stoneman observes, reflects greater satisfaction with computer usage than have some others, shows nonetheless that computers have not on average lived up to expectations in the United Kingdom. Deficiencies observed from Soviet experience should be interpreted in this light.

NOTES

NOTES TO CHAPTER 1

1 This account is taken chiefly from Holloway (1974), pp. 310–19.
2 A. I. Berg was then head of the Cybernetics Council of the Academy of Sciences, as already mentioned; A. I. Kitov is the author of numerous books on programming and computers; A. A. Lyapunov is a distinguished technical cyberneticist. An earlier brief reference is made in Bruk (1957) and see Belkin V. (1957). An interesting recent account of these early days is given in Tretyakova (1976), pp. 158–62.
3 The decree has also been linked with the foundation of TsEMI, of the Institute of Cybernetics of the Academy of Sciences of the Ukraine, and of TsNIITU, a research institute of the Ministry of Instrument Building (Yakovenko (1973), p. 39).
4 Academician Doroditsyn was, and is, director of the computer centre of the Academy of Sciences. Academician Fedorenko, a chemical engineer by training, is director of TsEMI and Academic Secretary of the Economics Section of the Academy of Sciences. Academician Glushkov is director of the Institute of Cybernetics of the Ukrainian Academy of Sciences, in Kiev.
5 Trapeznikov was director of the Institute of Automation and Remote Control (now renamed the Institute of Control Problems) and is a deputy chairman of the State Committee on Science and Technology.
6 (This phrase appears to indicate a stress upon the technical possibilities of information processing, within the same administrative framework. M. C.)
7 Other constituent parts of OGAS are lised in the glossary under the abbreviations, AIUS, ASFR, ASOI tsen, ASUNT, ASUS. Automated systems covering local government, health or education were also projected.
8 A head organisation in this context is one responsible for co-ordinating work in a particular field.
9 Among the more important reasons for the decision to replace the enterprise as the basic production unit are the desire to achieve economies of scale through specialisation and to bridge the science–production gap by establishing multi-plant firms with their own research and development facilities.
10 In the past *ob'edineniya* have been formed by grouping several smaller

enterprises around a single more advanced one. Since the latter is more likely to have an automated management system than the smaller enterprises it is absorbing, the reorganisation involved may not be very extensive. However the reorganisation does reduce the number of lower-level units from about 50,000 enterprises to a projected 7,000–8,000 production *ob'edineniya*. This obviously affects the automation targets.

NOTES TO CHAPTER 2

1 The problem of extending the study of information in structures to include both information which is neutral and that which is of a command character is taken up by Rakhmanin. His solution is for the super-ordinate members of the hierarchy to transmit to subordinates not only observations of the environment but also permissible ranges of their (the subordinates') decision variables. Such restrictions may be transmitted as variables of the decoding function (Fedorenko (1970), pp. 131 et seq.).
2 Kornai (1965). The model is developed and extended in Bagrinovskii (1973), pp. 11–29.
3 The author refers to the restoration in 1965 of a ministerial in place of a regional system of management.
4 Kornai (1971), pp. 39–42. Cf. Kornai's assessment of linear programming models of national economic planning. '[They], the models of the Kantorovich type, are fundamentally models of the real sphere. Of course, owing to the several simplifying assumptions (linearity, continuity, etc.) they do not faultlessly represent even the real sphere: however they approximate the solution of this problem to an acceptable extent. Yet they reflect almost nothing of the control sphere. The response functions of the control units, the information flows, etc. are missing' (ibid., p. 353).
5 For enterprise level see Fedorenko (1972a), p. 32; for branch level, see Fedorenko (1970), pp. 119–20; for the supply system, see Yakobi (1975), p. 25; for Gosplan level, see Problemy (1969a), p. 194.

NOTES TO CHAPTER 3

1 Unless otherwise stated, Gosplan refers to Gosplan USSR.
2 This approach to constructing a tree of goals has been described as deductive: i.e. 'based on logical-semantic analysis of concepts entering into the formulation of the development of the social–economic system as a whole'. The alternative approach is the inductive method, whereby we assume 'the existence of a fundamental structure of functional needs of the individual, refracted through the prism of technical capacities [i.e. the productive forces] and the totality of social institutions into a variable structure of goals of the social–economic system, which depends significantly on the basic, class–economic relations dominant in society'. The former approach is recognised as being more practical (Saltykov (1973), pp. 1035–6).
3 For details of the foreign trade system see Zakharov (1974); on the subsystem for Moscow, ASPR 'Moskva', see Chistyakov (1976).
4 See for example, the model used in the light industry section of Gosplan,

(Drogichinskii (1975a), pp. 372–3). Branch models are outlined in Chapter 5 below.

5 This coefficient operates in a way similar to a required rate of return for investment projects; it is used to evaluate investment projects in the USSR.

6 This illustrates the central and hitherto unresolved ambiguity in the notion of an inter-branch complex, that there is an almost limitless number of mutually exclusive criteria for forming such complexes out of ministries. This matter is well discussed in Zaimskikh (1977).

7 A whole issue of the journal *Mekhanizatsiya i Avtomatizatsiya Upravleniya* (No. 3, 1974) has been devoted to the system, and contains outlines of a number of sub-systems.

8 This shift can be seen in the 1974 edition of the methodological instructions for preparing the plan, where details on the use of mathematical methods are included in the main text. In the 1969 edition there is a special section on ASPR, which is not integrated into planning practice. See Metodicheskie (1969) and (1974). The process of integration is said to go further in the next edition under discussion in 1977 (Chistyakov (1977), pp. 87–8).

NOTES TO CHAPTER 4

1 In 1971 Gossnab and related organisations accounted for about two-thirds of total sales of producer goods.

2 These first two categories make up more than 70% of industrial output in value terms.

3 See for example an article entitled 'Why supply agents are turned into *tolkachy*' (Kharitonov (1974)).

4 In fact the complaint is often made that long-term direct links are arbitrarily breached by superior organisations, but the reasons are probably different from those cited here (Geronimus (1973), pp. 24–5; Glotov (1978)).

5 By contrast Kurotchenko, a Gossnab official, has challenged the conception of the supply system as merely a provider of services to customers and emphasised its directive or controlling function (Kurotchenko (1974), p. 12).

6 The problem of selecting appropriate levels of transport costs is a serious one. The 1974 edition of Gosplan's Methodological Instructions recommends use of figures calculated by Gosplan's Institute for Complex Transport Problems, or in their absence, actual rates charged (Metodicheskie (1974), p. 155). In principle, true transport costs should be based on the shadow price associated with capacity constraints in transport in an overall economy-wide maximisation problem, but this is an intractable problem (see Kovshov (1977)). For a detailed analysis of categories of transport costs appropriate to different kinds of decisions, conducted at the Institute of Complex Transport Problems, see Lugovoi (1973). The same approach to the treatment of transport costs is endorsed in the 1977 Standard Methodology for the development and location of industry, intended for use by ministries (see p. 138).

7 For example in ASU Metall the list of independent variables for the proposed regressions includes: the size and structure of national income,

output levels of branches using ferrous metals, structural changes in consuming branches, and price levels and price changes in ferrous metals and their substitutes (Protsenko (1973), p. 22).

8 In some cases columns are inserted for individual factories, and this alters the proportions of the table.

NOTES TO CHAPTER 5

1 This aspect is discussed on page 73 above. One important practical consideration is that the two levels of automated systems are developed by different organisations, which creates difficult problems of co-ordination; on this see Chapter 7 below.

2 In Soviet usage, automated management systems are divided into two parts, service and functional. The former comprises the information and computer systems, including software; the latter the sub-systems which perform the management operations, such as long-term planning or bookkeeping. This distinction is quite different from that between production and functional divisions of the ministry, the latter being concerned with an aspect of management common to all production units, the former with supervising a part of the ministry's production.

3 Minpribor is in a special position in that the Ministry as a whole is on a *khozraschet* basis. Its capital investment is determined not by allocations from the budget but from the residue of profit after payments have been made to the budget in specified amounts. Thus the limitation on capital investment as given in the programming model depends ultimately on the solution of the problem, since the latter determines the profit level of the branch.

4 Most iterative procedures are confined to altering the values of a single kind of variable, not several at once.

NOTES TO CHAPTER 6

1 I have not been able to identify the 1954 application of computers mentioned (Fedorenko (1973a), p. 11).

2 Soyuzsistemprom consists of a number of independent scientific research and design organisations (it includes no industrial enterprises). Each branch of the economy is allocated one of these organisations, to act as a co-ordinator, controlling the installation of ASUP.

3 These strictures clearly apply to all the Directing Materials for ASU and not merely those for ASUP.

4 I am heavily indebted to Dr Z. A. Siemaszko for help with this section.

5 'It is simply not obvious which improvements in process operation can be charged to the computer and which cannot' (Smith (1972), p. 11).

NOTES TO CHAPTER 7

1 In principle the problem is a great deal more complex as the level of investment undertaken should be fixed by achieving a balance between the

return on investment, for which the CRE stands as a proxy, and the social rate of time preference in consumption.

2 Recently the coefficient seems to have been reduced to 0.15, but it is not clear when this change takes effect.

3 Though where critical-path analysis was used, as at Gosplan for controlling the design of ASPR, the results were not conspicuously successful.

4 See for example TsEMI's replacement by a Gossnab institute as head organisation for the design of Gossnab's ASU (p. 99 above).

5 The change in the units of management, through the formation of *ob'edineniya*, is taken up below.

6 This interpretation suggests that the opposition of the ministries to the 1973 management changes, noted above, is misguided in the sense that they have not appreciated the scope for more effective control offered by a better information system, and are accordingly reluctant to lose the extra powers they wielded under the old pre-1973 régime. Alternatively, their own experience may have encouraged a sceptical attitude to the improvements made possible by the management automation programme.

NOTE TO APPENDIX II

1 For reasons of space only a few main references are cited in this appendix. Full references may be found in the work cited in the text (Amann (1977), pp. 377–406).

NOTE TO APPENDIX III

1 The best known expression of these worries is the fear, expressed by some economists in 1962, that by 1980 the whole Soviet labour force would be engaged in planning and administration (Zaleski (1967), pp. 54–5). It is interesting to note that the proportion of administrative, technical and clerical staff in British manufacturing increased by more than one half from 1953 to 1971, *Computers* (1972), p. 66.

BIBLIOGRAPHY

LIST OF ABBREVIATIONS OF PERIODICALS FREQUENTLY CITED
IN THE BIBLIOGRAPHY

The following abbreviations are used for periodicals frequently cited in the
bibliography.

Eko   Ekonomika i Organizatsiya Promyshlennogo Proizvodstva
              (Novosibirsk), Bimonthly.
Ekon. Gaz. Ekonomicheskaya Gazeta (Moscow), Weekly.
EMM   Ekonomika i Matematicheskie Metody (Moscow), Bimonthly.
MAU   Mekhanizatsiya i Avtomatizatsiya Upravleniya (Kiev),
              Bimonthly.
MTS   Material'no-tekhnicheskoe Snabzhenie (Moscow), Monthly.
Plan. Khoz. Planovoe Khozyaistvo (Moscow), Monthly.
PSU   Pribory i Sistemy Upravleniya (Moscow), Monthly.
Vest. Stat. Vestnik Statistiki (Moscow), Monthly.
Vop. Ekon. Voprosy Ekonomiki (Moscow), Monthly.

Abouchar (1972/3): A. Abouchar, 'The new Soviet standard methodology for
  investment allocation', Soviet Studies, 3 (1972/3), pp. 402–10.
Adamov (1972): P. G. Adamov and others, 'Avtomatizatsiya operativnogo
  upravleniya v "ASU-pribor"', *PSU*, 1 (1972), pp. 8–11.
  (1976): P. G. Adamov and others, 'Operativnoe upravlenie ostraslyu v
  usloviyakh funktsionirovaniya "ASU-pribor"', *PSU*, 1 (1976), pp. 8–10.
Adirim (1976): G. Adirim and Ya. A. Yanov, 'Opyt razrabotki i ispol'-
  zovaniya integrirovannoi modeli rosta narodnogo khozyaistva soyuznoi
  respubliki', *EMM*, 2 (1976), pp. 279–90.
Afanas'ev (1971): V. G. Afanas'ev, 'XXIV s'ezd KPSS i voprosy upravleniya
  sovetskim obshchestvom', *Voprosy Filosofii*, 12 (1971), pp. 3–16.
Aganbegyan (1969): A. G. Aganbegyan and others, *Optimal'noe Territorial'-
  no-proizvodstvennoe Planirovanie*, Novosibirsk (1969).
  (1972): A. G. Aganbegyan and others, *Sistema Modelei Narodnokhozyaistvennogo Planirovaniya*, Moscow (1972).
Amann (1977): R. Amann et al. (eds), *The Technological Level of Soviet
  Industry*, New Haven and London (1977).
Arrow (1972): K. J. Arrow, 'The value of and demand for information' in
  McGuire (1972), pp. 131–40.
ASPR (1973): 'ASPR: problemy i proektirovanie', *Vop. Ekon.*, 11 (1973),
  pp. 154–6.

(1974): 'ASPR – uslovie povysheniya nauchnoi obosnovannosti planov', *Plan. Khoz.*, 10 (1974), pp. 3–5.

Avtomatizirovannye (1974): 'Avtomatizirovannye sistemy upravleniya v narodnom khozyaistve Ukrainskoi SSR', *MAU* (1974), pp. 3–6.

Bachurin (1969): A. V. Bachurin, 'V. I. Lenin i sovremennye problemy planirovaniya narodnogo khozyaistva', *Plan. Khoz.*, 11 (1969), pp. 3–18.

(1972): A. V. Bachurin, 'Usilenie sistemnogo kompleksnogo podkhoda v planirovanii', *Plan. Khoz.*, 6 (1972), pp. 18–29.

(1974): A. V. Bachurin, 'Novaya struktura', *Ekon. Gaz.*, 35 (1974), p. 5.

(1975a): A. V. Bachurin, 'Planovoe upravlenie ekonomikoi i kontsentratsiya proizvodstva', *Plan. Khoz.*, 7 (1975), pp. 21–33.

(1975b): A. V. Bachurin, 'Proizvodstvennoe ob'edinenie – osnovnoe khozraschetnoe zveno promyshlennosti', *Eko.*, 4 (1975), pp. 3–21.

Bagrinovskii (1973): K. A. Bagrinovskii and E. L. Beryland (eds.), *Mathematicheskie Voprosy Formirovaniya Ekonomicheskikh Modelei*, Novosibirsk (1973).

Baibakov (1974): N. Baibakov, 'Dal'neishee sovershenstvovanie planirovaniya – vazhneishaya narodnokhozyaistvennaya zadacha', *Plan. Khoz.*, 3 (1974), pp. 5–13.

Baranov (1971): E. F. Baranov and others, 'O sisteme optimal'nogo perspektivnogo planirovaniya', *EMM*, 3 (1971), pp. 332–50.

(1976): E. F. Baranov and I. S. Matlin, 'Ob eksperimental'noi realizatsii sistemy modelei optimal'nogo perspektivnogo planirovaniya', *EMM*, 4 (1976), pp. 627–48.

Barskii (1975): L. A. Barskii and others, *Ispol'zovanie Ekonomiko-Matematicheskikh Modelei v Upravlenii i Planirovanii v Tsvetnoi Metallurgii*, Moscow (1975).

Basnin (1969): Yu. F. Basnin, 'Organizatsiya proektirovaniya i vnedreniya ASU MTS', *MTS*, 10 (1969), pp. 19–21.

(1974): Yu. F. Basnin, 'Nasushchnye voprosy MTS', *MTS*, 1 (1974), pp. 11–18.

Baumol (1964): W. Baumol and T. Fabian, 'Decomposition pricing for decentralisation and external economies', *Management Science*, September (1964), pp. 1–32.

Belkin, N. (1969): N. V. Belkin, 'Ekonomiko-matematicheskie metody i EVM v upravlenii snabzheniem', *MTS*, 10 (1969), pp. 2–6.

(1973): N. V. Belkin, 'Tekhnicheskaya baza ASU "Metall"', *PSU*, 8 (1973), pp. 1–2.

Belkin, V. (1957): V. Belkin, 'O primenenii elektronnykh vychislitel'nykh mashin v planirovanii i statistike narodnogo khozyaistva', *Vop. Ekon.*, 12 (1957), pp. 139–48.

Berg (1961): A. I. Berg and others, 'O vozmozhnostyakh avtomatizatsii upravleniya narodnym khozyaistvom', *Problemy Kibernetiki*, 6 (1961), pp. 83–100.

Bezrukov (1973): V. Bezrukov and V. Pryakhin, 'Ispol'zovanie ekonomiko-matematicheskikh metodov i EVM pri razrabotke planov po trudu i kadram', *Plan. Khoz.*, 7 (1973), pp. 93–9.

(1974): V. Bezrukov and D. Yurin, 'Operativnaya obrabotka ekonomicheskykh dannykh v usloviyakh ASPR', *Plan. Khoz.*, 10 (1974), pp. 28–32.

(1975): V. Bezrukov and V. Shekhovtsov, 'ASPR i ASU v sovershenstvovanii planirovaniya', *Vop. Ekon.*, 3 (1975), pp. 107–16.

(1976): V. Bezrukov, *Ispol'zovanie Ekonomiko-Matematicheskikh Metodov pri Planirovanii Truda*, Moscow (1976).

Birger (1978): E. S. Birger et al., 'Opyt postroeniya dinamicheskoi mezhotraslevoi modeli', *EMM*, 3 (1978), pp. 465–79.

Bobko (1976): I. M. Bobko, 'Ot ASU Barnaul k ASU Sigma', *Eko.*, 2 (1976), pp. 140–5.

Brudnik (1972): S. S. Brudnik, *Otsenka Ekonomicheskoi Effektivnosti ASUP*, Moscow, (1972).

Bruk (1957): I. Bruk, 'Elektronnye vychislitel'nye mashiny – na sluzhbu narodnomu khozyaistvu', *Kommunist*, 7 (1957), pp. 124–7.

Bryukharenko (1973): B. A. Bryukharenko and others, 'Primenenie ekonomiko-matematicheskikh metodov pri reshenii zadach po optimal'noi zagruzke listoprokatnykh stanov', *PSU*, 12(1973), pp. 17–19.

Budavei (1974): V. Budavei and others, 'Metodicheskie osnovy postroeniya ASPR', *Plan. Khoz.*, 11 (1974), pp. 21–31.

(1978): V. Budavei, 'Programmno-tselevoi metod v narodnokhozaistvennom planirovanii', *Vop. Ekon.*, 1 (1978), pp. 3–13.

Burkov (1973): V. N. Burkov and others, 'Problemy operativnogo upravleniya v ASU "Metall"', *PSU*, 8 (1973), pp. 8–10.

Burtseva (1972): L. D. Burtseva and others, 'Avtomatizatsiya tekhniko-ekonomicheskogo planirovaniya v "ASU-pribor"', *PSU*, 1 (1972), pp. 12 –14.

Bystrov (1966): V. Bystrov, 'O printsipakh postroeniya kompleksnoi avtomatizirovannoi sistemy upravleniya material'no-tekhnicheskim snabzheniem', *MTS*, 5 (1966), pp. 50–9.

Chernyak (1963): Yu. Chernyak, 'Sovnarkhozam – avtomatizirovannuyu sistemu informatsii', *Plan. Khoz.*, 8 (1963), pp. 52 – 6.

(1974): Yu. Chernyak, *Informatsiya i Upravlenie*, Moscow (1974).

Cheshenko (1973): N. Cheshenko, 'Obshchii yazik elektronnykh mashin', *Ekon. Gaz.* (1973), p. 10.

Chistyakov (1976): E. Chistyakov, 'Avtomatizatsiya planirovaniya ekonomicheskogo i sotsial'nogo razvitiya goroda', *Plan. Khoz.*, 5 (1976), pp. 53–9.

(1977): E. Chistyakov, 'Sovershenstvovanie metodiki razrabotki narodnokhozyaistvennykh planov', *Plan. Khoz.*, 6 (1977), pp. 81–9.

Chizhikova (1974): E. I. Chizhikova, 'Voprosy postroeniya i funktsionirovaniya sistemy SPU', *EMM*, 4 (1974), pp. 687–93.

Computers (1972): *Computers in Offices*, HMSO, London (1972).

Constable (1972): C. J. Constable, 'Managerial problems associated with process control computer applications', *International Journal of Production Research*, 2 (1972), pp. 129–39.

Danilov-Danil'yan (1977): V. I. Danilov-Danil'yan, 'Tselevye programmy i optimal'noe perspektivnoe planirovanie', *EMM*, 5 (1977), pp. 1150–63.

Dantzig (1961): G. Dantzig and P. Wolfe, 'A decomposition algorithm for linear programming', *Econometrica* (1961), pp. 767–78.

Davis (1978): N. C. Davis and S. E. Goodman, 'The Soviet bloc's unified

system of computers', *Computing Surveys*, 2 (1978), pp. 93–122.
Dorfman (1958): R. Dorfman and others, *Linear Programming and Economic Analysis*, New York, (1958).
Doroditsyn (1964): A. Doroditsyn and others, 'O nekotorykh problemakh kibernetiki', *Izvestiya*, 6 September (1964), p. 4.
Drogichinskii (1972): N. P. Drogichinskii, 'Zvenya upravleniya', *Ekon. Gaz.*, 41 (1972), p. 7.
  (1974): N. P. Drogichinskii, 'Ob optovoi torgovle v sredstvami proizvodstva', *Vop. Ekon.*, 4 (1974), pp. 25–35.
  (1975a): N. P. Drogichinskii (ed.), '*Sovershenstvovanie Mekhanisma Khozyaistvovaniya v Usloviyakh Razvitogo Sotsialisma*, Moscow (1975).
  (1975b): N. P. Drogichinskii, 'Proekty general'nykh skhem upravleniya otraslevymi sistemami', *Plan. Khoz.*, 5 (1975), pp. 6–17.
Dudkin (1971): L. Dudkin and V. Ulyanov, 'Ob otraslevykh avtomatizirovannykh sistemakh upravleniya', *Vop. Ekon.*, 8 (1971), pp. 64–76.
Dyagalets (1976): I. D. Dyagalets, 'Ekonomicheskie problemy sozdaniya ASUP', *Eko.*, 6 (1976), pp. 183–9.
Eckstein (1971): A. Eckstein (ed.), *The Comparison of Economic Systems*, Berkeley, Cal. (1971).
Effektivnost' (1973): 'Effektivnost' ASU', *Ekon. Gaz.*, 23 (1973), p. 22.
Ekonomiko-matematicheskie (1967): 'Ekonomiko-matematicheskie metody v praktiku material'no-tekhnicheskogo snabzheniya', *MTS*, 3 (1967), pp. 52–65.
Ellman (1971): M. Ellman, *Soviet Planning Today*, Cambridge (1971).
  (1973): M. Ellman, *Planning Problems in the USSR*, Cambridge (1973).
Fedorenko (1967): N. P. Fedorenko and B. Geronimus, 'Problemy sozdaniya avtomatizirovannoi sistemy upravleniya snabzheniem', *MTS*, 2 (1967), pp. 57–66.
  (1968): N. P. Fedorenko, *O Razrabotke Sistemy Optimal'nogo Funktsionirovaniya Ekonomiki*, Moscow (1968).
  (1969a) N. P. Fedorenko (ed.), *Optimal'noe Planirovanie i Sovershenstvovanie Upravleniya Narodnym Khozyaistvom*, Moscow (1969).
  (1969b): N. P. Fedorenko, 'The role of economic–mathematical methods in the planning and management of the economy of the USSR', *Journal of Development Planning*, 1 (1969), pp. 39–106.
  (1970): N. P. Fedorenko (ed.), *Voprosy Proektirovaniya OASU*, Moscow (1970).
  (1971): N. P. Fedorenko, 'Sovenshenstvovat' sistemu sotsialisticheskogo planirovaniya', *EMM*, 4 (1971), pp. 484–517.
  (1972a): N. P. Fedorenko (ed.), *Informatsiya i Modeli Struktur Upravleniya*, Moscow (1972).
  (1972b): N. P. Fedorenko (ed.), *Problemy Optimal'nogo Funktsionirovaniya Sotsialisticheskoi Ekonomiki*, Moscow (1972).
  (1972c): N. P. Fedorenko and others, 'Sistema kompleksnogo planirovaniya', *EMM*, 3 (1972), pp. 323–41.
  (1973a): N. P. Fedorenko (ed.), *Otraslevye Avtomatizirovannye Sistemy Upravleniya*, Moscow (1973).
  (1973b): N. P. Fedorenko (ed.), *Yazyki Ekonomicheskogo Upravleniya i Proektirovaniya Sistem*, Moscow (1973).

(1973c): N. P. Fedorenko, 'Planirovanie i sistemnyi podkhod', *Nauka i Zhizn'*, 5 (1973), pp. 2–7.

(1974a): N. P. Fedorenko (ed.), *Kompleksnoe Narodnokhozyaistvennoe Planirovanie*, Moscow (1974).

(1974b): N. P. Fedorenko and V. V. Karibskii (eds.), *Spravochnik Proektirovshchika ASUP*, Moscow (1974).

(1975): N. P. Fedorenko (ed.), *Sistema Modelei Optimal' nogo Planirovaniya*, Moscow (1975).

Feinstein (1967): C. H. Feinstein (ed.), *Socialism, Capitalism and Economic Growth*, Cambridge (1969).

Figurnov (1975): E. Figurnov, 'Podsistema ASGS "balans narodnogo khozyaistva"', *Vest. Stat.*, 6 (1975), pp. 323–41.

Fisher (1973): L. Fisher, *The Diffusion of Technological Information*, Research Report, Polytechnic of Central London (1973).

Ganin (1975): V. Ganin and V. Loginov, 'Prognozirovanie potrebnosti narodnogo khozyaistva v produktsii priborostroeniya', *MTS*, 1 (1975), pp. 28–33.

Geronimus (1972): B. L. Geronimus and A. D. Khmel'nitskii, 'O svyazakh ASU otraslyami promyshlennosti s ASU Gossnabom SSSR', *PSU*, 4 (1972), pp. 3–5.

(1973): B. L. Geronimus, *Puti Sovershenstvovaniya Planirovaniya Material'- no Tekhnicheskogo Snabzheniya*, Moscow (1973).

Glotov (1978): V. Glotov and I. Sadreeva, 'Plan i dol'gosrochnye svyazi', *Ekon. Gaz.*, 13 (1978), p. 11.

Glushchenko (1976): K. P. Glushchenko, 'Problemy planirovaniya i organizatsii razrabotok ASU', *EMM*, 3, 1976, pp. 505–14.

Glushkov (1969): V. M. Glushkov and S. O. Petrovskii, 'Avtomatizirovannoe upravlenie proizvodstvom–neobkhodimost' i real'nost''', *MAU*, 3 (1969), pp. 2–3.

(1973): V. M. Glushkov and others, 'Obshchegosudarstvennaya avtomatizirovannaya sistema (OGAS)', *Algorithmy i Organizatsiya Resheniya Ekonomicheskykh Zadach*, 2 (1973), pp. 5–25.

(1974): V. M. Glushkov, 'Problemy OGAS na sovremennom etape', *Algorithmy i Organizatsiya Resheniya Ekonomicheskykh Zadach*, 6 (1974), pp. 5–14.

(1975a): V. M. Glushkov, 'ASU-pervye uroki', *Literaturnaya Gazeta*, 5 (1975), pp. 10–11.

(1975b): V. M. Glushkov, 'ASU-sostoyanie i perspektivy', *MAU*, 1 (1975), pp. 3–7.

(1975c): V. M. Glushkov, 'Strategiya avtomatizatsiya', *Izvestiya*, 13 May (1975), p. 3.

Golosov (1972): O. Golosov, 'Proektnyi tsentr mekhanizatsii ucheta i vychislitel'nykh rabot', *Vest. Stat.*, 12 (1972), pp. 51–60.

Goreux (1973): L. Goreux and A. Manne (eds.), *Multi-level Planning*, Amsterdam (1973).

Gorshunov (1972): M. D. Gorshunov and V. V. Sokolov, 'Problemy sozdaniya avtomatizirovannoi sistemy normativov v narodnom khozyaistve', *Plan. Khoz.*, 3 (1972), pp. 70–8.

(1974): M. D. Gorshunov and V. V. Sokolov, *Normirovanie Raskhoda*

Material'nykh Resursov s Primeneniem EVM, Moscow (1974).

Goryachev (1977): F. G. Goryachev, 'Primenenie ekonomiko-matematicheskikh metodov i EVM v upravlenii predpriyatami', *EMM*, 3 (1977), pp. 602–7.

Graham, (1973): L. Graham, *Science and Philosophy in the Soviet Union*, London, (1973).

Grebnev (1974): E. Grebnev and others, 'Analiz effektivnosti mezhotraslevykh ASU', *Vop. Ekon.*, 12 (1974), pp. 35–42.

Grenbek (1972): G. V. Grenbek, 'Sovershenstvovanie upravleniya i ASU', *Eko.*, 2 (1972), pp. 28–38.

Holloway (1974): D. Holloway, "Innovation in science – the case of cybernetics in the Soviet Union', *Science Studies*, 4 (1974), pp. 299–337.

Hurwicz (1969): L. Hurwicz, 'On the concept and possibility of informational decentralisation', *American Economic Review Papers and Proceedings*, (1969), pp. 513–24.

(1972a): L. Hurwicz, 'On informationally decentralised systems', in McGuire (1972), pp. 297–336.

(1972b): L. Hurwicz, 'Centralisation and decentralisation in economic processes', *Jahrbuch der Wirtschaft Osteuropas*, Band 3 (1972), pp. 87–113.

Integrirovannye (1970): *Integrirovannye Sistemy Obrabotki Dannykh*, Moscow (1970).

Iotkovskii (1974): A. A. Iotkovskii and N. D. Fasolyak (eds.), *Ekonomika, Organizatsiya i Planirovanie Snabzheniya i Sbyta* (2nd ed.), Moscow (1974).

Isaev (1974): O. Isaev and E. Belotelov, 'Tipizatsiya kak osnova v metodologii sozdaniya ASU Gossnaba SSSR', *MTS*, 11 (1974), pp. 72–7.

Ishkov (1976): A. A. Ishkov, 'Kurs – na maksimal'nuyu kontsentratsiyu', *Ekon. Gaz.*, 30 (1976), p. 10.

Issledovanie (1968): *Issledovanie Potokov Ekonomicheskoi Informatsii*, Moscow (1968).

Kalinin (1977): I. Kalinin, 'Ob ulushchenii sbalansirovannosti planov na osnove sovershenstvovaniya sistemy natural'nykh i stoimostnykh balansov', *MTS*, 10 (1977), pp. 79–92.

Kalinina (1978): V. Kalinina and R. Manilovskii, 'Raschety optimal'nogo proizvodstvennogo plana predpriyatiya i ob'edineniya v mashinostroenii', *Plan. Khoz.*, 2 (1978), pp. 81–8.

Kandaurov (1974): N. N. Kandaurov and A. M. Shimanskii, *Printsipy Sozdaniya Otraslevykh ASU*, Minsk (1974).

Kantorovich (1969): L. V. Kantorovich, 'Vystuplenie na aktive Gossnaba SSSR', *MTS*, 10 (1969), pp. 68–71.

(1972): L. V. Kantorovich, 'O matematicheskom obespechenii ASU "Metall"', *PSU*, (1972), pp. 8–10.

(1978): L. V. Kantorovich et al., 'Ob ispol'zovanii optimizatsionnykh raschetov v ASU otraslyami narodnogo khozyaistva', *EMM*, 5 (1978), pp. 821–34.

Karibskii (1970): V. V. Karibskii, 'Opyt avtomatizatsii upravleniya predpriyatami v otrasli', *Eko.*, 2 (1970), pp. 128–37.

(1972): V. V. Karibskii, 'Sovershenstvovanie metodov postroeniya i razrabotki ASU promyshlennimi predpriyatami', *PSU,* 5 (1972), pp. 2–4.

Karnovskii (1976): Yu. Karnovskii and I. Kurtynin, 'Khozyaistvennyi raschet promyshlennykh ob'edinenii', *Plan. Khoz.,* 7 (1976), pp. 33–9.

Karpachev (1974): D. Karpachev, 'Sovershenstvovanie raboty v soyuzglavtsvetmete', *MTS,* 7 (1974), pp. 28–32.

Kazz (1971): S. Kazz, 'Upravlyat' pomogaet avtomatika', *MTS,* 3 (1971), pp. 87–8.

Khaninev (1974): B. Khaninev, 'K voprosu sozdaniya obshchesoyuznykh klassifikatorov', *Plan. Khoz.* (1974), pp. 105–11.

(1976): B. T. Khaninev, *Kodirovanie Ekonomicheskoi Informatsii v Usloviyakh ASPR,* Moscow (1976).

Kharitonov (1974): N. Kharitonov, 'Pochemy snabzhentsy prevrashchayutsya v "tolkachei"'*Ekon. Gaz.,* 10 (1974), p. 7.

Khmel'nitskii (1974): A. Kheml'nitskii and L. Yakovlev, 'Nekotorye problemy proektirovaniya ASU MTS', *MTS,* 8 (1974), pp. 65–9.

Khorinzhii (1970): L. Khorinzhii, 'Avtomatizirovannaya sistema upravleniya ekonomikoi (ASU)', *Vop. Ekon.,* 12 (1970), pp. 112–21.

Khrutskii (1973): E. A. Khrutskii, 'Na edinoi sisteme', *MTS,* 3 (1973), pp. 68–73.

(1974a): E. A. Khrutskii, *ASU i Material'no-tekhnicheskoe Snabzhenie,* Moscow (1974).

(1974b): E. A. Khrutskii and B. L. Geronimus, 'Problemy optimizatsii planirovaniya material'no-tekhnicheskogo snabzheniya', *EMM,* 3 (1974), pp. 505–20.

(1974c): E. A. Khrutskii and E. Grebnev, 'A esli resultat za predelami vedomstva?', *Ekon. Gaz.,* 23 (1974), p. 7.

Kilin (1972): L. Kilin, 'K voprosu o pokozatelyakh deyatel'nosti snabzhencheskikh organizatsiyakh', *MTS,* 11 (1972), pp. 74–7.

King (1972): J. R. King, 'Production planning and control by computer', *The Production Engineer,* October (1972), pp. 333–6.

Kirichenko (1978): V. Kirichenko, 'Programmnyi podkhod v perspektivnom narodnokhozyaistvennom planirovanii', *Plan. Khoz.,* 1 (1978), pp. 35–43.

Kirilyuk (1972): N. N. Kirilyuk and others, *Proektirovanie i Vnedrenie ASUP,* Kiev (1972).

(1974): N. N. Kirilyuk and others, 'Avtomatizirovannaya sistema planovykh raschetov Ukrainskoi SSSR', *MAU,* 3 (1974), pp. 3–11.

Kisilev (1976): M. Kisilev and others, 'Sovershenstvovanie otraslevogo planirovaniya pri ASPR', *Plan. Khoz.,* 9 (1976), pp. 125–36.

Kodya (1973): D. Kodya and others, 'Razrabotka klassifikatorov dlya ASU "Tsvetmet"', *MTS,* 5 (1973), pp. 62–7.

Kolosov (1973): Yu. Kolosov and others, 'Ierarkhicheskaya skhema resheniya zadachi zagruzki prokatnykh stanov i prikrepleniya k nim potrebitelei', *PSU,* 8 (1973), pp. 7–9.

Kopelovich (1972): A. P. Kopelovich and others, 'Ob osnovakh unifikatsii ASU predpriyatami', *PSU,* 4 (1972), pp. 1–3.

Kornai (1965): J. Kornai and T. Liptak, 'Two-level planning', *Econometrica,* (1965), pp. 141–69.

(1970): J. Kornai, 'A general descriptive model of planning processes', *Economics of Planning,* 1–2 (1970), pp. 1–19.

(1971): J. Kornai, *Anti-Equilibrium*, Amsterdam (1971).

Korobkov (1976): I. Korobkov and others, 'Vnedrenie v Soyuzglavkhime sistemy raschetov mezhproduktovogo balansa', *MTS*, 9 (1976), pp. 3–15.

Kossov (1971): V. V. Kossov, 'Vnedrenie EMM kak vazhneishii put' sovershenstvovaniya narodnokhozyaistvennogo planirovaniya', *EMM*, 3 (1971), pp. 327–31.

(1974): V. V. Kossov and V. Pugachev, 'Mnogostupenchataya sistema optimizatsionnykh raschetov perspektivnykh narodnokhozyaistvennykh planov', *Plan. Khoz.*, 10 (1974), pp. 12–20.

Kostakov (1970): V. G. Kostakov and P. P. Litvyakov, *Balans Truda*, Moscow (1970).

Kotov (1976): V. Kotov and V. Pryakhin, 'ASPR v planirovanii sebestoimosti i pribyli', *Plan. Khoz.*, 5 (1976), pp. 59–68.

Kovalenko (1973): V. Kovalenko, 'V positsii nablyudatelei', *Sotsialisticheskaya Industriya*, 2 June (1973), p. 2.

Kovshov (1977): G. N. Kovshov, 'Transport v sisteme modelei perspektivnogo planirovaniya narodnogo khozyaistva', *EMM*, 5 (1977), pp. 1033–53.

Kozlov (1973): S. I. Kozlov, 'Elektronnye upravlayushchie', *Pravda*, 11 July (1973), p. 4.

Kozlova (1972): O. V. Kozlova (ed.), *Avtomatizirovannaya Sistema Upravleniya*, Vol. 1, Moscow (1972).

Krasavin (1976): A. N. Krasavin and S. A. Emelyanov, 'Osobennosti avtomatizatsiya upravleniya komplektatsiei v "ASU-pribor"', *PSU*, 2 (1976), pp. 49–51.

Krivtsov (1976): A. M. Krivtsov, 'Sotsial'nye problemy sozdaniya ASU', *Eko.*, 2 (1976), pp. 145–52.

Kruchinin (1977): I. A. Kruchinin, 'ASUP i ekonomicheskaya effektivnost' proizvodstva', *PSU*, 5 (1977), pp. 4–5.

Krushevskii, (1973): A. V. Krushevskii, *Avtomatizirovannye Sistemy Upravleniya Otraslyu*, Kiev (1973)

Kul'ba (1973): V. V. Kul'ba and A. D. Tsviruki, 'Modeli i metody proektirovaniya ASU (iz opyta ASU "Metall")', *PSU*, 3 (1973), pp. 3–5.

Kurotchenko (1974): V. Kurotchenko, 'ASU snabzheniem narodnogo khozyaistva', *MTS*, 6 (1974) pp. 3–17.

(1978): V. Kurotchenko, 'O problemakh sovershenstvovaniya upravleniya snabzheniem', *MTS*, 2 (1978), pp. 8–14.

Lagutkin (1970): V. M. Lagutkin (ed.), *Nekotorye Problemy Sovershenstvovaniya Material'no-tekhnicheskogo Snabzheniya*, Moscow (1970).

(1971a): V. M. Lagutkin (ed.), *Ekonomiko-matematicheskie Metody v Snabzhenii*, Moscow (1971).

(1971b): V. M. Lagutkin, 'Sovershenstvovat' snabzhenie na osnove nauchno-tekhnicheskogo progressa', *MTS*, 7 (1971), pp. 3–14.

(1975): V. M. Lagutkin, *ASU Material'no-tekhnicheskim Snabzheniem*, Moscow (1975).

Lange (1967): O. Lange, 'The computer and the market', pp. 158–61 of Feinstein (1969).

Lapshin (1975): Yu. Lapshin, 'Sozdanie i razvitie obshchegosudartvennoi avtomatizirovannoi sistemy sbora i obrabotki informatsii', *Vop. Ekon.*, 2 (1975), pp. 121–9.

(1977): Yu. Lapshin, *Razvitie Avtomatizirovannykh Sistem Upravleniya v*

Promyshlennosti, Moscow (1977).

Laptev (1972): V. K. Laptev, 'Nekotorye osobennosti i spetsifika razrabotki i vnedreniya ASU "Metall"', *PSU*, 12 (1972), pp. 4–6.

Larionov (1974): A. M. Larionov (ed.), *Edinaya Sistem EVM*, Moscow (1974).

Lebedinskii (1973): N. Lebedinskii, 'ASPR – odno iz osnovnykh napravlenii sovershenstvovaniya planirovaniya', *Plan. Khoz.*, 9 (1973), pp. 6–13.

(1974): N. Lebedinskii, 'Vzaimodeistvie i sovmestimost' ASPR Gosplana SSSR i ASU Gossnaba SSSR', *MTS*, 1 (1974), pp. 3–11.

(1977): N. Lebedinskii, 'ASPR – vazhnyi instrument planirovaniya', *Plan. Khoz.*, 5 (1977), pp. 8–17.

Leibkind (1973): Yu. R. Leibkind and others, 'K metodike razrabotki kompleksnykh narodnokhozyaistvennykh programm', *EMM*, 4 (1973), pp. 651–8.

(1974): Yu. R. Leibkind, 'Problemy programmno-tselevogo planirovaniya', *EMM*, 3 (1974), pp. 449–54.

Lemeshev (1973): M. Ya. Lemeshev and A. I. Panchenko, *Kompleksnye Programmy v Planirovanii Narodnogo Khozyaistva*, Moscow (1973).

Lewin (1974): M. Lewin, *Political Undercurrents in Soviet Economic Debates*, London (1974).

Loskutov (1973): V. Loskutov and Yu. Lapshin, 'Vychislitel'naya tekhnika v planirovanni i upravlenii', *Plan. Khoz.*, 9 (1973), pp. 31–8.

Lototskii (1973): V. A. Lototskii and A. S. Mandel', 'O zadache upravleniya zapasami v ASU "Metall"' *PSU*, 12 (1973), pp. 22–4.

Lugovoi (1973): P. A. Lugovoi and others, *Osnovy Tekhniko-ekonomicheskikh Raschetov na Zhelezhnodorozhnom Transporte*, Moscow (1973).

Lyapin (1970): I. Lyapin, 'Stadii razrabotki ASU MTS', *MTS*, 10 (1970), pp. 75–7.

McGuire (1972): C. B. McGuire and R. Radner (eds.), *Decision and Organisation*, Amsterdam (1972).

McRae (1971): T. W. McRae (ed.), *Management Information Systems*, Harmondsworth (1971).

Maiminas (1971): E. Z. Maiminas, *Protsessy Planirovaniya v Ekonomike* (2nd ed.), Moscow (1971).

Maiorov (1973): E. V. Maiorov, *Kodirovanie Ekonomicheskoi Informatsii i Mashinochitaimye Dokumenty*, Moscow (1973).

Makhnova (1973): V. I. Makhnova, 'Planirovanie proizvodstva i khozyaistvennye svyazi', *Eko.*, 4 (1973), pp. 58–69.

Makhrov (1974): N. V. Makhrov and others, *Parametry Razrabotki Sovremennykh Avtomatizirovannkyh Sistem Upravleniya Predpriyatami*, Moscow (1974).

Maksarev (1973): R. Maksarev, 'S positsii novoi tekhniki', *Sotsialisticheskaya Industriya*, 15 September (1973), p. 2.

Maksimenko (1974): V. Maksimenko, 'Faktory effektivnosti', *Ekon. Gaz.*, 16 (1974), p. 8.

(1977): V. I. Maksimenko and others, 'Chto pokazalo obsledovanie?', *Eko.*, 2 (1977), pp. 61–70.

Mamikonov (1972): A. G. Mamikonov, 'Osnovy postroeniya ASU "Metall"', *PSU*, 12 (1972), pp. 6–7.

Marshak (1975): V. D. Marshak, 'O podkhode k postroeniyu modeli formirovaniya otraslevogo plana', *EMM*, 5 (1975), pp. 923–30.

'Materialist' (1953): 'Materialist', 'Komy sluzhit kibernetika', *Voprosy Filosofii*, 5 (1953), pp. 210–19.

Materialy (1971): *Materialy XXIV S'ezda KPSS*, Moscow (1971).

(1976): *Materialy XXV S'ezda KPSS*, Moscow (1976).

Mergelov (1972): G. S. Mergelov, 'Ekonomicheskaya reforma v priboorstroitel'noi promyshlennosti', *PSU*, 12 (1972), pp. 47–9.

(1975): G. S. Mergelov, 'Tsentralizirovannye fondy i rezervy vsesoyuznykh promyshlennykh ob'edinenii', *Plan. Khoz.*, 8 (1975), pp. 87–97.

Metodicheskie (1969): *Metodicheskie Ukazaniya k Sostavleniyu Gosudarstvennogo Plana Razvitiya Narodnogo Khozyaistva SSSR*, Moscow (1969).

(1972): *Metodicheskie Polozheniya Optimal'nogo Otraslevogo Planirovaniya v Promyshlennosti*, Novosibirsk (1972).

(1974): *Metodicheskie Ukazaniya k Razrabotke Gosudarstvennogo Plana Razvitiya Narodnogo Khozyaistva SSSR*, Moscow (1974).

Mikhalevich (1974): V. S. Mikhalevich and others, 'Metodicheskoe obespechenie ASPR respubliki', *MAU*, 3 (1974), pp. 11–16.

Mikhalevskii (1967): B. N. Mikhalevskii, 'Sistema modelei dlya rascheta sbalansirovannogo srednesrochnogo plana', *EMM*, 5 (1967), pp. 711–28.

(1972): B. N. Mikhalevskii, *Sistema Modelei Srednesrochnogo Narodnokhozyaistvennogo Planirovaniya*, Moscow (1972).

Mikhlin (1974): M. Mikhlin, 'Raschety vedut EVM', *MTS*, 7 (1974), pp. 33–40.

Mikhno (1971): M. Mikhno and L. Lobanova, 'O modelirovanii osnovnykh protsessov upravleniya metallosnabzheniem', *MTS*, 12 (1971), pp. 16–20.

Mironetskii (1972): N. B. Mironetskii and I. M. Romanova, 'ASU "Barnaul" v deistvie', *Eko.*, 3 (1972), pp. 61–89.

Modelirovanie (1972): *Modelirovanie Ekonomicheskikh Protsessov*, Moscow (1972).

Modin (1963): A. A. Modin, 'Developing inter-branch balances for economic simulation', *Economics of Planning*, 2 (1963), pp. 104–16.

(1970): A. A. Modin and others, *Sistemnyi Analiz i Matematicheskoe Modelirovanie v OASU*, Moscow (1970).

(1972): A. A. Modin and E. G. Yakovenko, *Organizatsiya i Upravlenie Proizvodstvennom Protsessom na Promyshlennom Predpriyatiem*, Moscow (1972).

(1974): A. A. Modin and E. G. Yakovenko, 'Parametry deistvuyushchikh sistem', *Eko.*, 6 (1974), pp. 97–104.

(1978): A. A. Modin, 'Razvitie metodicheskikh osnov sozdaniya ASUP', *EMM*, 5 (1978), pp. 835–44.

Moiseev (1974): N. N. Moiseev, 'Upravleniyu – programmnyi podkhod', *Eko.*, 1 (1974), pp. 24–43.

Montias (1963): J. M. Montias, 'On the consistency and efficiency of central plans', *Review of Economic Studies* (1963), pp. 283–90.

Mosin (1972): V. Mosin, 'O sozdanii avtomatizirovannoi sistemy planirovaniya', *Vop. Ekon.*, 11 (1972), pp. 28–39.

Movshits (1971): V. Movshits and A. Krivitskaya, 'Razrabotka i vnedrenie avtomatizirovannoi sistemy obrabotki dannykh', *MTS*, 7 (1971), pp. 87–90.

Myasnikov (1974): V. A. Myasnikov, 'Opyt, uroki, perspektivy', *Eko.*, 6 (1974), pp. 89–96.
Napravleniya (1976): 'Napravleniya proektirovaniya ASPR', *Plan. Khoz.*, 5 (1976), pp. 3–8.
National (1972): National Computer Centre, *Analysis of Computer Usage in the U. K. in 1971*, Manchester (1972).
  (1973): National Computer Centre, *Computerguide 9: Production Control*, Manchester (1973).
Nauchno-tekhnicheskii (1974): *Nauchno-tekhnicheskii Progress i Organizatsiya Proizvodstva, Truda, Upravleniya*, Moscow (1974).
  (1977): *Nauchno-tekhnicheskii Uroven' Avtomatizirovannykh Sistem Upravleniya Ob'edineniyami i Predpriyatami*, Moscow (1977).
Nemchinov (1964): V. S. Nemchinov (ed.), *The Use of Mathematics in Economics*, Edinburgh (1964).
Neuberger (1966): E. Neuberger, 'Libermanism, computopia and the visible hand', *American Economic Review Papers and Proceedings* (1966), pp. 131–44.
Nikulin (1976): N. V. Nikulin and S. A. Emelyanov, 'Upravlenie material'notekhnicheskim snabzheniem v "Asu-pribor"', *PSU*, 2 (1976), pp. 48–9.
Nove (1972): A. Nove and D. Nuti (eds.), *Socialist Economics*, Harmondsworth (1972).
Novick (1973): D. Novick (ed.), *Current Practice in PPBS*, London (1973).
Novikov (1974): D. Novikov, 'Otsenka effektivnosti vnedreniya ASU', *MTS*, 8 (1974), pp. 69–75.
  (1976): E. D. Novikov, Yu. M. Samokhin, *Kompleksnye Narodnokhozyaistvennye Programmy*, Moscow, 1976.
Novitskii (1977): L. Novitskii, 'Na raznykh "yazikakh"', *Pravda*, 25 July (1977), p. 2.
Nurbagandov (1974): A. Nurbagandov, 'Problemy sozdaniya ASN', *MTS*, 6 (1974), pp. 17–24.
Obshcheotraslevye (1977): *Obshcheotraslevye Rukovodyashchie Metodicheskie Materialy po Sozdaniyu Avtomatizirovannykh Sistem Upravleniya Predpriyatami i Proizvostvennymi Ob'edineniyami*, Moscow (1977).
Obsuzhdenie (1973): 'Obsuzhdenie metodicheskikh voprosov razrabotki dolgosrochnogo plana razvitiya SSSR', *EMM*, 3 (1973), pp. 365–9.
Odess (1973): V. I. Odess and B. M. Goldengorm, 'Avtomatizirovannaya sistema upravleniya metallosnabzheniem osnovannaya na printsipakh khozrascheta', *PSU*, 12 (1973), pp. 19–21.
Oganesyan (1975): E. Oganesyan and M. Borimechkov, 'Printsip "vedushchego zvena" v raschetakh mezhotraslevogo balansa', *Plan. Khoz.*, 4 (1975), pp. 87–96.
O rabote (1964): 'O rabote tsentral'nogo ekonomiko-matematicheskogo instituta', *Vestnik Akademii Nauk*, 10 (1964), pp. 3–14.
Otsenka (1973): 'Otsenka ekonomicheskoi effektivnosti', *Ekon. Gaz.*, 38 (1973), p. 22.
Pashkevich (1972): B. V. Pashkevich and others, 'Planirovanie i analiz truda i zarabotnoi platy v "ASU-pribor"', *PSU*, 7 (1972), pp. 54–6.
Pervaya (1976): 'Pervaya ochered' ASGS prinyata', *Vest. Stat.*, 3 (1976), pp. 3–6.

(1977): 'Pervaya ochered' ASPR', *Plan. Khoz.*, 5 (1977), pp. 3–7.
Pirogov (1963): G. Pirogov, 'Shire ispol'zovat' ekonomicheskuyu kibernetiku', *Plan. Khoz.*, 8 (1963), pp. 48–52.
Plenum (1969): 'Plenum nauchnogo soveta AN SSSR po kompleksnoi probleme "Optimal'noe planirovanie i upravlenie narodnym khozyaistvom"', *EMM*, 3 (1969), pp. 472–7.
Pokrovskii (1976): A. I. Pokrovskii, 'Glavnoe – ne poteryat' perspektivu', *Eko.*, 2 (1976), pp. 122–36.
Polonskii (1964): M. Polonskii and M. Ippa, 'Na putyakh k edinoi sisteme', *Ekon. Gaz.*, 6 (1964), p. 42.
Polyak (1976): S. V. Polyak and Yu. L. Shon, 'Metody avtomatizatsiya upravleniya finansovoi deyatel'nosti otrasli', *PSU*, 2 (1976), pp. 51–2.
Popov (1967): G. Kh. Popov, *Problemy Teorii Upravleniya* (1st ed.), Moscow (1967).
(1974): G. Kh. Popov, *Problemy Teorii Upravleniya* (2nd ed.), Moscow (1974).
(1977): G. Kh. Popov, 'Programmno-tselevoi podkhod v upravlenii', *Vop. Ekon.*, 2 (1977), pp. 57–65.
Portes, (1971): R. D. Portes, 'Decentralised planning procedures and centrally-planned economies', *American Economic Review Papers and Proceedings* (1971), pp. 422–9.
Povyshat' (1974): 'Povyshat' effektivnost' snabzheniya', *MTS*, 5 (1974), pp. 3–34.
Primenenie (1968): *Primenenie Matematicheskikh Metodov v Razmeshchenii Proizvodstva*, Moscow (1968).
Problemy (1969a): *Problemy Funktsionirovaniya Bol'shikh Ekonomicheskikh Sistem*, Moscow (1969).
(1969b): 'Problemy sozdaniya avtomatizirovannykh sistem planovykh raschetov', *EMM*, 5 (1969), pp. 783–90.
(1970a): *Problemy Metodologii Sistemnogo Issledovaniya*, Moscow (1970).
(1970b): *Problemy Sozdaniya Avtomatizirovannoi Sistemy Upravleniya Material'no-Tekhnicheskym Snabzheniem*, Moscow (1970).
(1972): *Problemy Sovershenstvovaniya Material'no-tekhnicheskogo Snabzheniya*, Moscow (1972).
(1974): *Problemy Planirovaniya i Prognozirovaniya*, Moscow (1974).
(1975): 'Problemy razvitiya avtomatizirovannykh sistem upravleniya proizvodstvom', *EMM*, 1 (1975), pp. 165–82.
Proskurov (1966): V. S. Proskurov and O. N. Yun, 'Avtomatizatsiya razrabotki planovogo balansa denezhnykh dokhodov i raskhodov naseleniya', *EMM*, 4 (1966), pp. 496–509.
(1975): V. S. Proskurov, *Informatsiya v ASPR*, Moscow (1975).
Protsenko (1973): O. D. Protsenko and S. L. Novikova, 'Podsistema prognozirovaniya potrebnosti v ASU "Metall"', *PSU*, 12 (1973), pp. 21–2.
Pugachev (1964): V. G. Pugachev, 'Voprosy optimal'nogo planirovaniya narodnogo khozyaistva s pomoshchyu edinoi gosudarstvennoi seti vychislitel'nykh tsentrov', *Vop. Ekon.*, 7 (1964), pp. 18–25.
(1977): V. F. Pugachev et al., 'Mnogootraslevoi kompleks v mnogostupenchatoi sisteme optimizatsii perspektivnogo planirovaniya', *EMM*, 2 (1977), pp. 213–23.

Rakovskii (1967): M. Rakovskii, 'Ekonomiko-matematicheskie metody – v praktiku planirovaniya', *Plan. Khoz.*, 3 (1967), pp. 18–25.
  (1977): M. Rakovskii, '"Syurprizy" elektronnykh mashin', *Pravda*, 2 March (1977), p. 2.
  (1978): M. Rakovskii, 'Planomernost' i sblansirovannost'', *Ekon. Gaz.*, 23 (1978), p. 14.
Rayatskas (1972a): R. Rayatskas, *Integrirovannaya Sistema Planirovaniya Narodnogo Khozyaistva Soyuznoi Respubliki*, Vilnius (1972).
  (1972b): R. Rayatskas and S. Zhemetaitaitite, *Informatsiya-Prognoz-Plan*, Moscow (1972).
  (1972c): R. Rayatskas, 'Sozdanie edinoi avtomatizirovannoi sistemy planirovaniya i upravleniya narodnym khozyaistvom soyuznoi respubliki', *Plan. Khoz.*, 11 (1972), pp. 88–93.
  (1976): R. Rayatskas, *Sistema Modelei Planirovaniya i Prognozirovaniya* Moscow (1976).
Resheniya (1968 & 1970): *Resheniya Partii i Pravitel'stva po Khozyaistvennym Voprosam*, Moscow, Vol. 4 (1968), Vol. 7 (1970).
Romanov (1978): I. Romanov, 'O primenenii optimal'nykh ekonomiko-matematicheskikh modelei v ASPR', *Plan. Khoz.*, 10 (1978), pp. 49–56.
Rudnev (1972): K. N. Rudnev and others, 'Avtomatizirovannaya sistema upravleniya priborostroitel'noi promyshelennosti i perspektivy ee razvitiya', *PSU*, 1 (1972), pp. 1–5.
  (1977): K. N. Rudnev, 'Priborostroitel'naya promyshelennost' k yubileyu Velikogo Oktyabrya', *PSU*, 10 (1977), pp. 1–2.
Rudnik (1972): I. Rudnik and V. Liberman, *ASU 'Sistema-Frezer'*, Moscow (1972).
Saltykov (1973): B. G. Saltykov and V. L. Tambovtsev, 'K probleme postroeniya dereva tselei sotsial'no-ekonomicheskoi sistemy', *EMM*, 6 (1973), pp. 1029–38.
Samborskii (1974): G. Samborskii and V. Simchera, 'Put' povysheniya effektivnosti vychislitel'noi tekhniki', *Vop. Ekon.*, 7 (1974), pp. 79–89.
Sazonov (1975): S. Sazonov, 'Sozdanie ASGS – vazhneishaya zadacha organov gosudarstvennoi statistiki', *Vest. Stat.*, 6 (1975), pp. 3–8.
Schroeder (1968): G. Schroeder, 'The Soviet economic "reforms" – a study in contradictions', *Soviet Studies*, 1 (1968), pp. 1–21.
  (1972): G. Schroeder, 'The reform of the supply system in Soviet industry', *Soviet Studies*, 1 (1972/3), pp. 97–119.
Segedov (1977): R. S. Segedov et al., 'Aspekty sozdaniya ASUP na baze EVM tret'ego pokoleniya', *PSU*, 5 (1977), pp. 1–3.
Selivanov (1969): A. I. Selivanov, 'Problemy razrabotki ASU soyuzglavkhima', *MTS*, 10 (1969), pp. 15–19.
  (1971): A. I. Selivanov and B. L. Geronimus, 'Ot eksperimenta k vnedreniyu', *MTS*, 6 (1971), pp. 28–31.
  (1975): A. I. Selivanov, 'Planomerno razvivat' pryamye dlitel'nye svyazi', *MTS*, 1 (1975), pp. 11–18.
Seminar (1970): 'Seminar po nauchno-metodicheskim voprosam razrabotki i vnedreniya ASPR', *EMM*, 5 (1970), pp. 784–90.
Shatalin (1971): S. Shatalin, 'Ekonomiko-matematicheskie metody v planirovanii i upravlenii', *Vop. Ekon.*, 7 (1971), pp. 15–24.

Shatilov (1974): N. F. Shatilov, 'Modeli mezhotraslevogo balansa v avto-matizirovannoi sisteme planovykh raschetov', *MAU*, 3 (1974), pp. 41–3.
Shorin (1972): V. G. Shorin (ed.), *Aktual'nye Problemy Upravleniya*, Moscow (1972).
(1973): V. G. Shorin (ed.), *Avtomatizirovannye Sistemy Upravleniya*, Moscow (1973).
Siemaszko (1976): Z. A. Siemaszko, 'Industrial Process Control in the Soviet Union', Birmingham University, PhD Thesis (1976).
Silin (1977): V. Silin and A. Tolkachev, 'O metodakh i pokaʐatelyakh otsenki effektivnosti ASPR', *Plan. Khoz.*, 8 (1977), pp. 73–80.
Simakova (1975): G. Simakova, 'Vzaimodeistvie ASGS i ASPR', *Vest. Stat.*, 6 (1975), pp. 50–5.
Sinavina (1970): V. Sinavina, *Mekhanizatsiya i Avtomatizatsiya Upravleniya Otraslyu*, Moscow (1970).
Sinyak (1972): V. S. Sinyak, 'Osnovnye problemy razvitiya otraslevykh avtomatizirovannykh sistem upravleniya', *PSU*, 5 (1972), pp. 4–7.
(1973a): V. S. Sinyak, 'ASU-pribor v nastoyashchem i budushchem', *Nauka i Tekhnika*, 10 (1973), pp. 7–8.
(1973b): V. S. Sinyak, 'Tekhnicheskaya baza i perspektivy ASU', *Ekon. Gaz.*, 28 (1973), p. 8.
(1978a): V. S. Sinyak et al., 'Avtomatizatsiya upravleniya kachestvom produktsii v otrasli priborostroeniya', *PSU*, 1 (1978), pp. 1–4.
(1978b): V. S. Sinyak et al., 'Sovremennoe sostoyanie i osnovnye napravleniya razvitiya ASU-pribor', *EMM*, 5 (1978), pp. 845–56.
Siroyezhin (1968): I. M. Siroyezhin, 'Man-machine systems in the USSR', *Management Science*, Series B, 2 (1968), pp. 1–10.
Sistemy (1967): *Sistemy Ekonomicheskoi Informatsii*, Moscow (1967).
Smirnov (1971): K. Smirnov, 'Voprosy razrabotki ASU snabzheniem podshipnikovoi produktsii', *MTS*, 1 (1971), pp. 63–70.
Smith (1972): C. L. Smith, *Digital Computer Process Control*, Scranton, Pa., 1972.
Smolinski (1974): L. Smolinski, 'Towards a socialist corporation', *Survey*, Winter (1974), pp. 24–35.
Sobolev (1974): V. A. Sobolev and A. L. Tamarkin, *Avtomatizirovannaya Sistema Upravleniya na Minskom Traktornym Zavode*, Moscow (1974).
Soviet (1973): *Soviet Economic Prospects for the Seventies*, Washington, DC (1973).
Sozdanie (1972): 'Sozdanie ASPR – zadacha obshchegosudarstvennaya', *Plan. Khoz.*, 8 (1972), pp. 3–8.
Spivakovskii (1973): L. I. Spivakovskii and others, 'Metodicheskie i organizatsionnye osnovy optimal'nogo planirovaniya proizvodstva i raspredeleniya produktsii trubnoi promyshlennosti', *PSU*, 8 (1973), pp. 5–7.
Spravochnik (1974): *Spravochnik po Material'no-tekhnicheskomy Snabzheniyu i Sbytu*, Moscow (1974).
Starovskii (1965): V. Starovskii, 'Gosudarstvennaya statistika v novykh usloviyakh', *Pravda*, 18 December (1965), p. 2.
(1971): V. Starovskii, 'XXIV S'ezd KPSS i zadachi sovetskoi statistiki', *Vest. Stat.*, 5 (1971), pp. 5–12.
Stefani (1978): E. P. Stefani and V. I. Gritskov, 'Puti povysheniya effektivnosti

rabot po sozdaniyu ASU TP', *PSU*, 3 (1978), pp. 1–4.

Stephenson (1970): G. G. Stephenson, 'A hierarchy of models for planning in a division of ICI', *Operations Research Quarterly*, 1970, No. 2, pp. 221–45.

Stewart (1971): R. Stewart, *How Computers Affect Management*, London (1971).

Stoneman (1976): P. Stoneman, *Technological Diffusion and the Computer Revolution*, Cambridge (1976).

Suprunyuk (1972): V. S. Suprunyuk, 'Opyt organisatsiya informatsionnogo obespecheniya "ASU-pribor"', *PSU* 1 (1972), pp. 15–16.

Syrov (1974): Yu. Syrov, 'Osnovy ekonomiki i upravleniya proizvodstvom i material'no-tekhnicheskim snabzheniem', *MTS*, 3 (1974), pp. 81–90.

Telegin (1976): N. A. Telegin and L. A. Buyanovskii, 'Podsistema tekhniko-ekonomicheskogo planirovaniya', *PSU*, 1 (1976), pp. 6–8.

Theil (1967): H. Theil, *Economics and Information Theory*, Amsterdam (1967).

Tikhonenko (1974): L. N. Tikhonenko and Yu. G. Bondarenko, 'Sovershenstvovanie i unifikatsiya dokumentov v otraslevykh ASU', *Mekhanizatsiya i Avtomatizatsiya Proizvodstva*, 1 (1974), pp. 46–7.

Tipovaya (1977): 'Tipovaya metodika raschetov po optimizatsii razvitiya i razmeshcheniya proizvodstva na perspektivy', *EMM*, 6 (1977), pp. 1137–49.

Trapeznikov (1964): V. A. Trapeznikov, 'Za gibkoe ekonomicheskoe upravlenie predpriyatami', *Pravda*, 17 August (1964), pp. 3–4.

(1966): V. A. Trapeznikov, 'Avtomaticheskoe upravlenie i ekonomika', *Avtomatika i Telemekhanika*, 1 (1966), pp. 5–22.

(1972): V. A. Trapeznikov, 'Nauchnye aspekty razrabotki ASU "Metall"', *PSU*, 12 (1972), pp. 3–5.

Treml (1972): V. Treml and J. Hardt (eds.), *Soviet Economic Statistics*, Durham, NC (1972).

Tretyakova (1976): A. Tretyakova and I. Birman, 'Input–output analysis in the USSR', *Soviet Studies*, 2 (1976), pp. 157–86.

Urinson (1975): Ya. M. Urinson, 'Mezhotraslevye modeli v svodnykh ekonomicheskikh raschetakh', *EMM*, 5 (1975), pp. 865–75.

(1978): Ya. Urinson, 'Povyshenie effektivnosti ispol'zovaniya ekonomiko-matematicheskikh modelei v ASPR', *Plan. Khoz.*, 6 (1978), pp. 59–66.

Vainshtein (1974): B. S. Vainshtein and M. K. Dubovoi, 'Nadezhdy i real' nost', *Eko.*, 6 (1974), pp. 120–7.

Vasil'ev (1971): I. I. Vasil'ev, *Nash Opyt Organizatsiya i Mekhanizatsiya Upravleniya Proizvodstvom*, Leningrad (1971).

Vazhnyi (1973): 'Vazhnyi etap rabot po sozdaniyu ASPR', *Plan. Khoz.*, 9 (1973), pp. 3–5.

Velikotskii (1972): A. N. Velikotskii and others, 'Avtomatizatsiya perspektivnogo planirovaniya v ASU-pribor', *PSU*, 1 (1972), pp. 5–7.

(1976): A. N. Velikotskii and others, 'Avtomatizatsiya protsessa formirovaniya perspektivnykh planov razvitiya otrasli', *PSU*, 1 (1976), pp. 3–6.

V Gosplane (1973): 'V Gosplane SSSR', *Plan. Khoz.*, 9 (1973), pp. 157–8.

(1974): 'V Gosplane SSSR', *Plan. Khoz.*, 11 (1974), pp. 155–6.

(1978): 'V Gosplane SSSR', *Plan. Khoz.*, 6 (1978), pp. 156–8.

Volchkov (1970): B. A. Volchkov, *Avtomatizirovannaya Sistema Planovykh Raschetov*, Moscow (1970).
(1974): B. A. Volchkov and I. P. Romanenko, *Osnovy Razrabotki Avtomatizirovannykh Sistem Planirovaniya*, Moscow (1974).
Volodarskii (1978): L. M. Volodarskii, 'Avtomatizirovannaya sistema gosudarstvennoi statistiki', *Ekon. Gaz.*, 26 (1978), p. 5.
Vorob'ev (1972): B. Vorob'ev, 'O tekhnicheskom zadanii na razrabotky ASPR', *Plan. Khoz.*, 8 (1972), pp. 16–21.
(1973): B. Vorob'ev, 'O primenenii mezhotraslevogo balansa v praktike planirovaniya, *Plan. Khoz.*, 7 (1973), pp. 55–8.
Vremennaya (1973): 'Vremennaya metodika opredeleniya ekonomicheskoi effektivnosti ASUP', *Ekon. Gaz.*, 8 (1973), p. 22.
(1975): *Vremennaya Metodika Opredeleniya NTU ASUP*, Moscow (1975).
Vsesoyuznoe (1974): 'Vsesoyuznoe soveshchanie po voprosam avtomatizirovannykh sistem upravleniya', *Plan. Khoz.*, 6 (1974), pp. 142–3.
Ware (1965): W. H. Ware and W. B. Holland (eds.), *Soviet Cybernetics Technology: V. Process Control Computers*, Rand Corp., Santa Monica (1965).
Wasowski (1970): S. Wasowski (ed.), *East-West Trade and the Technology Gap*, New York (1970).
Weitzman (1970): M. Weitzman, 'Iterative multi-level planning with production targets', *Econometrica* (1970), pp. 50–65.
XXII S'ezd (1962): *XXII S'ezd KPSS – Stenograficheskii Otchet*, Vol. 3, Moscow (1962).
Yakobi (1975): A. Yakobi and others, 'Ot elementov k sisteme', *MTS*, 9 (1975), pp. 22–34.
Yakovenko (1973): E. G. Yakovenko and others, *Osnovy Avtomatizirovannykh Sistem Upravleniya*, Moscow (1973).
Yakovlev (1972): V. V. Yakovlev, 'Effektivnost' ASU – kak ee povysit'', *Eko.*, 4 (1972), pp. 38–50.
Yasin (1970): E. G. Yasin, *Teoriya Informatsii i Ekonomicheskie Issledovaniya*, Moscow (1970).
(1971): E. G. Yasin, 'Ob effektivnosti ASOD i probleme izmereniya tsennosti dannykh', *EMM*, 3 (1971), pp. 389–96.
(1972): E. G. Yasin, 'K probleme postroeniya sistemy ekonomicheskykh klassifikatsii', *Ekonomiko-Matematicheskie Modeli*, Sbornik 4 (1972), pp. 139–58.
(1974): E. G. Yasin, *Ekonomicheskaya Informatsiya*, Moscow (1974).
Yun (1978): O. Yun, 'Napravleniya sovershenstvovaniya planirovaniya pri sozdanii vtoroi ocheredi ASPR', *Plan. Khoz.*, 10 (1978), pp. 42–9.
Zaimskikh (1977): A. N. Zaimskikh, 'Problemy formirovaniya i funktsii mezhotraslevykh narodnokhozyaistvennykh kompleksov', *Izvestiya Akademii Nauk SSSR, Seriya Ekonomicheskaya*, 3 (1977), pp. 39–52.
Zaitsev (1974): B. Zaitsev and Yu. Urinson, 'Razrabotka avtomatizirovannoi sistemy svodno-ekonomicheskikh raschetov', *Plan. Khoz.*, 10 (1974), pp. 20–7.
Zakharov (1974): S. Zakharov and V. Sulyagin, 'Sistema ASOP-Vneshtorg; tseli, zadachi, struktura', *Plan. Khoz.*, 12 (1974), pp. 39–47.

Zaleski (1967): E. Zaleski, *Planning Reforms in the USSR 1962–66*, Chapel Hill, NC (1967).

Zauberman (1975): A. Zauberman, *The Mathematical Revolution in Soviet Economics*, London (1975).

Zenchenko (1972): N. Zenchenko, 'Primenenie setevykh metodov pri sostavlenii naradnokhozyaistvennogo plana', *Plan. Khoz.*, 8 (1972), pp. 22–8.

(1976): N. Zenchenko, 'Razrabotka plana i setevye metody', *Eko.*, 1 (1976), pp. 31–44.

Zhemetaitaitite (1975): S. A. Zhemetaitaitite and others, 'O postroenii modeli sbalansirovannogo rosta narodnogo khozyaistva soyuznoi respubliki', *EMM*, 5 (1975), pp. 892–9.

Zherebin (1968): V. M. Zherebin, 'Yazik ekonomicheskoi sistemy i otsenka informatsii', *EMM*, 5 (1968), pp. 751–62.

Zhichkin (1971): A. Zhichkin, 'Obshchesoyuznyi klassifikator produktsii', *Plan. Khoz.*, 11 (1971), pp. 20–5.

Zhimerin (1972): D. G. Zhimerin et al. (eds.), *Avtomatizirovannye Sistemy Upravleniya*, Moscow (1972).

(1974a): D. G. Zhimerin, 'Itogy i perspektivy', *Ekon. Gaz.*, 2 (1974), p. 8.

(1974b): D. G. Zhimerin, 'ASU: ekonomicheskaya sluzhba', *Pravda*, 9 June (1974), p. 3.

(1974c): D. G. Zhimerin, 'Tekhnicheskii progress i sovershenstvovanie upravleniya', *Ekon. Gaz.*, 27 (1974), p. 10.

(1976a): D. G. Zhimerin, 'ASU: problemy i perspektivy', *Pravda*, 17 February (1976), p. 3.

(1976b): D. G. Zhimerin, 'Nauchno-tekhnicheskii progress i upravlenie', *Ekon. Gaz.*, 14 (1976), p. 7.

(1978): D. G. Zhimerin, 'Kachestvennyi novyi etap', *Ekon. Gaz.*, 22 (1978), p. 7.

Zigmund (1973): M. Zigmund and Yu. Berezhkin, 'Opyt vnedreniya ASU v soyuzglavkomplektavtomatike', *MTS*, 8 (1973), pp. 72–7.

INDEX

Academy of Sciences
  and cybernetics, 1
  and early automation plans, 7, 11
  and the economic return to auto-
    mation, 162, 171
  role in overall automation project of,
    176, 177
accounting, independent, see *khozraschet*
ASPR
  see Gosplan
association, see *ob'edinenie*
ASU-Metall
  see metal products
ASU-pribor
  see Ministry of Instrument-Building
Automated System of Normatives
  (ASN) ix, 72, 80, 117–8, 130
automation, targets for, 13, 15, 22, 173,
  175, 176

Barnaul Radio Factory, 159, 166
Berg, A. I., 1, 3, 199
Brezhnev, L. I., 12, 13, 16, 183

Central Economic Mathematical Institute, see TsEMI
Central Statistical Administration, see
  TsSU
chemical products, automated supply
  system for, 114–7
classification of products
  need for multi-level system of, 101
  Unionwide Product Classifier (OKP),
    44, 119, 177, 185–8
coding
  compatability and uniformity in, 119,
    177, 185–8
  developing systems of, 4
  examples of, 144, 185–8
  optimal, theory of, 44–5

problems of, 82, 79, 131
coefficient of relative effectiveness (CRE)
  use of in investment planning, 73–4,
    137
  see also economic return to auto-
    mation
Committee for Popular Control, 131,
  164, 186
computer centres
  for joint use, 18–22, 95, 132–3
  State Network of (GSVTs), 2–13,
    45–6, 175
computers
  low utilisation of, 18
  Soviet stock of, 11, 190
  use of Western, 98, 112
  see also computer technology
computer technology
  level in USSR of, 2, 189–91
  second generation, 2, 15, 131–2
  third generation, 15, 132
compatibility, problems of 14–15, 19,
  117–18, 129–30, 177–8
consistency
  of balances, 91
  of data, 117–18, 127–8
critical path analysis, 76, 175, 203
cybernetics
  impact in USSR of, 1–2, 3, 5, 41
  Institute of (Kiev), 6, 10, 79, 106, 109,
    154, 177, 199

decentralisation
  concepts of, 30, 182
  of authority, 29–30
  of information, 28
  opposition to, 12, 85
decentrally-planned commodities, 90
decomposition methods 9, 26, 31, 60–1,
  85, 182